The Politics of Latino Education

THE POLITICS OF
LATINO EDUCATION

EDITED BY

David L. Leal

Kenneth J. Meier

Teachers College
Columbia University
New York and London

Published by Teachers College Press, 1234 Amsterdam Avenue, New York, NY
10027

Library of Congress Cataloging-in-Publication Data

The politics of Latino education / edited by David L. Leal, Kenneth J. Meier.
    p. cm.
  Includes bibliographical references and index.
    ISBN 978-0-8077-5142-8 (pbk. : alk. paper) — ISBN 978-0-8077-5143-5
(hardcover : alk. paper) 1. Hispanic Americans—Education—Political aspects.
2. Education and state—United States. I. Leal, David L. II. Meier, Kenneth J.,
1950–
  LC2669.P65 2010
  371.829'68073—dc22

                                                              2010036668

ISBN 978-0-8077-5142-8 (paperback)
ISBN 978-0-8077-5143-5 (hardcover)

Printed on acid-free paper
Manufactured in the United States of America

18 17 16 15 14 13 12 11   8 7 6 5 4 3 2 1

Contents

Acknowledgments

David would like to acknowledge the support of the National Academy of Education and the Spencer Foundation. This book began as a conference held at the University of Texas at Austin as a component of his National Academy of Education/Spencer Foundation postdoctoral fellowship. Neither the conference nor the book would have transpired without the support of the program and its staff. He also would like to thank the University of Texas at Austin for its role in supporting the conference and volume, specifically the Irma Rangel Public Policy Institute, the College of Liberal Arts, and the Department of Government. He particularly appreciates the assistance of Jill Strube (Project Coordinator of the Irma Rangel Institute), Luis F.B. Plascencia (the previous Project Coordinator), John Higley and Gary Freeman (past and present chairs of the Department of Government), Jennifer Lamm (Graduate Research Assistant of the Irma Rangel Institute), and the GRAs who staffed the conference and otherwise assisted with the project.

Ken acknowledges the support of the Carlos Cantu Hispanic Education and Opportunity Endowment at Texas A&M University as well as the Spencer Foundation.

The Politics of
Latino Education

Introduction

David L. Leal

Education may be the most critical public policy issue facing Latino populations in the United States today. It is strongly associated with political activism and engagement, financial and career success, immigrant integration, and a host of other factors. The issue of educational attainment will help to determine whether millions of Latinos take a central place in American economic and civic life or remain marginalized on the fringes of society. Education is a foundational issue for Latinos because statistics in other policy areas—such as employment, health care, housing, and criminal justice—are unlikely to improve without greater educational progress.

The education of Latinos is also a key issue for America in the 21st century. As the Latino population expands rapidly, the number and percentage of Latino students in the public schools has considerably increased. According to Fry (2006), Latinos constitute almost two thirds of the increase in public school enrollments—3 million of 4.7 million students—from 1993 to 2003. This trend is even more pronounced in public elementary schools, where the Latino student population increased by 155 percent while Anglo (non-Hispanic white) enrollments declined. The educational success of Latino students will therefore have far reaching implications for the economic, cultural, and political future of the nation. According to the National Council of La Raza (2007), "ensuring that our nation's public schools and universities improve their capacity to adequately serve Latinos students . . . is one of our country's most significant challenges" (p. 13).

The U.S. Supreme Court ruling in *Plyler v. Doe* (1982) guaranteed a free public education for all children in the United States, regardless of citizenship status. Public schooling is therefore one of the most accessible and widely available government services for the Latino community. Immigration officials do not check student documents and schools do not report suspected undocumented children to the authorities. In an era when noncitizens (including legal permanent residents) have been losing access to government programs, education is the most significant and broad-based Latino-serving government institution.

The transformative potential of education for Latinos is impossible to exaggerate. For many Latinos, a public school is their first introduction to American life. Schools teach not only a formal curriculum but also about less tangible factors like community and national values and can be a key part of the acculturation process. Despite some claims to the contrary, Latino parents take seriously the education of their children (see Moreno & Valencia, 2004; Pew, 2004; San Miguel, Jr., 1987),[1] and the beginning of public education can bring a great deal of optimism and hope to both parents and students. Nevertheless, achievement data are alarming, and many worry that schools are failing Latino students. Such facts feed back into the policy stream; for instance, the disparity between white and minority students was part of the logic behind the No Child Left Behind legislation.

Not only is education key for Latinos as individuals and as a community, but recognition is growing that it is crucial for the future health of the U.S. economy. As the Latino population grows, so does the Latino percentage of the workforce. In testimony before the U.S. House of Representatives Committee on Education and the Workforce, Tomás Arciniega, President Emeritus of California State University, Bakersfield, stated that "Current U.S. Department of Labor studies show that Hispanics, who currently represent about 13% of the U.S. work force and make up one of every three new workers, are projected to provide one of every two new workers by 2025." He also noted that, "Advanced technical and scientific skills are becoming essential to future earnings and career achievement in areas necessary to the nation's economic strength, security and position within the world economy."[2] It is therefore increasingly important for Latinos to not only finish the K–12 path but to also receive undergraduate and graduate degrees. Dr. Arciniega further pointed out that the educational achievement of Latinos is important for not only the economy but also for the government and public sector.

According to a report by the National Academies (2006), *Multiple Origins, Uncertain Destinies: Hispanics and the American Future*, the education of Latinos is crucially important for U.S. prosperity as the "baby boomer" generation moves into retirement. By 2030, 26 million children of Spanish-speaking immigrants may live in the United States, most of whom will participate in the labor force: "Underinvesting in their education would compromise the quality of their lives and, in all likelihood, U.S. competitiveness. . . . They also face some conditions that other waves of immigrants did not, such as a global marketplace that increasingly relies on well-educated employees."[3]

This issue will be particularly acute in states with large and growing Latino populations. According to a recent strategic plan for the Texas Workforce Commission (2004), "As the Texas population continues to grow, it is also becoming more ethnically diverse. Sometime between 2004 and 2005, Texas is projected to be less than half Anglo, with Hispanics continuing to be the faster growing ethnic group in the state. The trend of historically lower educational attainment among the fastest growing ethnic group must be reversed for Texas to maximize potential." However, such states are not necessarily well prepared to meet this challenge. As noted by the NCLR (2007), Texas is one of the states where "school districts with the highest percentage of minority children receive significantly less funding than districts with the fewest minority children" (p. 9).

LATINOS, EDUCATION, AND POLITICS

While some believe education should be nonpolitical—with teachers simply teaching and students simply learning—education has long been intertwined with political dynamics. This is not always well recognized by the research literature, however. According to Meier and Stewart (1991), "The overwhelming bulk of educational literature goes to great lengths to avoid discussing politics" (pp. 4–5). These authors argued that it is "a fiction" to contend that a public school system that consumes hundreds of billions of taxpayer dollars per year should be above politics. Political scientists, in contrast, have been more willing to explore the political dynamics of education (for example, see Chubb & Moe, 1990; Clarke, Hero, Sidney, Fraga, & Anhalt Erlichson, 2006; Henig, 1994; Henig, Hula, Orr, & Pedescleaux, 1999; Henig, 2004; Hess, 1999; Howell & Peterson, 2002; Katznelson & Weir, 1985; Loveless, 2000; and Stone, Henig, Jones, & Pierannunzi, 2001).

From the earliest conception of the common school to the Progressive Movement to the market-based reforms of today, public education has been inexorably influenced by the values of communities, political institutions, and political actors. In recent decades, public education has experienced several well-discussed waves of reform efforts—from "excellence" to "restructuring" to "standards" (Fuhrman & Lazerson, 2005). Not everyone is happy with this reality. As Wirt and Kirst (2001) noted, "Many education professionals believe politics should have no role in their work" (p. 3). But the idea of public education without any public accountability—just teachers teaching behind an opaque classroom door—would raise a host of other problematic questions.

The historic lack of research on educational politics reflects, as suggested above, a desire by many to separate education from politics. The creation of independent school districts, the use of nonpartisan school board elections, and the holding of school board elections and bond referenda in political "off-years" were just some of the strategies with the ostensible purpose of keeping politics at arms length from schools.

However, many of these reforms were designed not to remove politics from schools but to remove particular groups from school politics. The Progressives saw "good government" as one where immigrants and the urban poor had little choice but to defer to the policy decisions of an upper-class establishment. We might therefore be skeptical of reform plans—then and now—that are supposed to help a group but without the political input of that group. For Latinos, as for the Irish and Italians before them, politics is an important way to have a voice in how their children are educated.

An antipolitics perspective is not unique to education policy, however. According to Stone (2001), the "new field of policy science, supposedly devoted to improving governance, was based on a profound disgust for the ambiguities and paradoxes of politics. By and large, the new science dismissed politics as an unfortunate obstacle to clear-headed, rational analysis and good policy (which were the same thing)" (p. xi). Stone argued that politics is inescapably connected to policymaking and cannot be a purely rational and objective process: "The fields of public policy and policy analysis worship objectivity and determinate rule. . . . I argue that each of the analytic standards we use to set goals, define problems, and judge solutions is politically constructed" (p. xii).

For Latinos, it is clear that the history and legacy of educational problems are a result of political decisions made largely by non-Latinos. As Olivas (1983) noted, "it may be impossible to disentangle the educational problems stemming from Hispanic political disenfranchisement, inasmuch as educational policy is political both at local and higher levels" (p. 112). For example, Meier and Stewart (1991) found that Latino school board representation was related to a wide range of educational outcomes. School districts with fewer Latino board members had lower Latino graduation rates, fewer Latino students in gifted classes, more Latinos assigned to special education and bilingual classes, and higher levels of corporal punishment, suspensions, and expulsions. Politics, it was shown, was at the heart of longstanding Latino educational problems. Politics must therefore be central to their amelioration.

Given the alarming statistics about low Latino educational achievement, it is perhaps not surprising that a growing number of scholars and reformers are turning their attention to how and what Latino children are taught. However, the political nature of education raises questions as to whether the system has the capacity to meet the many needs of Latino students. As

Hess (1999) observed, a great deal of "policy churn" takes place in education reform, and much of it is short-lived, driven by fads, and not always in the best interests of students or teachers. Will an education system with such a history be able to develop and implement meaningful reforms, or will Latino students be buffeted by one trendy reform wave after another?

Furthermore, history suggests that Latino education reform will not be the consensus recommendation of experts. Instead, it will emerge (or not emerge) from a highly political process that involves interest groups, legislators, thinks tanks, academics, business executives, parties, school administrators, teachers, philanthropists, parents, and voters. In this regard, it resembles all education reform. Those interested in Latino education must therefore pay attention to the political dynamics of overall school reform as well as to the policymaking and political processes relevant to Latinos in particular. To complicate the issue further, assessing the progress of Latino students is difficult because "Latino" conflates many different groups. As discussed below, aggregate data about rising or declining Latino educational achievement may reflect multiple and varying trends. To better understand such myriad political and statistical dynamics is a key task for researchers, parents, stakeholders, and politicians.

The chapters in this volume, therefore, cover a wide range of subjects, collectively providing a better understanding of the multiple ways in which politics affects Latino education dynamics. The authors are an interdisciplinary group, with contributions from political scientists and education scholars. They use a variety of methodological approaches, ranging from quantitative to qualitative methods, and they bring to bear a great deal of collective experience in the study of education politics.

DEMOGRAPHICS

It is sometimes said that if you want to see the demographic future of America, the best place to look is the public schools. According to a report by Richard Fry (2006) of the Pew Hispanic Center, the number of children in the public schools increased by 4.7 million from the 1993–1994 to the 2002–2003 school years. The majority of this increase, 64%, was due to growing Hispanic enrollments. These 3 million new Latino students significantly outnumbered the new 1.1 million African American students and half a million Asian American students. By contrast, Anglo public school enrollment dropped by 35,000 students. Such dynamics are especially evident in elementary schools. According to Fry, while Anglo enrollment in such schools declined during the 10-year period by 1.2 million students, Latino enrollment increased by 1.6 million. These figures reflect changes in the ethnic makeup of the United States as a whole. By 2050, the

Census Bureau estimates that non-Hispanic whites (Anglos) could constitute about half of the U.S. population. In 2004, four states were "majority
minority," where the total number of minorities was larger than the total
number of Anglos—California, Texas, Hawaii, and New Mexico (Pear,
2005).

More generally, Fry (2003) noted that Latinos were the fastest-growing
youth population in the United States during the 1990s. For the 16–19-year-
old Latino population, this decade saw a 57% increase in immigrant youth
and a 55% increase in native-born youth. By contrast, the growth rates
of the Anglo (3%), African-American (7%), and Asian/Pacific Islander
(29%) youth populations were considerably lower. In the late 1990s, Latinos became the largest minority population in the public school system.
Such numbers are only likely to increase. For instance, according to census
data, Latinos were responsible for 70% of the growth in the population of
children under the age of five from 2004 to 2005 (Cohn & Bahrampous,
2006).

In the state of Texas, a prime destination for immigrants from Mexico
and Central America, the Latino student percentage increased during the
1990s from 35.5% to 43.8%. Such growth is not just a phenomenon of the
Rio Grande Valley or border regions. In the central Texas area, the Latino
school presence is growing not only in the capital city of Austin (from 37.7%
to 53.1%) but also in outlying school districts such as Round Rock (from
13.6% to 21.1%), Pflugerville (from 18.3% to 29.7%), Del Valle (from
50.6% to 69%), and Hayes (from 36.9% to 52.3%) (Moscoso, 2006).

The Latino presence in schools is growing in every region of the nation.
While the percentage of Latinos in K–12 education in the West grew from
15% to 39% from 1972 to 2004, the population also grew in the South
from 5% to 17%, in the Northeast from 6% to 14%, and in the Midwest
from 2% to 7% (NCLR, 2007).

One dynamic in public education is a renewed tendency toward segregation by race and ethnicity. According to a report by the Harvard Civil
Rights Project (Frankenberg, Lee, & Orfield, 2003), the last 3 decades have
seen the growing segregation of Latino students. In 1970, about 44% of the
classmates of the average Latino student were non-Hispanic, a figure that
dropped to 28.5% for the 2000–2001 school year.[4] The reasons include a
combination of demographics and politics, such as residential separation
by race and class, the focus on neighborhood schools, lower birth rates for
Anglos, and courts, policymakers, and voters who oppose the use of race-
conscious remedies for segregation (Mollison, 2003).

Some of these dynamics are also evident in data on those schools most
affected by increased Hispanic enrollments. The Pew Hispanic Center
(2004) reported that two thirds of new Hispanic students entered existing
schools, whereby only one third entered new schools. According to Harry

Pachon, President of the Tomás Rivera Policy Institute, this is likely because immigrants often settle in older urban areas (Moscoso, 2006). By contrast, while Anglo student enrollment declined by 2.6 million from 1993–94 to 2002–03, 2.5 million students in the new schools were white. Such figures are important because new schools are smaller and serve more affluent families.

In addition, there are troubling statistics for those schools that saw the largest Hispanic enrollment; such schools not only grew by 25% (while schools with few new Hispanic enrollments did not increase), but the percentage of poor students increased and the declines in student-teacher ratios were the slowest. Such schools also saw a large drop in the share of Anglo students (from 60% to 38%) in contrast to a slower decline in schools less affected by new Hispanic students (from 71% to 66%).

STUDENT ACHIEVEMENT

The broad outline of Latino educational problems is well known but bears some discussion. If Latino students were performing well in school, then research on political and policymaking questions would be less pressing. It is also important to identify where the conventional wisdom is correct and incorrect. Some areas of educational failure are more complicated than they seem at first glance, and there are some areas of improvement. This section will therefore discuss Latino educational outcomes, particularly the key issues of dropout rates and disproportionately low test scores.

According to Valencia (2004a), "School failure among Chicano students refers to their *persistently, pervasively, and disproportionately, low academic achievement*" (p. 4; emphasis in original). He noted that research suggests the two most important indicators are testing (particularly reading) and holding power (graduation); this section will review Latino achievement in these areas. Valencia (2004b) also discussed 15 educational conditions and outcomes for Latinos, ranging from standardized testing to the teacher workforce to school stress. He found the resulting profile "disturbing" but noted that the contributors to his volume were optimistic that Latino educational success is possible. Corcoran and Goertz (2005) found that such disparities are large by global standards: "Results from the Program for International Student Assessment (PISA) conducted in 2000 by the Organization for Economic Co-Operation and Development show that the United States has among the largest disparities in achievement among the 32 participating nations" (p. 30).

There are two key problems with Latino educational outcomes: not only is Latino educational achievement low, but it is typically lower than comparable statistics for other racial and ethnic groups. If Latinos are to realize their full economic, personal, and civic potentials, they must receive adequate education along both measures.

Some of these problems reflect the challenges facing Latino communities and families. While some claim that Latinos do not value education, there is a growing body of contrary evidence. Latino parents believe it is very important for their children to graduate from high school and college, as parents are aware that education is a ticket to a better life and the American dream. One problem is that Latino parents are not always able to help their children in the same way as native-born parents. As J. Berger wrote in *The New York Times*, "Parental involvement is a buzzword in education, a recommended cure for high dropout rates, poor test scores and almost everything else that ails schoolchildren" (p. A23). However, as Pedro Noguera noted in the article, the problem is that many immigrant parents are busy at work, have limited English skills, are anxious about their legal status, and are often from a culture that emphasizes deference to teachers (Berger, 2006).

A related issue is the socioeconomic status of Latino families and communities. Frankenberg, Lee, and Orfield (2003) found that Latino students attend schools that are not only highly segregated but also very poor:

> These consistent trends towards increasing segregation for the nation's minority students should be considered in the context of segregation's strong correlation to poverty. High poverty schools have been shown to increase educational inequality for students in these schools because of problems such as a lack of resources, a dearth of experienced and credentialed teachers, lower parental involvement, and high teacher turnover. Almost half of the students in schools attended by the average black or Latino student are poor or near poor. By contrast, less than one in five students in schools attended by the average white student is classified as poor. (p. 35)

Frankenberg, Lee, & Orfield (2003) further found that Latinos and African Americans constitute a disproportionate share—85.8%—of students in very high poverty schools (where 50% to 100% of the students are poor). According to Hochschild and Scovronick (2005), "The worst-off students and schools have a completely different educational experience from the best off, and the outcomes are predictably very different. . . . The pattern is clear. Those segments of the population that are growing most rapidly— Latinos, and immigrants and their children—are likely to live in school districts that can offer them only the poorest quality of education" (p. 313).

Another issue is English language ability, both for students and their parents. Fry (2003) found that "A lack of English-language ability is a prime characteristic of Latino dropouts. Almost 40% do not speak English well. The 14% of Hispanic 16–19-year-olds who have poor English language skills have a dropout rate of 59%" (p. v).

Dropouts

The Pew Hispanic Center investigated the "status" dropout rate, in this case the percentage of youths ages 16–19 who are either not enrolled in high school or not a graduate. Using 2000 census data, they found an overall 10% dropout rate, with Latinos at a relatively high 21%, followed by Native Americans and Alaska Natives at 16%, Native Hawaiians and Pacific Islanders at 11%, African Americans at 12%, Anglos at 7%, and Asian Americans at 4%. These figures suggest a 14-point gap between Latinos and Anglos, and the gap is even higher for some Latino national-origin groups. The dropout rates are 35% for Guatemalans, 33% for Hondurans, 28% for Salvadorans, and 25% for Mexicans. The national-origin groups with the lowest dropout rates are Panamanian (4%), Venezuelan (5%), Chilean and Peruvian (6%), and Colombian and Argentinean (7%). The dropout rate also varies by gender. According to the NCLR (2007), there is a 10-percentage point gap between boys and girls, with the latter more likely to graduate.

Dropout data are complex, however, because there are a number of ways to present the data, including snapshots, trends, completion vs. graduation, "status" vs. "event" dropouts, and comparisons by race and ethnicity, age, immigrant status, and national-origin group. For example, the "completion" rate includes the percent of the 18–24-year-old population that either graduated from high school or obtained a credential such as the General Educational Development (GED) credential. According to the National Center for Educational Statistics (2003), completion rates were 64% for Latinos, 84% for African Americans, and 92% for Anglos. However, the GED is not an equivalent credential to a high school diploma. Some wage data suggests little difference between high school dropouts and those who received a GED.

There is also some debate about the accuracy of high school dropout data. Most importantly, the "status" dropout rate includes individuals who never took part in the American educational system yet are counted as dropouts (see Fry, 2003). An individual who migrates to the United States from Mexico at the age of 17 and does not attend school in the United States may not possess a high school degree, but this person is not a "dropout" as the word is commonly used. This is important because dropout data are often seen as a reflection of the quality of public schooling in America.

The U.S. Department of Education and the Pew Hispanic Center studied this issue and found more encouraging educational data. As the Pew Hispanic Center (2004) noted, "A significant proportion of teen Hispanic school dropouts are recently arrived immigrants who have never enrolled in school in the U.S." (pp. 1–2). The report estimated that one third of such dropouts never attended an American school. Taking this into account lowered the 16–19-year-old Latino status dropout rate in 2000 from 21% to 15%. Fry (2003) noted that "Latino youth who are educated abroad [about 8% of

Latino youth] are nearly all high school dropouts" (p. 6), and that it makes little sense to consider them dropouts from the American educational system.

Using the National Education Longitudinal Study of 1988, the U.S. Department of Education (NCES, 2003) tracked eighth graders from 1988 to 1994 and compared the educational attainment of Latinos and Asian Americans by immigration status. It found that the Latino dropout rate in 1994 was 27.6% for immigrants, 28% for second-generation students, and 27.7% for the third generation and beyond. While these figures are still high—and much higher than the corresponding figures for Asian Americans (14.5, 7.3, and 7.5, respectively), they do suggest that immigration alone cannot explain Latino education attainment.

Second, there are also problems with how some dropout data are collected. Jay Greene, a contributor to this volume, has estimated that graduation rates are much lower than are commonly reported by districts. For the high school class of 1998, Greene (2002) estimated an overall graduation rate of 71%, with 78% for white students, 56% for African Americans, and 54% for Latinos. These data show some notable state variations. For example, Montana had an 82% graduation rate, followed by Maryland and Louisiana at 70%. The overall Latino figure is very close to the estimate of the National Council of La Raza, which reported that only 50% of Hispanic children will graduate from high school (Berger, 2006).

Discrepancies are evident at the district and state levels. The heavily Hispanic Dallas Independent School District (DISD) reported a 1.3% dropout rate, but Greene calculated a 52% graduation rate. While DISD data were based on a methodology that attempts to track individual students, Greene (2002) found this implausible, asking "If only 1.3% of students drop out each year, how is it that Dallas had 9,914 students in eighth grade in 1993 but only 5,659 graduates in 1998 while the total student population in the district went up by 10.5%?" (p. 8).

Similarly, Greene (2002) calculated a dropout rate of 32% for the state of Texas, whereas the state itself reported a 1.6% annual dropout rate. Again, he asked, "If it is true that only 1.6% of students in Texas drop out of school each year, what explains the fact that there were 274,208 eighth graders in Texas in 1993 and only 197,186 graduates in 1998 while the state's student population increased by 5.9%?" (p. 9). While districts may legitimately argue that a student who transfers to another high school outside of the district is not a dropout, Greene observed that some districts take too many liberties: "Because school systems and their officials are under strong pressure not to have high dropout rates, they have incentives to assume that students moved out of town or fell into some other category that exempted them from being called dropouts" (p. 8).

There are some encouraging dropout data, however. A Pew Hispanic Center report (Lowell & Sura, 2002) found that more Hispanic immigrants were graduating from high school and earning college degrees, although the educational gap between immigrants and the native born was still significant. From 1970 to 2000, the percentage of Hispanics over the age of 25 with a high school diploma increased for immigrants (28% to 59%) and the native born (53% to 87%).

In addition, Fry (2003) found that between 1990 and 2000, the dropout rates for native-born Latinos declined by 1.2 percentage points, while the percentage of the 18–19-year-old population that completed high school rose by 5.3 percentage points for the native-born and 6.1 percentage points for immigrants. In addition, according to the Pew Hispanic Center (2004), 12% of Hispanics aged 15–19 are not attending high school, compared to 5% for Anglos, 7% for African Americans, and 2% for Asian Americans (Berger, 2006).

Test Scores

While dropout rates are the most discussed Latino educational statistic, other factors are equally notable. For instance, the National Center for Educational Statistics (2003) found that Latino students were somewhat more likely than Anglos to have been held back a grade from kindergarten through 12th grade (13% vs. 9%). In 1999, 20% of Latinos in grades 7–12 had ever been suspended or expelled, versus 15% for Anglos. Reported absenteeism is also higher for Latinos than Anglos among students in both 8th grade and 12th grade.

In the world of standardized testing, the gold standard is the National Assessment of Educational Progress (NAEP). Reading, mathematics, and science scores were discussed by the NCES (2003). The results generally showed improvement over the last 2 decades, although gaps remained between Latino and Anglo test scores. In some cases, the size of the gap decreased, but other cases saw no change; in only one case (9-year-olds in math) did the gap increase.

Reading scores were first reported by Hispanic ethnicity in 1975, and the data show improvement by 1999 for the 9-, 13-, and 17-year-olds tested. There was still a gap between Latino and Anglo scores, however (13% for 9-year-olds, 9% for 13-year-olds, and 8% for 17-year-olds). The size of the gap decreased for the 17-year-olds, but not for the 9- and 13-year-olds. There were also Anglo-Latino reading score gaps even when comparing students with similar levels of parental education. For example, there was a 21-point gap between Anglo and Latino 12th graders whose parents had attended college.

In math, Latino student scores were higher in 1999 than in 1973 in all three age groups, although there were still gaps between Latino and Anglo scores. This gap decreased over time among 13- and 17-year-olds, although there was some increase among 9-year-olds. As with reading scores, there were achievement gaps even when comparing students with similar levels of parental education (with the exception of one grade level).

For science, scores across the three age groups increased from 1977 to 1999. However, the gaps have not generally changed, and gaps still exist according to parental education.

Implications of Latino Education Outcomes

As stated by the National Council of La Raza (2007), data such as the above indicate that:

> the status of Latino education suggests a number of missed opportunities from early childhood education through higher education. Compared to their peers, Latinos are more likely to start school later and leave school earlier. Especially concerning is that Latinos are the second-largest student population enrolled in our nation's schools, and improved educational outcomes for Latinos have not kept pace with their rapid growth. (p. 13)

Furthermore, educational achievement data are important not only for the individuals who comprise the statistics but also for larger political debates.

An example of the former—the implications for individuals—is the relationship between education and wages. A report by the Federal Reserve Bank of Dallas discussed the educational and wage gaps between Latinos and Anglos in 2000 (Orrenius, 2004). First generation Mexican-American males earn about 60% lower wages than do Anglo native males, which declines to a 29% gap for third generation Mexican Americans and Anglo native males. Most of this gap is explained by Anglo-Latino education gaps. When education is controlled, the Anglo-Mexican wage gap is reduced to 11-percentage points.

An example of the latter—the implications for politics—is how educational trends can be cited in the debate about immigration reform. In his controversial article "The Hispanic Challenge," Samuel Huntington (2004) refers to Latino high school graduation rates in a section called "Sidebar: Failure to Assimilate." For this side of the immigration debate, dropout data are another argument in favor of restrictionist immigration reform, a "law and order" approach or reform of legal immigration. As Fraga and Segura (2006) note, this can be akin to blaming the victim:

> Economic and social outcomes of marginalized groups are not useful indicators of the group's adherence to values and norms. Such a claim assumes that the groups possess an unexpected amount of power to negotiate their place within contemporary American society, an assumption at odds with the prevailing research and common understanding. . . . Such an understanding completely

discounts the many barriers Latinos have historically faced in attaining upward mobility in the United States. (p. 284)

THE CONTENTS OF THIS BOOK

The chapters in this volume collectively address a range of political and policy topics important to Latino education. In doing so, the book contributes in a unique way to the growing literature on Latino education. For many decades, Latinos were of little interest to most social scientists. As Meier and Stewart (1991) noted, while the educational attainment of African Americans has long been the subject of scholarly interest, few paid any attention to Latinos. As a conquered people after the Mexican-American War, regionally isolated in the southwest and increasingly marginalized in terms of politics and economics, Latinos had become the "forgotten people" by the end of the 19th century (Sanchez, 1940) and the objects of discrimination and neglect throughout much of the 20th.

While renewed immigration at various times in the last century brought new attention to this group, the result was not always positive in terms of policy outcomes. Latinos were often underserved by government, disenfranchised at the polls, misunderstood by policymakers and elected officials, and more likely to be the subject of negative attention (for instance, by journalists and police officials) than treated with respect. Contemporary educational disparities are only one legacy of a history in which the civic place of Latinos in the United States was equivocal and tenuous. As Carter (1970) noted, "in the past the plight of this group was little known and there was small desire to correct it" (p. 9).

Fortunately, this is changing. Historians like Guadalupe San Miguel, Jr. began to uncover the history of educational struggles by Mexican-American individuals and organizations. Education scholars like Thomas Carter and Roberto Segura critiqued "cultural deprivation" theory and explored the significant problems faced by Latinos in the public schools (see Carter, 1970; Carter & Segura, 1979; and San Miguel Jr., 1990, 2001). This neglect has given way to an emergent literature. A growing number of important and well-known works about Latinos and education discuss subjects such as improving Latino educational achievement and encouraging high performance (Conchas, 2006; Garcia, 2001; Nieto, 1999; Noguera and Wing, 2006; Pizarro, 2005; Reyes, Scribner, & Scribner, 1999; Valencia, 2004; and Valenzuela, 1999), immigrant children and education (Flores, 1996; Suárez-Orozco & Suárez-Orozco, 2001; and Valdés, 1996), and the learning of civics and citizenship (Baldi, Perie, Skidmore, Greenberg, Hahn et al. 2001; Luktus, Weiss, Campbell, Mazzeo, & Lazer, 1999; and Rippberger & Staudt, 2003). The first four chapters of this book address school reform, a perpetually important and politically charged issue in America. They discuss standardized testing, social promotion, and charter schools.

The first two chapters of this book take on the subject of standardized high-stakes testing, the signature education reform of the new century. The implications of such reforms for Latinos and other racial and ethnic groups are an increasingly important topic for researchers.

In Chapter 1, Angela Valenzuela and Brendon Maxcy address the subject of who is tested and the implications of this for the overall accountability regime. Throughout the 1980s and 1990s, states increasingly adopted performance accountability systems to spur reform and increase achievement. Their chapter contributes to the accountability discussion by examining both the expressed logic and politics behind performance accountability systems with respect to the testing (or nontesting) of *Limited English Proficient* (LEP) youth. Through an examination of schooling conditions for LEP youth and a debate regarding Texas' exemption policy during the 77th regular legislative session in 2001, the authors develop a framework that challenges the alleged virtue of *public-ness* in Texas' market-based model of accountability. They suggest that by placing test-challenged LEP youth into non-tested categories, Texas-style accountability not only relegates these students to a second-class status but is contrary to the logic of public accountability.

In the second chapter, Kathy Staudt investigates how high-stakes accountability tests in Texas affect the civic learning of Latino students as measured in state accountability and NAEP-type testing instruments. The setting is three Texas middle schools located in one of the 10 largest urban districts on the U.S.-Mexico border. She concludes that the tests—and the way they drive the curriculum and instructional strategies to increase rote memorization—undermine the potential for civic engagement among Latino students. In addition, social studies testing in Texas is unlikely to reduce participation gaps between Latino and Anglo adults, thereby failing to increase diverse voices in U.S. democracy.

In Chapter 3, Jay Greene and Marcus Winters provide a different perspective on school testing than do the two previous contributions. They evaluate the effects of a Florida policy that requires students to reach a minimum threshold on the state's standardized reading test in order to be promoted to the fourth grade. Proponents claim that students must possess basic skills in order to succeed in higher grades, while opponents claim that retention harms academic growth. Their study examines the gains made on math and reading tests by students in the first cohort of third graders who were subject to the retention policy. It compares those who scored below the threshold with students in the prior year who had the same low test scores but for whom the policy was not yet applicable. The study also evaluates potential differences in program effectiveness by race and ethnicity. They find that after 1 year, students subject to the retention policy made greater reading and math gains than did students not subject to the policy. Because some students subject to the policy obtained special exemptions and were promoted despite their scores, the study also uses regression analysis to measure the effects of actually being retained. Those who were retained made greater reading and math gains than those who were promoted. The study finds similar gains in math and reading for Hispanic, Anglo, and African-American students.

In Chapter 4, Robert Wrinkle and his coauthors contribute to the charter school literature by studying the effects of such schools in Texas. They first test whether charter schools have a negative effect on public school enrollment, contain a disproportionate share of minority students, and lead to changes in public school student performance. The regression results for the effects of charters are mixed. While charters do not reduce public school enrollment or have a disproportionate minority enrollment, there were some relationships between charter schools and Latino student achievement in the public schools.

The two chapters that follow address immigrant education. This is an increasingly important subject because of the continuing growth in the number of Latino immigrants, the immigrant share of the overall Latino population, and the diversity of the Latino immigrant population.

Chapter 5 examines the Latino student-teacher gap, specifically the factors that structure the availability of Latino teachers. Paru Shah and Melissa Marschall show that as the Latino K–12 population rises due to the immigration surge that began in the 1990s, the number of Latino teachers has not kept pace. This is important because the presence of minority teachers can have a positive effect on school policies and practices that affect minority students, and these teachers can also serve as cultural brokers between the home and school environments of Latino students. Using the 1999–2000 National Center for Education Statistics' Schools and Staffing Survey, Shah and Marschall investigate the factors that structure the availability of Latino teachers. They find that several demographic and political factors are at work. For the former, the percentage of Latinos aged 25 or older with a bachelor's degree, Latino citizenship status, and Latino attachments to their local community are all positively related to the availability of Latino teachers. This suggests that the New Gateway Areas—which lack these demographic characteristics—will continue to have a short supply of Latino teachers. Some factors subject to community influence can increase the presence of Latino teachers, however, including political and school governance factors, such as the election of Latinos to school boards. In addition, while general teacher incentive programs are unlikely to reduce the gap, programs designed specifically to recruit Latino teachers have promise.

Ted Hamann further contributes to our understanding of the growing Latino presence in regions—and therefore local schools—where they were hitherto almost unknown. As the NCLR (2007) noted, "although Latino students are still concentrated in 'traditional' Latino states, such as Texas and California, their presence is growing in nontraditional states in the Midwest and Southeast" (p. 1). In Chapter 6, Hamann explores the response of Anglo educational and community leaders in Dalton, GA to a rapidly growing Latino school population. By using Suárez-Orozco's (1998) concept of pro-immigration and anti-immigration "scripts," he examines how the well-intentioned educational response of Dalton—which brought together business elites, school officials, and a Mexican university—was formulated, implemented, contested, and ultimately defeated.

Chapters 7 and 8 discuss the educational representation of Latinos, particularly on school boards. These are among the nation's most local political institutions, and board members are responsible for a wide range of educational policymaking with direct implications for Latino students and families.

In Chapter 7, Kenneth J. Meier and his coauthors examine how the dynamics of Latino representation have changed over a two-decade period. Meier and Stewart (1991) used a school board survey from the 1980s to examine the causes and educational consequences of Latino school board representation. They found that electoral structures influenced the number of Latinos elected, and that officials elected under different systems were differentially associated with the implementation of policies beneficial to Latino students. This chapter reexamines those 130 districts with contemporary data to see how such dynamics—as well as how the districts themselves—have changed. The chapter finds not only significant growth in the Latino student population, but also that an increase in ward electoral systems has tended to increase Latino representation. They then study the causes and consequences of Latino board representation over the past 2 decades, finding a declining effect of population on representation but a growing substantive effect of board representation on the Latino presence in school bureaucracies.

Rene Rocha examines whether inter-minority ("rainbow") governing coalitions are feasible in school politics, an increasingly important subject in an increasingly diverse America. Analyzing urban school board data from the 2001 National Latino Education Study, Chapter 8 examines whether the descriptive representation of one group affects the substantive representation of another group. He finds that the descriptive representation of Latinos is not associated with the substantive representation of African Americans. However, African-American descriptive representation is negatively associated with Latino substantive representation. His study therefore offers a cautionary note about the possibility of minority board members working together in order to achieve positive educational outcomes.

Chapters 9 and 10 address bilingual education, a policy issue that has long been central to the Hispanic community. According to Guadalupe San Miguel Jr. (1987), Latino activists in the 1970s came to see it as "the most appropriate instrument for attaining equality in society" (p. 215). Not only was the program considered important for Spanish-speaking children, but it also "implied a fundamental reassessment of the support, governance, administration, and content of the public schools" (p. 215).

In Chapter 9, Regina Branton and her coauthors investigate the 1998 California vote for Proposition 227, the anti–bilingual education ballot initiative. This initiative reflected a reaction to the growing Latino population in California in the 1990s, and unlike its cousin Proposition 187 in 1994, it was upheld by the courts. Branton and coauthors note that research on such initiatives usually discusses the effect of ethnic context on voting behavior but overlooks how geospatial factors can influence how context structures the vote. Their chapter accounts for distance from the U.S.-Mexico border, finding that individuals residing closer to the border are more likely to support the proposition. In addition, the role of geography varies by partisanship; while distance from the border slightly reduces the likelihood of Republicans voting for the proposition, Democratic support declines considerably as distance increases.

David Leal and Frederick Hess then examine the determinants of bilingual education expenditures in the nation's largest urban school districts. Using a database built from a Council of Urban Boards of Education (CUBE) survey, Chapter 10 examines how political and structural factors affect the funding of such programs. After a brief review of the history of bilingual education, they present regression results showing that political factors do play a role. A key variable is Latino representation on school boards: the more Latinos, the greater the per-pupil funding. This is further evidence that the election of Latinos to such boards—whose determinants were discussed in two previous chapters in this volume—is of substantive as well as symbolic importance. In addition, they find that Asian-American board representation is positively associated with bilingual education expenditures, as are several other structural and political factors.

The next two chapters look at two aspects of the Latino educational pipeline. In Chapter 11, Carl Doerfler identifies policies, procedures, programs, and pedagogical practices in public school districts in Texas that increase levels of college preparation among Latino students. He identifies these practices by interviewing school administrators at 22 school districts throughout the state. These districts were selected by using education production function models to identify the highest and lowest performing school districts on a variety of college preparation measures. His chapter uses three short case studies to illustrate the differences between schools that suffer from low and high student achievement, drawing lessons about what works, what does not work, and how schools can improve.

In Chapter 12, Alisa Hicklin discusses the importance of politics in Latino higher education. This is a consequential subject because "Although Latino enrollment in institutions of higher education has increased, Latinos are still less likely than non-Latinos to be enrolled in or graduate from college" (NCLR, 2007, p. 10). She notes that far more attention is paid to Latino K–12 education than to Latinos in higher education, and the attention that does exist is more likely to examine court decisions and, to some degree, facets like budgeting and oversight. Her chapter examines several state and institutional factors that affect the enrollment of Latinos in higher education, including minority legislators, bureaucratic structure, judicial interventions, and university-specific characteristics. She concludes that political dynamics do play a role. This is not to diminish the responsibility of the K–12 system but to point out how political representation, court rulings on affirmative action, college selectivity, and tuition costs help to structure the Latino presence in colleges and universities. She also discusses how state governments can help to improve Latino college matriculation.

Taken together, these chapters describe the political and policymaking dynamics that affect Latino education. As with any other public policy field, a wide variety of political factors—ranging from elected officials to electoral structures to voters—play central roles. This volume thereby contributes to an expanding literature that seeks to better understand the Latino educational experience. Such research will hopefully be of use to all stakeholders who seek to promote equal opportunity in America and are concerned about the educational, economic, and political future of the nation.

NOTES

1. In his book *One Nation, One Standard* (2006), Herman Badillo wrote that "Education is not a high priority in the Hispanic community . . . Hispanics have simply failed to recognize the overriding importance of education." However, according to the 2004 Pew Hispanic Center/Kaiser Family Foundation "National Survey of Latinos: Education," 95% of Latinos, 94% of African Americans, and 78% of Anglos responded "very" to the following question: "How important is it to you that your child get a college education?"

2. *Testimony of Tomás Arciniega, President Emeritus, California State University-Bakersfield, and member of the HACU governing board, on behalf of the Hispanic Association of Colleges and Universities (HACU) and Hispanic-Serving Institutions.* Written testimony for submission to the record on HR 761, "Expanding

opportunities for graduate study at Hispanic–Serving Institutions." To the Subcommittee on Select Education of the House Committee on Education and the Workforce. At a field hearing at the University of Texas Pan American, May 2, 2005. Retrieved June 16, 2010, from http://www.hacu.net/hacu/Arciniega_testimony_HR_761_EN.asp?SnID=2

3. *Publication Announcement: Prudent Investments in Education and Training For Nation's Hispanic Population Would Benefit U.S. Society.* http://www8.nationalacademies.org/onpinews/newsitem.aspx?RecordID=11314

4. For African-American students, the corresponding figures are 32% in 1970, 36% in 1980, and 31% in 2000.

REFERENCES

Badillo, H. (2006). *One nation, one standard.* New York: Penguin.

Baldi, S., Perie, M., Skidmore, D., Greenberg, E., & Hahn, C., et al. (2001). *What democracy means to ninth-graders: U.S. results for the international IEA civic education study.* Washington, DC: National Center for Educational Statistics.

Berger, J. (2006, November 1). For hispanic parents, lessons on helping with the homework. *New York Times*, p. A23.

Carter, T. P. (1970). *Mexican Americans in school: A history of educational neglect.* Princeton, NJ: College Entrance Examination Board.

Carter, T. P., & Segura, R. D. (1979). *Mexican Americans in school: A decade of change.* Princeton, NJ: College Entrance Examination Board.

Chubb, J., & Moe, T. (1990). *Politics, markets, & America's schools.* Washington, DC: Brookings Institution Press.

Clarke, S. E., Hero, R. E., Sidney, M. S., Fraga, L., & Anhalt Erlichson, B. (2006). *Multiethnic moments: The politics of urban education reform.* Philadelphia: Temple University Press.

Cohn, D. V., & Bahrampous, T. (2006, May 10). Of U.S. children under 5, nearly half are minorities. *Washington Post*, p. A10.

Conchas, G. Q. (2006). *The color of success: Race and high-achieving urban youth.* New York: Teachers College Press.

Corcoran, T., & Goertz, M. (2005). The governance of public education. In S. Fuhrman & M. Lazerson (Eds.), *Institutions of American democracy: The public schools.* Oxford, UK: Oxford University Press.

Flores, J. L. (Ed.). (1996). *Children of la frontera.* Charleston, WV: ERIC Clearinghouse on Rural Education and Small Schools.

Fraga, L. R., & Segura, G. M. (2006). Culture clash? Contesting notions of American identity and the effects of Latin American immigration. *Perspectives on Politics, 4*, 279–287.

Frankenberg, E., Lee, C., & Orfield, G. (2003, January 16). *A multiracial society with segregated schools: are we losing the dream?* Cambridge, MA: Civil Rights Project.

Fry, R. (2003). Hispanic youth dropping out of U.S. schools: Measuring the challenge. Washington, DC: Pew Hispanic Center.

Fry, R. (2006). The changing landscape of American public education: new students, new schools. Washington, DC: Pew Hispanic Center.

Fuhrman, S., & Lazerson, M. (2005). Introduction. In S. Fuhrman & M. Lazerson (Eds.), *The public schools*. New York: Oxford University Press.

Garcia, E. (2001). *Hispanic education in the United States: Raíces y alas*. Lanham, MD: Rowman & Littlefield.

Greene, J. P. (2002). High school graduation rates in the United States. New York: Manhattan Institute. Retrieved June 16, 2010, from http://www.manhattan-institute.org/html/cr_baeo.htm

Henig, J. (1994). *Rethinking school choice: Limits of the market metaphor*. Princeton, NJ: Princeton University Press.

Henig, J. (2004). *Mayors in the middle: Politics, race, and mayoral control of urban schools*. Princeton, NJ: Princeton University Press.

Henig, J., Hula, R., Orr, M., & Pedescleaux, D. (1999). *The color of school reform: Race, politics, and the challenge of urban education*. Princeton, NJ: Princeton University Press.

Hess, F. M. (1999). *Spinning wheels: The politics of urban school reform*. Washington, DC: Brookings Institution Press.

Hochschild, J., & Scovronick, N. (2005). Demographic change and democratic education. In S. Fuhrman & M. Lazerson (Eds.), *The public schools*. New York: Oxford University Press.

Howell, W., & Peterson, P., with Wolf, P., & Campbell, D. (2002). *The education gap: Vouchers and urban schools*. Washington, DC: Brookings Institution Press.

Huntington, S. P. (2004, March/April). The Hispanic challenge. *Foreign Policy*.

Katznelson, I., & Weir, M. (1985). *Schooling for all: Class, race, and the decline of the democratic ideal*. New York: Basic Books.

Loveless, T. (2000). *Conflicting missions? Teachers unions and educational reform*. Washington, DC: Brookings Institution Press.

Lowell, B. L., & Suro, R. (2002). The improving educational profile of Latino immigrants. Washington, DC: Pew Hispanic Center. Retrieved June 16, 2010, from http://pewhispanic.org/report.php

Lutkus, A. D., Weiss, A. R., Campbell, J. R., Mazzeo, J., & Lazer, S. (1999). NAEP 1998 Civics report card for the nation. Washington, DC: National Center for Educational Statistics.

Meier, K. J., & Stewart, J. (1991). *The politics of Hispanic education*. Albany, NY: State University of New York Press.

Mollison, A. (2003, January 19). Study: Desegregation losing ground. *Austin American-Statesman*.

Moreno, R., & Valencia, R. (2004). Chicano families and schools: Myths, knowledge, and future directions for understanding. In R. Valencia (Ed.), *Chicano school failure and success*. New York: Routledge Falmer.

Moscoso, E. (2006, October 6). Hispanic propel surge in number of U.S. schoolchildren. *Austin American-Statesman*.

National Academies. (2006). *Prudent investments in education and training for nation's hispanic population would benefit U.S. society*. Retrieved January 4, 2007, from http://www.nationalacademies.org/morenews/20060301b.html

National Center for Education Statistics. (1998). Generational status and educational outcomes among Asian and Hispanic 1988 eighth graders. Washington,

DC: U.S. Department of Education. Retrieved July 5, 2010, from http://nces. ed.gov/pubs99/1999020.pdf

National Center for Education Statistics. (2003). Status and trends in the education of Hispanics. Washington, DC: U.S. Department of Education. Retrieved July 5, 2010, from http://nces.ed.gov/pubs2003/2003008.pdf

National Council of La Raza (Kohler, A., & Lazarín, M.). (2007). Hispanic Education in the United States: Statistical Brief. Washington, DC: Author.

National Council of La Raza. (1999). A force overlooked: Achieving full representation of Hispanics in the department of defense workforce. Washington, DC: Author.

Nieto, S. (1999). *The light in their eyes: Creating multicultural learning communities.* New York: Teachers College Press.

Noguera, P., & Wing, J. Y. (2006). *Unfinished business: Closing the racial achievement gap in our schools.* San Francisco: Jossey-Bass.

Olivas, M. A. (1983). Research and theory on Hispanic education: Students, finance, and governance. *Aztlan, 14,* 111–146.

Orrenius, P. (2004, May/June). Immigration assimilation: Is the U.S. still a melting pot. Southwest Economy. Federal Reserve Bank of Dallas.

Pear, R. (2005). Racial and ethnic minorities gain in the nation as a whole. *The New York Times.* August 11, 2005. Retrieved May 12, 2009, from www.mona.uwi. edu/liteng/courses/e21h_2007/documents/Texas%20now%20minority%20 majority.doc

Pew Hispanic Center Fact Sheet. (2004, January). Latino teens staying in high school: A challenge for all generations. Washington, DC. Author.

Pizarro, M. (2005). *Chicanas and Chicanos in school: Racial profiling, identity battles, and empowerment.* Austin, TX: University of Texas Press.

Plyler v. Doe, 457 U.S. 202 (1982).

Reyes, P., Scribner, J., & Scribner, A. P. (Eds.). (1999). *Lessons from high-performing Hispanic schools.* New York: Teachers College Press.

Rippberger, S., & Staudt, K. (2003). *Pledging allegiance: Learning nationalism at the El Paso-Juárez border.* New York: Routledge Falmer.

San Miguel, G. Jr. (1987). *'Let All of Them Take Heed': Mexican Americans and the campaign for educational equality in Texas, 1910–1981.* Austin, TX: University of Texas Press.

San Miguel, G. Jr. (2001). *Brown, not white: School integration and the Chicano movement in Houston.* College Station, TX: Texas A&M University Press.

Sanchez, G. I. (1940). *Forgotten people.* Albuquerque, NM: University of New Mexico Press.

Stone, C., Henig, J., Jones, B., & Pierannunzi, C. (2001). *Building civic capacity: The politics of reforming urban schools.* Lawrence, KS: University Press of Kansas.

Stone, D. (2001). *Policy paradox: The art of political decision making.* New York: Norton.

Suárez-Orozco, C., & Suárez-Orozco, M. M. (2001). *Children of immigrants.* Cambridge, MA: Harvard University Press.

Suárez-Orozco, M. M. (1998). State terrors: Immigrants and refugees in the post-national space. In Y. Zou & E. T. Trueba (Eds.), *Ethnic identity and power: Cultural contexts of political action in school and society* (pp. 283–319). Albany: State University of New York Press.

Texas Workforce Commission. (2004, July). *Strategic plan: For the fiscal years 2005–09 period*. Retrieved January 4, 2007, from http://www.twc.state.tx.us/twcinfo/stratplan/twc05_09plan.pdf

Valdés, G. (1996). *Con respeto: Bridging the distance between culturally diverse families and schools*. New York: Teachers College Press.

Valencia, R. R. (2004a). *Chicano school failure and success: Past, present, and future*. New York: Routledge Falmer.

Valencia, R. R. (2004b). The plight of Chicano students: An overview of schooling conditions and outcomes. In R. Valencia (Ed.), *Chicano school failure and success*. New York: Routledge Falmer.

Valenzuela, A. (1999). *Subtractive schooling: U.S.-Mexican youth and the politics of caring*. Albany, NY: State University of New York Press.

Wirt, F. M., & Kirst, M. W. (2001). *The political dynamics of American education* (2nd ed.). Richmond, CA: McCutchan Publishing Corporation.

CHAPTER 1

Limited English Proficient Youth and Accountability: All Children (Who Are Tested) Count

Angela Valenzuela and Brendan Maxcy

As we composed this chapter, a category 5 hurricane named Katrina struck the U.S. gulf coast just to the east of Texas. The following day, two levees gave way, flooding New Orleans. News crews pouring in to record the devastation found thousands stranded at the Superdome, at the Convention Center, on their roofs and in their attics. The viewing public discovered that most of those citizens—predominantly poor and black—did not choose to ride out the storm, but were left behind as their neighbors, including many public servants, headed for higher ground. Many were shocked to find tens of thousands of residents of a major American city lacked both the means to evacuate as a hurricane bore down and a safety net to rescue them from the floodwaters rising in its wake. Katrina seemed to force the New Orleans "underclass" into view.

Perhaps—to borrow from Ralph Ellison's *Invisible Man*—they were never really out of sight, but were deemed so unworthy of attention as to become unreal. Attention is costly. As Nobel laureate Herbert Simon noted, information "consumes" people's attention: "Hence, a wealth of information creates a poverty of attention, and a need to allocate that attention efficiently among the overabundance of information sources that might consume it" (cited in Varian, 1995, p. 200). With information abundant and attention scarce, political expedience dictates that the most relevant and socially critical issues, individuals, and communities should receive the most attention. To help discover and manage information, Varian (1995) calls for information managers, "specialists in manipulating information . . . to locate, filter, organize and summarize it" (p. 200).

In an era in which public information is produced and disseminated as a means to drive and direct school reform, the character and consequences of information management is of great concern to policy makers, parents, educators, students and anyone else with a stake in public education. Accepting information management as necessary but problematic, we must ask about the ends and interests served in its management. In a profound and disturbing way, Katrina brought to light a relationship between political power, information management, and public services, a relationship critically dependent on our public servants' attention to the public's problems and the public's perceptions. More generally, the management of public information to direct public attention reveals much about public priorities.

In this chapter, we turn attention to the Texas Education Agency (TEA) and its information management regarding English language learners, mostly Mexican immigrant children, who—albeit from a deficiency perspective—are officially identified as *Limited English Proficient* (LEP) youth. We contribute to a discussion on accountability in public schooling by examining both the expressed logic and the politics behind performance accountability systems with respect to the testing (or nontesting) of LEP youth. We argue that the management of information through the state's Academic Excellence Indicator System (AEIS) reflects and affects which students count more and which students count less in Texas schools. We identify a *hierarchy of public-ness* whereby presentation of data results in focusing attention on certain performances and performers to the exclusion of others. Moreover, we argue that resources flow accordingly as an intended consequence of the system-established hierarchy.

We contend that the central concern of politics—"who gets what, when and how" (Laswell, 1936)—depends critically on one's position in that hierarchy. A priori decisions to place entire segments of test-challenged, LEP youth into the *nontested* categories of Texas' accountability system not only relegate them to "second-class status," but also defy the expressed logic of public accountability. More insidiously, our review of state-level decision making reveals the way that nonuniform, nonuniversalistic applications of accountability suggest the enforcement and policing of preferential status (i.e., *tested student*) to preserve the legitimacy of the accountability system itself.

We explore the current educational logic of Texas-style accountability (TSA), its implications for the schooling of LEP youth, and the debate surrounding the state's test exemption policy. From this, we offer and illustrate a framework challenging TSA's alleged virtue of data public-ness. Specifically, the debate between lawmakers and various stakeholders in the 2001 Texas 77th Legislative Session centered on the number of years LEP youth should be exempt from the annual state assessments and, to a lesser extent, on the definition of LEP youth. We demonstrate how performance pressures worked through a hierarchical structure of public accounting to marginalize these historically underserved students.

THE LARGER CONTEXT OF EDUCATION
FOR LEP STUDENTS

There is little doubt that limited English proficiency is a barrier to academic achievement when instruction is primarily conducted in English. A 7-year cohort study of over 250,000 students given exit-level exams found that, of the non-LEP group, 78% and 80% passed the reading and math portions, respectively (TEA, 2002). Only 61% and 66% of their LEP peers passed the same tests. Beyond communication difficulties, LEP students often face additional struggles. The General Accounting Office (1994) found that LEP youth are nearly twice as likely to live in poverty, they often have significant health and emotional needs, and they tend to move in and out of schools more often. Further, the study found that language issues inhibited parental involvement in schools.

The needs of LEP youth are unlikely to be met given current enrollment and staffing trends reflecting declining teacher quality vis-à-vis language minority youth. Consistent with their Southwestern counterparts, TEA (1998) finds enrollments of LEP students in Texas schools far outpace overall enrollment growth. Between the 1997–1998 and 2003–2004 school years, LEP enrollment grew one-third faster than that of overall enrollments. By 2003–2004, over 15% of all students enrolled in Texas public schools were identified as LEP. While the proportion of non-Hispanic white students has fallen below 40%, non-Hispanic white teachers continue to make up over 70% of the state's full-time teaching force (TEA, 2004). A corresponding scarcity of trained and certified teachers combines with a limited knowledge base of how to best educate LEP students (Ruiz de Velasco, 2005; Ruiz de Velasco, Fix, & Clewell, 2000).

Rising enrollments and troublesome staffing patterns emanating from variation among individual schools and districts pose challenges for LEP students. While pockets of excellence no doubt exist, proper identification of the instructional needs of LEP students based on principles of language acquisition varies significantly throughout Texas and the U.S. According to TEA (2002), the availability and quality of special language services varies according to "Official district policies and informal practices, school climate, degree of community involvement, community expectations, and availability and allocation of resources" (p. 21). Unfortunately, the needs of LEP children will continue to be neglected because bilingual education policy "does not lend itself to the majoritarian politics that characterize state legislatures" (McDonnell & Hill, 1993, p. 32). Ostensibly, while LEP youth should benefit from efforts to reduce the performance variation among student groups through performance accountability systems like those instituted in Texas, their exclusion from the system prevents this from occurring. Paradoxically, a pervasive systemic "blind spot" regarding the needs of LEP youth may be juxtaposed to a high-level awareness of their potential to jeopardize the school ratings central to TSA.

TEXAS-STYLE ACCOUNTABILITY

"Texas-style accountability" (TSA; see Valenzuela, 2005) emerged as educational administration (particularly) and public administration (generally) suffered a "crisis of legitimacy" in the 1970s and 1980s (Cibulka, 1997; Foster, 1980). By the late 1990s "performance accountability"—of which TSA is one form—emerged as the dominant state reform model (Cibulka & Derlin, 1998). By design, these systems direct "the flow of fiscal, human, and material resources" to state-defined performance goals (Fuller & Johnson, 2001, p. 280). TEA's performance monitoring includes three main objectives:

- Promote action within and across all sectors of the system that is directed to the tangible outcomes established by the indicators;
- [Provide] parents . . . better information about how their children's schools compare to other schools [so that] they will pressure weak schools to improve; and
- Create conditions that facilitate the use of indicators in planning and decision making so that the data have a direct, rather than an indirect, influence on policy. (TEA, 1996, pp. 8–9)

In order to offer an effective steering system for public education, TSA utilizes publicly available data in an attempt to promote accountability and a good decision-making environment. The problematic "hierarchy of public-ness" in TSA resulting from how TEA manages information and attention is discussed below.

A HIERARCHY OF PUBLIC-NESS IN STATE DATA

An apparent hierarchy of public-ness troubles citizen use of available accountability data. In Orwellian double-speak—and as the case of LEP youth suggests—some data appear to be "more public" than others. Data that are the most readily available to the public tend to be the most consequential to the teachers and administrators in Texas' 1,041 school districts. We argue that the measures that are most public are the school and district ratings, followed closely by the passing rates in reading, writing, and math. These ratings are disaggregated according to school and ethnicity and are the basis of school and district ratings. Newspapers throughout the state routinely report these data, rather than other less prominent, if still open, data that may reveal disparities in performance and opportunities to learn among schools and districts. The public-ness of these data is not solely determined by visibility, but also by positive and negative sanctions accruing to schools, districts and individual children based on them. A drop in a school or district rating may precipitate intense public pressure for change, establishing the intended effect noted above.

School and district ratings are based on a formula combining *base indicators* determined by the students' tested performance in reading, writing, and math and the overall dropout rate (TEA, 2001). Test-related indicators are based on average passing rates for the *accountability subset* of tested students in grades three to eight and ten. To the degree that Texas schools face: 1. high stakes associated with test-dominated performance ratings, 2. uncertainties about effective practices for less typical students, and 3. limited resources to address the different educational needs of these students, organizational cheating through selective inclusion of students in the accountability subset becomes an increasingly attractive strategy (Bohte & Meier, 2000). Given an average passing rate of 15 points below their non-LEP peers (TEA, 2000), TSA creates perverse incentives for school officials to exclude greater numbers of LEP students from the accountability subset. Consistent with this logic, Sloan (2005) found that the LEP students in one district were increasingly viewed as liabilities with a corresponding rise in "deficit thinking" (Valencia, 1997) among teachers as ratings pressures mounted.

In short, information and attention management combined with performance pressures in Texas have dramatic implications for LEP students. We demonstrate below the influence of the hierarchy of public-ness on the exemption debate in the legislature. This illustration conflicts with the rhetoric that all children count. Within the logic of the accountability system itself, *tested* students are more consequential than the *nontested*, shaping the flow of resources at the expense of test-exempt LEP youth. Stated differently, our emerging framework points to the unintended consequence that LEP youth may be further marginalized as schools pursue public recognition for student performance by manipulating their state-defined accountability subset. We turn now to a debate among policy makers regarding the place of LEP youth within that subset.

AN IMPORTANT CAVEAT

Before proceeding, we want to make clear that we are not advocates for a blanket policy of testing all students. Such indiscriminate policies are invalid when linguistic, physiological, or neurological circumstances preclude meaningful interpretation of student scores. Further, we oppose reliance on high-stakes, test-centered performance accountability systems to stimulate reform. Our intent is to hold up for scrutiny one such system against the legitimating, high-sounding claims of many politicians, scholars, and school officials that these systems ensure "all children count." Our inquiry raises troubling questions about the efforts of state education leaders, particularly administrators, to exclude certain student groups perceived to jeopardize school ratings.

THE INCLUSION/EXEMPTION DEBATE IN THE TEXAS LEGISLATURE

The lead author served as a consultant to the Mexican American Legal Defense and Education Fund (MALDEF) during the 77th Legislative Session, primarily on legislation calling for the use of multiple criteria in assessment (i.e., grades in core subjects, teacher recommendation, and so forth, where any of these could compensate for poor test performance). This experience brought her into the circle of policy makers who then called upon her to share her expertise and testify on the state's exemption policy, as well as other legislation. Through this experience, she found herself conducting an ethnography of public policy drawing from informal conversations with several individuals central to this debate: four directors of bilingual education programs in four major Texas districts, one state representative and his chief of staff, as well as the chief of staff of another representative.

In addition, field notes regarding commentaries from key experts have been incorporated into this study. These experts include several individuals from the Intercultural Development Research Association (IDRA), a non-profit Latino advocacy organization in San Antonio, the chief of staff of a senator representing Laredo, a State Board of Education (SBOE) member, and the lead attorney for MALDEF. Analyses of field notes from the 2001 legislative session, conversations with expert witnesses and bill sponsors, transcriptions of Public Education Committee hearings in both the House and Senate Education Committee, and documentary data (Texas statutes, TEA reports, and newspaper coverage during the past session) form the corpus of data for this analysis. Specific attention was paid to commentary in public testimony on the effects of testing on both the children and the educational processes, as well as ways that public officials, policy makers, and advocates addressed test exemptions.

English Language Education Practices in Texas

Immigrant students in Texas have historically been placed within the LEP status category to minimize their impact on school performance ratings by moving them outside the accountability subset. Efforts toward their greater inclusion were, to a large extent, prompted in 1994 with the reauthorization of the federal Title I program. This reauthorization required states to submit plans for including all students into their accountability programs by the 2000–2001 school year.

Along with the federal mandate, abuses of the state's exemption policy of LEP (and Special Education) youth in many districts spawned internal pressure from the State Legislature. State Representative Domingo García from Dallas assumed leadership on this issue. In the 1999 legislative session, García amended Senate Bill 103. That bill—signed into law on June 8, 1999—would go into effect during the 2002–2003 school year. The García amendment, scheduled to go into effect immediately, reduced the schools' latitude to exempt LEP youth for a maximum of 3 years to 1 year only. Pressure on TEA and the SBOE, primarily from predominantly Mexican-origin, South Texas Valley school districts requesting additional time for implementation, yielded a 1-year postponement. The SBOE ruled that this policy would go into effect during the 2000–2001 academic year, which coincided with the 2001 biennial legislative session.

Appalling dropout statistics among Mexican-origin students in the Dallas Independent School District (DISD) motivated García's press for limiting exemptions. In 1999, 18.1% of the entire DISD student population was exempted from the state assessments, a rate three times higher than the state as a whole. Half of these students were LEP students and disproportionately Latino. García noted, "I saw who was dropping out and who was not being tested and I decided to do something about it."

Although his later legislation incorporated a more diagnostic view of that original assessment, García initially construed accountability as primarily a monitoring system along the lines of TSA. García learned that many students had never been tested in elementary school, only to drop out by the time they reached middle school. He felt confident that LEP children needed to be included in the accountability subset in order to receive instructional attention. Making schools accountable by testing the majority of the students, he reasoned, would reduce the dropout rate.

Anticipating enactment of the García amendment, DISD tested the LEP population in 1999–2000, exempting only those in the country for 12 months or less. Inclusion of these previously untested LEP students in DISD's accountability subset resulted in a dramatic increase in "low-performing" schools from 9 in 1998–1999 to 28 in 1999–2000. Early in the 2001 session, Dallas-area superintendents and various state administrator associations lobbied the legislature for revocation of the García amendment in favor of a return to a version of the previous, time-honored, 3-year exemption policy. García believed they saw what happened in Dallas and were afraid that "[their] political and bureaucratic careers were at stake if the 1-year exemption was to remain" (personal communication with A. Valenzuela, July 11, 2001). He also noted that superintendents and school board members mainly testified at the pivotal March 13, 2001 hearing of the dueling proposals before the House Committee on Public Education. "It's all part of the cover-up," he concluded: "This goes back to Edgewood. It's easier to not teach to this population and hide their scores than it is to suggest taking money away from rich districts that do not have any of these kinds of children in them to give to poor districts that do have them."

In sum, historically excluded LEP students were on the verge of near-total inclusion in the accountability subset until a turnabout in the 2001 legislative session.

Competing Legislative Proposals

Three bills heard on March 13, 2001 reflected two variations—more and less inclusive—in the exemption of LEP youth. State Representative Domingo García (Dallas) authored the more inclusive H.B. 2487. Senator Judith Zaffirini (Laredo) sponsored the contrasting S.B. 676, a companion to H.B. 1374 authored by State Representative Ron Oliveira (Brownsville). State Representative Pete Gallego (Uvalde) offered H.B. 1787, largely consistent with the Zaffirini bill. The day prior to the March 13 hearing before the House Committee on Public Education, Zaffirini's Senate bill passed unanimously. Worded identically, S.B. 676 was thus laid out in lieu of H.B. 1374, the Oliveira companion. The success of S.B. 676 thus shifted the balance of forces away from García's more inclusive proposal.

Each proposal departed from the original, 3-year LEP exemption policy administered by the Language Proficiency Assessment Committee (LPAC) that failed to distinguish either recency of migration or nativity. The broadness of the LEP definition meant that many immigrant and U.S.-born students alike were chronically labeled as LEP and were thus never tested. Moreover, many of these students were then neglected or ignored. For example, the director of the bilingual education program in DISD referred to the practice of taking already scarce bilingual teachers out of the bilingual classrooms to help children in the all-English classrooms prepare for the state test.

Notwithstanding the egregious practices that compounded the problem of their low academic performance, this administrator suggested that if these children were failing in later years, at least part of the explanation was attributable to too few opportunities for the children needing bilingual education to take the test. To curb such testing abuse, a narrower definition of the "testable" LEP population, born out of contentious discussion and debate, was adopted—though ambiguities in definition prevailed because of the lack of specificity in the actual language of the Zaffirini/Oliveira bill.

All proposals concurred on a seemingly narrower definition of LEP youth, which held that recent arrivals and "unschooled" immigrants are the categories of youth to whom the exemption policy should appropriately apply. *Unschooled immigrants* was defined as immigrant youth who have received an insufficient educational foundation in their own country to assist their learning of the state curriculum. The primary point of contention (which was eventually ironed out) was whether the conditions of being a recent and an unschooled immigrant were to hold together or whether they could apply separately. Because of an apparent mistrust of the school-level LPAC committee, legislators ended up curtailing the Committee's decision-making latitude by adopting the definition of the unschooled immigrant that already appears in the Texas Administrative Code. According to this definition, both conditions of being immigrant and unschooled must jointly hold.

This redefinition of which categories of LEP youth count for testing purposes suggests greater inclusion, or accountability, of the LEP populations. That is, the U.S.-born population, even if indeed LEP, must now take the state's English or Spanish assessment with no hope for exemption. So must long-term immigrants who have been in the U.S. longer than 3 years. Without an explicit verification procedure on the application of the law, however, it was feared that practices could still distort outcomes. For example, a Texas Federation of Teachers (TFT) lobbyist offered testimony at the March 13 hearing in favor of auditing schools to be sure that only recent immigrants are given the exemption, saying, "I'd be a little bit nervous that we're stepping back and regressing into what we used to have, and that is a lack of accountability."

In response to this continuing concern over potential abuse, Oliveira referred to language in his and Zaffirini's bill requiring the state to report the annual performance change in the percentage of LEP students exempted from the exam. Oliveira's response implied that in the absence of test score data, this information would satisfy the monitoring aspect of accountability. Within an existing hierarchy of public-ness in state data, however, this indicator is less powerful and thus less consequential than outright inclusion of the students in the accountability subset.

The less detailed Gallego bill (H.B. 1787) largely aligned with the Zaffirini bill. Both called for a 3-year maximum exemption of recent immigrants who were LEP as determined by their scores on TEA's newly devised Reading Proficiency Test in English (RPTE). That is, immigrants with 3 or fewer years in the U.S. would be exempt as long as they scored poorly on the RPTE and were, thus, not proficient in English.

The RPTE is a reading test that contains test items in English mirroring the state assessments. The RPTE was developed after the 76th legislature (1999) mandated TEA to fully incorporate LEP youth into the accountability system. Beginning in the 2000–2001 school year, the TEA implemented the RPTE to assess student readiness for the state assessment in English (it was field-tested in 1999–2000). The test is administered to all LEP students in grades 3–12 regardless of whether they are in bilingual or ESL classes. Students scoring at the advanced level of proficiency are deemed ready to be tested in English thereafter.

The Zaffirini proposal called for an automatic, 1-year exemption for recent immigrants if the student is LEP. The child could also receive up to 2 years of additional exemptions if: 1. the student had already received the 1-year exemption and was a recent, unschooled immigrant, or 2. if the student was in a grade with no assessment in the students' primary language.

Prior to the Zaffirini bill, the SBOE fully established the RPTE as a performance indicator within the Academic Excellence Indicator System (AEIS) system. It therefore doubles as a basis for determining exemptions from state assessments and as a performance indicator itself. As a performance indicator, it purports to measure the progress toward English language acquisition; however, the population taking the test changes from year to year, making it a dubious measure of performance or progress. Given these limitations, the García proposal to use the actual state assessment in either English or Spanish promised a more meaningful annual measure of progress.

The García bill required immigrant students to take the actual state test in their second year of U.S. residency pursuant to a 1-year postponement. The test would be taken in the language of instruction—depending on the judgment of the LPAC—but the scores would be exempted from the rating system. The test would therefore serve only a diagnostic purpose. Additional research evidence indicating that multiple attempts improved test performance convinced García that LEP students would benefit from inclusion in testing in the second year, but their scores would be excluded from the rating system until the third under his system.

All three bills were left pending after the March 13 hearing. A persistent issue that day was defining "recent, unschooled immigrant" due to the concern that ambiguity would lead to continued abuses in the law. By March 27, the issue was resolved. Zaffirini amended her bill to include the SBOE's dual definition. With this resolved, the bill passed quickly through both houses and was signed into law on April 11, 2001, in time to preempt the previously scheduled mass testing of immigrant, LEP youth called for in the original García proposal.

Actors in the Policy Debate

Administrator and teacher associations, civil rights groups, and Mexican-American advocacy organizations were the primary actors in the policy debate that played out in both legislators' offices and in the pivotal March

13 Committee on Public Education hearing. The teacher organizations included the Texas Association for Bilingual Education (TABE), the Bilingual ESL Association of the Metroplex (BEAM) representing bilingual and ESL teachers in 25 Dallas and Fort Worth school districts, and the Texas Federation of Teachers (TFT). Superintendents represented various districts throughout Texas (especially from the Dallas and Brownsville areas). The South Texas Association of Schools (STAS), Harlingen Consolidated ISD, and Lyford Consolidated ISD represented the Rio Grande Valley. The Texas Association of School Boards (TASB), a nonprofit, statewide educational association representing school districts in the legislature, and the Texas Association of School Administrators (TASA) also testified.

Advocacy organizations consisted of MALDEF (with whom the lead author consulted as an expert witness) and IDRA, a nonprofit, education advocacy organization for Texas' Mexican-American community (GI Forum Image De Tejas v. Texas Education Agency, 87 F. Supp 667, W.D. Tex. 2000). Indeed, the state's Mexican-American educational leadership (primarily from the Dallas and Brownsville areas) largely conducted the public debate. TEA participated less overtly, favoring the Zaffirini/Oliveira proposal.

The Substance of the Policy Debate: Differing Meanings of Accountability

The debate centered as much around differences between, as well as aspects within, the several legislative proposals. Concerns involved the maximum time LEP children should be exempted from testing and the means to ensure accountability when they are excluded, as well as the need to narrow the definition of LEP youth for testing purposes.

Although working at cross-purposes, two distinct meanings of accountability surfaced in this discussion. One referred to pedagogically valid uses of the state assessment. The other referred to its monitoring function. The conflation of these resulted in a perceived trade-off. The favored Zaffirini proposal would sacrifice monitoring power for pedagogical soundness. Given the undue influence of the administrators on the outcome, however, and the extent to which they benefited from this alleged "sacrifice" in monitoring, pedagogical clarity and administrative largesse were perhaps most motivated by status-driven concerns connected to school ratings.

The hierarchy of public-ness entered into the debate in three ways. First, reporting the percentage of LEP students exempted from testing from 1 year to the next was proposed in order to assure monitoring. Reporting exemption percentages in data that are merely "open" to the public is hardly as powerful as either an explicit verification process or as an integral measure within the most "public" and consequential data connected to school ratings, however. That is, relegated to a lower position in the hierarchy, these data are less likely to capture the public's attention and thus less likely to provoke public pressure.

Second, the notion that the RPTE is a performance indicator akin to the state test scores was a stretch. As an available—but lower-status—indicator, the RPTE simultaneously served to obscure LEP student achievement as measured by the rating determining state assessments while responding to the demands of both governmental edicts and special interest calls for greater inclusion in the state accountability system. A lack of transparency in performance indicators limits their public use (and runs counter to the state's accountability rhetoric).

Third, and as embodied in the García proposal, allowing LEP youth an opportunity to take the state assessments without including their scores into the accountability subset was dismissed by TEA representatives as problematic because it did not make sense to administer the test and not "make it count." Their concern would seem to be addressed in the language of the bill analysis itself. That is, this test would be used for diagnostic purposes and to give children practice taking the exam. Interestingly, TEA did not explain their opposition to the García bill using either a pedagogical or a monitoring definition of accountability. For example, they could have offered a pedagogical explanation regarding the merits of the RPTE over the state assessment.

From a hierarchy of public-ness perspective, the state's concern became clear. The García proposal would have resulted in available test-score data that could be made fully public and thus become consequential. For instance, these scores might be used to direct attention to a performance gap for LEP students and thus underpin an argument to direct action and channel resources to closing that gap. Because the consequentiality of these data was imminent, a separate accountability subset apart from the primary one for the state was deemed nonsensical.

The explanation for this lack of agreement on the diagnostic potential of the test reflects not only how accountability is more a testing than an assessment system, but more importantly, about how open data could expose deficiencies, garner public attention, and give rise to new demands. García provided one interpretation of TEA's position:

> They wanted to continue the cover-up regarding the true [state assessment] scores. They don't want to be held accountable to their scores. So this was a disingenuous way to hide the problem. It's just like what they've [TEA] done with the dropout rate. Rather than address the true dropout problem, they play with the definition of who's a dropout.

In addition to the lack of monitoring accountability and the definitional problems associated with the unschooled immigrant language in the Zaffirini/Oliveira bill, much of the testimony given at the March 13 hearing reflected the positions of the teacher and administrator organizations. The former accorded emphasis to pedagogical concerns and conditions under which testing LEP youth is appropriate. They noted, for example, the inadequacies in the services and human resources that certain districts are able to provide due to a lack of bilingual teachers. The latter referred to the trauma incurred on recently arrived, under-schooled immigrant children confronting an opprobrious testing situation.

The BEAM group from the Dallas-Fort Worth area did not agree with García's original legislation or the newer version. Indeed, their mobilization sparked a great deal of the impetus for change toward a more exclusionary testing policy. While they understood well the abuses that García was attempting to curtail, this group nevertheless felt compelled to support the Zaffirini proposal because of their experience with great resource disparities. On the subject of resources, the DISD bilingual education director cited earlier offered the following:

> There are not enough teachers for pre-K–3 [pre-Kindergarten through third grade]. There are 18 fourth- through sixth-grade bilingual education teachers in the entire district! We're having to ask them to teach the younger grades because we are getting them [LEP students] in such huge numbers. We're piloting newcomer schools right now, schools that will specifically serve the LEP population.

> We're not where Houston ISD is right now. We don't have the personnel, the resources that they have. HISD gives stipends for bilingual and ESL teachers. We only do so for bilingual teachers and we're in such a desperate situation that we're moving these elementary teachers to teach pre-K–3. Houston, on the other hand, has a bilingual program that goes through to the fifth grade. And I applaud them for that. The hard cold reality for us here is that we're not there yet.

The fate of LEP children in the Dallas area, with its more limited history of leadership and program development in bilingual education, is apparently more circumscribed than it is in other areas of the state. Including the Dallas LEP students into the accountability system would have thus been to their detriment as the DISD would be in jeopardy of losing already too scarce resources.

The TASB and the Valley superintendents raised concerns emphasizing the traumatic effects of testing in a language that the children do not command. To make this point, one Anglo Dallas-area superintendent representing TASB and TASA referred the Public Education Committee members to a page from a state test translated into Greek. When the superintendent attempted to demonstrate just how traumatic such a test would be for an American eighth grader who had lived in Greece for less than a year but was required to take the test in Greek, all the representatives laughed. Valley superintendents corroborated his point, including an administrator from Harlingen ISD in south Texas, who referred to the trauma that LEP students experience when taking a test in a foreign language. Another superintendent representing the South Texas Association of Schools similarly spoke up in favor of the Zaffirini bill, referring to his own loss of self-esteem as a child when subjected to tests that he could not pass.

In a subsequent conversation with Representative García, he took issue with the superintendent's position:

> Those who testified were suggesting that the children were being traumatized by having to take the [state exams] in English. How much more traumatized can you get than a 70% dropout rate? Brownsville has the largest dropout rate than any school district in Texas!

A spokesperson for the Intercultural Development Research Association (IDRA) supported García's bill, saying that either the RPTE or the state assessment could legitimately be offered in the second year. She further expressed concern over "the danger of [districts] exempting students, playing with the labels and categories so that students can maintain the exemption." She emphasized the importance of multiple criteria in lieu of a single indicator for high-stakes decisions on students' behalf, especially decisions on retention, promotion, and graduation.

Woven throughout the teacher representative testimonies was recognition that the practice of exempting large numbers of LEP youth was widely known to serve the purpose of raising passing rates and school ratings. For example, a TABE spokesperson proposed that testing instruments in various languages be made available for greater inclusion of LEP youth in the accountability system. The DISD's director of bilingual education said:

> We exempted tons of LEP students in our state [prior to the one-year exemption]. Out of 55,000 LEP Students, there was a huge pocket— between one third and one fourth—that we didn't test. When you don't test kids, they're not a front-burner issue. Once the children were tested, principals started paying attention, providing tutoring to the children.

This same individual earlier argued that the state should not test LEP children too soon, which attests to the dual operant meaning of accountability.

When asked whether this "attention" consisted of a quality educational experience, the director responded, "Testing policies are what's driving our instruction. There's no making any bones about that!" While sympathetic to a concern Valenzuela raised regarding excessive teaching to the test that could result from with greater inclusion, the director suggested that to deny testing opportunities in the current accountability context is to prepare LEP youth poorly for the future. She further suggested that, minimally, students need multiple opportunities to take the state tests so that they can get the same practice that other students get. Moreover, to test them alongside other students is to treat them equitably (see Black & Valenzuela, 2004 for more details regarding this call for "equal access to mandated testing" in their examination of public policy development for LEP children in Texas).

García's analysis of the introduced version of his bill (H.B. 2787) mirrored these equity concerns: "In the past, some school districts have placed LEP students in special education courses so that they would not have to take the [state] test." A document circulated by his office, "Possible Revisions to S.B. 103 (76th Texas Legislature–1999)," asserted, "Under the old 3-year waiver rule, LEP children were treated as second-class kids who were not tested and who fell into a black education 'neverland.'"

Representative García echoed the bilingual education director's views that children need more practice. His approach would have served a diagnostic function. Moreover, schools would have more complete information, relative to the RPTE, on which areas to target for improvement. In essence, García felt that greater accountability in terms of both better pedagogy and monitoring could be ensured without LEP children suffering the consequences that accrue to lower test performance.

Although García's bill explicitly excluded the scores of LEP youth from the school and district rating system, this less-public, yet open information, could still have been exposed by an inquisitive citizen, researcher, or newspaper reporter. Particularly in instances showing school and district ratings discrepant with LEP test results, public exposure of this information could have called the integrity of the entire system into question. The deeper meaning here is that to construct an accountability subset with LEP test-score information that stands apart from the primary accountability data is to risk its credibility. The only remaining option, therefore, was to predetermine which children's scores would count.

This latter interpretation becomes transparent in an exchange that occurred in the March 13 hearing between State Representative Rene Oliveira and Rene Lara, the TFT lobbyist. The focus was a TFT concern about potential abuses of the exemption process. Specifically, Lara was concerned that no loopholes exist that would allow exemptions of ineligible students. The following exchange reveals the hierarchy of public-ness and the consequences that are subsequently attached to them:

Rep. Oliveira: You are aware that the percentage change in what you report is a performance indicator. So that operates as a disincentive for a district to wholesale these kids into LEP status . . .

Lara: Um, representative, we are supportive of that but I, I think that what is most important especially in the accountability system is the designation of whether a school district or a school campus is rated low performing. And I think that that is the most public, uh, accountability or rating and certainly anything that relates to that accountability rating takes priority over any other type of reporting procedure.

Rep. Oliveira: This is not just a reporting procedure. It becomes a performance indicator. It's part of the grade. It's part of the data you review to grade the schools or the district. That is in this bill.

Since the test scores that inform school ratings "take priority," then the existence of additional test data on unschooled, immigrant LEP youth under an open system of accountability would have risked making the results fully public and thus consequential.

CONCLUSIONS

Though this battle in the legislature took place mostly between Mexican-American officials and state educational leaders in 2001, the debate on the exemption policy took place within the conceptual rubric of the accountability system itself. It occurred on preestablished terms as part of a history of educational policy development in Texas and in the nation that dates back to the early 1980s in Texas (see McNeil, 2000). Just as the political agendas of the school superintendents were driven by their need to preserve their ratings—accomplished to some degree by excluding LEP students from the accountability system—so, too, is the discourse of possibility for Latinos within education framed by subordinating their needs to bureaucratic exigencies.

Submerged in this debate was discussion on how testing and accountability work in tandem as agents of "subtractive cultural assimilation" that, in ironic fashion, compromises the very achievement that both sides seek. Subtractive cultural assimilation refers to a schooling process that divests youth of their culture and language in an assimilationist fashion (Valenzuela, 1999). Rather than promoting bilingualism and biliteracy, most U.S. schooling subtracts children's bilingual and bicultural competencies. The blanket administering of the RPTE to immigrant, under-schooled youth in grades three through six supports this claim of subtractive cultural assimilation. It violates research-based understandings regarding assessment. According to one district administrator in the Houston ISD:

I don't agree with testing the children annually with the RPTE because this is testing them in a language that is not the language of instruction. This is inappropriate. Principals—even the Spanish ones—are doing away with their bilingual education programs because you're looking at the RPTE that the kids have to take at the end of the year and it is in English.

In addition, the 3-year exemption policy is illogical when language minority youth require 5 to 7 years to acquire native-like English proficiency (Thomas and Collier, 1997). The framing of the issue in the legislature squelched discussion of a more appropriate policy in light of this research. The suggested alternative—a multiple-criteria system meeting the demands of both the pedagogical and monitoring aspects of accountability—also failed to resonate as an option (Valenzuela, 2002).

Defending the monitoring dimension of TSA, Scheurich and Skrla (2001) marshal civil rights rhetoric to hail the "top-down" framework that "just like the top-down civil rights laws and Title IX, has pushed and forced schools, districts, administrators, teachers, and community leaders to attend more strongly to the educational needs of children of color" (p. 325). Their analysis does not attend to the perverse incentives to exclude test-challenged students like LEP youth from the most public aspects of the accountability system, however. The legislative debate reveals a priori manipulation of the accountability subset relegating entire segments of test-challenged, LEP youth to nontested categories—and thereby to second-class status—that undercuts rhetoric that no child is to be left behind. More insidiously, the nonuniform, nonuniversalistic imposition of TSA suggests preferred categories (i.e., tested) may be enforced and policed to preserve the legitimacy of the accountability system itself.

Analogizing the development and implementation of accountability systems to civil rights legislation is only appropriate if the demand for higher achievement—like the demand for the integration of public lunch counters, jobs, and schools—were issued to those who control the resources, namely, higher-level administrators. Inasmuch as tests measure higher achievement, it cannot simply be commanded into existence by teachers who possess no control over the very resources that determine the outcomes (Dye, 2002). Likewise, integration was demanded not of the employees or the patrons, but of the bosses in control of the resources.

In theory, the state's performance monitoring system provides the public with the tools they need to "promote action," enable school comparisons, and pressure weak schools to improve. The legislative account suggests something different. That is, school and district ratings are consequential not because they are public but because they are more public in a hierarchy of public-ness as established by education policy. Within this hierarchical public policy space, LEP youth can at once "count" and "not count." Limited English Proficient youth count to the extent that they are included in the AEIS generally, but do not count to the extent that they are excluded from the most public of test score data—primarily through their historic over-representation in the exempted status category. Moreover, the case of LEP youth clearly demonstrates their differential opportunities to learn the state curriculum due to widespread differences in resources, including access to bilingual programs and bilingually certified teachers. The reporting of data in the AEIS does not in itself create the conditions for reforms that are more attuned to students' needs.

We reiterate that our aim here is not to suggest that all LEP youth should be tested. Rather we seek to use this case to show how levels of public-ness are conveniently manipulated to make some children count more than others. We do not deny the possibility that changes made during the 2001 legislative session may result in much greater inclusion and hence, accountability, than has been the case historically for LEP youth. Such an outcome would still hardly negate the larger issue that surfaces in this account, namely, the ability of those in power to "game" the system as well as the inability of those who lack power to re-frame the debate in more culturally- and assessment-relevant terms, at least for the present.

REFERENCES

Black, W. R., & Valenzuela, A. (2004). Educational accountability for English language learners in Texas: A retreat from equity. In L. Skrla, & J. J. Scheurich (Eds.), *Educational equity and accountability: Paradigms, policies and politics* (pp. 215–234). New York: Routledge Falmer.

Bohte, J., & Meier, K. (2000). Goal displacement: Assessing the motivation for organizational cheating. *Public Administration Review, 60*, 173–182.

Cibulka, J. (1997). Two eras of urban schooling: The decline of the old order and the emergence of new organizational forms. *Education and Urban Society, 29*(3), 317–341.

Cibulka, J., & Derlin, R. (1998). Accountability policy adoption to policy sustainability: Reforms and systemic initiatives in Colorado and Maryland. *Education and Urban Society, 30*(4), 502–515.

Dye, J. (2002). *A natural yet overlooked feature of accountability in public education: Accountability is supposed to go both ways.* Unpublished manuscript. University of Rochester, New York.

Foster, W. P. (1980). Administration and the crisis in legitimacy: A review of habermasian thought. *Harvard Educational Review, 50*(6), 496–505.

Fuller, E. J., & Johnson, J. F. (2001). Can state accountability systems drive improvements in school performance for children of color and children from low-income homes? *Education and Urban Society, 33*(3), 260–283.

General Accounting Office. (1994). *Limited English proficiency: A growing and costly educational challenge facing many School Districts* (No. HEHS-94-38). Washington, DC: Government Printing Office.

Laswell, H. (1936). *Politics: Who gets what, when and how.* New York: McGraw Hill.

McDonnell, L. M., & Hill, P. T. (1993). *Newcomers in American schools: Meeting the educational needs of immigrant youth.* Santa Monica: Rand Corporation.

McNeil, L. M. (2000). *Contradictions of school reform: Educational costs of standardized testing.* New York: Routledge.

Ruiz de Velasco, J. (2005). Performance-based school reforms and the federal role in helping schools that serve language-minority students. In A. Valenzuela (Ed.), *Leaving children behind: How Texas-style accountability fails Latino youth.* Albany, NY: SUNY Press.

Ruiz de Velasco, J., Fix, M., & Clewell, B. C. (2000). *Overlooked and underserved: Immigrant students in U.S. secondary schools.* Washington, DC: The Urban Institute.

Scheurich, J. J., & Skrla, L. (2001). Continuing the conversation on equity and accountability: Listening appreciatively, responding responsibly. *Phi Delta Kappan, 83*(4), 322–326.

Sloan, K. (2005). Playing to the logic of the Texas accountability system: How focusing on "ratings"—not children—undermines quality and equity. In A. Valenzuela (Ed.), *Leaving children behind: How Texas-style accountability fails Latino youth* (pp. 153–178). Albany, NY: SUNY Press.

Texas Education Agency (TEA). (1996). *The development of accountability systems nationwide and in Texas* (Statewide Texas educational progress study no. 1). Austin, TX: Author.

(TEA). (1998). *Academic achievement of elementary students with limited English proficiency in Texas public schools* (Policy research report no. 10 [Document no. GE8 600 03]). Austin, TX: Author.

(TEA). (2000). *Study of possible expansion of the assessment system for limited English proficient students: A report to the 77th Texas Legislature from the Texas education agency.* Austin, TX: Author.

(TEA). (2001). *2001 Accountability manual: The 2001 accountability rating system for Texas public schools and school districts and blueprint for the 2002 through 2005 accountability.* Austin, TX: Author.

(TEA). (2002). *Program participation and academic progress of second language learners: Texas middle school update* (Policy Research Report No. 15 [Document no. GE02 600 01]). Austin, TX: Author.

(TEA). (2004). Academic excellence indicator system: 2003–2004 state performance report. Austin, TX: Author.

Thomas, W. P., & Collier, V. P. (1997). *School effectiveness for language minority students.* Washington, DC: Educational Resources Information Center.

Valencia, R. R. (1997). *The evolution of deficit thinking: Educational thought and practice* (Vol. 19). Washington, DC: Falmer Press.

Valenzuela, A. (1999). *Subtractive schooling: U.S. Mexican youth and the politics of caring.* Albany, NY: SUNY Press.

Valenzuela, A. (2002). High-stakes testing and U.S.-Mexican youth in Texas: The case for multiple compensatory criteria in assessment. *Harvard Journal of Hispanic Policy, 14,* 97–116.

Valenzuela, A. (Ed.). (2005). *Leaving Children Behind: How Texas-style Accountability fails Latino youth.* Albany, NY: SUNY Press.

Varian, H. (1995). The information economy. *Scientific American, 273*(3), 200–202.

CHAPTER 2

Texas Accountability Tests:
Standardizing Civic Disengagement for Latinos?

Kathleen Staudt

The eyes of the nation have been focused on Texas and its now more than decade-old, high-stakes accountability testing system. Once touted as a model program, it was signed into law nationally in 2002 under nomenclature that some consider misleading: No Child Left Behind. Standardized testing regimes now dominate education in the United States, but the system's critics see a need for more extensive national standards and testing (Ravitch, 1995, 2010) as well as for multiple assessment methods (Kohn, 2000; Valenzuela, 2005). School districts have invested extensive resources in test preparation, the tests themselves, and the public visibility of test results. For example, the Texas Education Agency (TEA) posts data regarding campus, district, region, and state tests results for content area, grade level, test language (Spanish and English), English proficiency, and student demographics (ethnicity, gender, and economic disadvantage) on its Web site.

A flourishing democracy depends on the consent and participation of the governed, whatever their gender, ethnicity, or income. Are Latinos and Latinas participating fully in U.S. democracy? What bearing might social studies education have on that participation? I assume that the connections between youth civic education and political participation are strong, although many intervening variables influence the strength of those relationships. Early political socialization research, focused on how children learn about politics, also made such assumptions, but only a few longitudinal studies among youth activists support this connection.

This chapter discusses a study that analyzed the civic knowledge of Latino and Latina students as measured in state accountability and national civics testing instruments, to assess the instruments themselves, and to examine nuanced atmosphere-specific and leadership differences on school campuses. To do so, I analyzed the test questions, the test results, the campus climates, and the students' attitudes in three Texas middle schools located in El Paso's Ysleta Independent School District (YISD) on the U.S.-Mexico border. This chapter contends that the tests and the way state tests drive the curriculum and instructional strategies increase the emphasis on rote memorization and undermine the potential for civic engagement among Latino and Latina students. As such, social studies testing in Texas will not likely reduce participation gaps between Latino and Anglo (non-Hispanic white) adults, thereby failing to increase the diversity of voices in U.S. democracy.

PARTICIPATION:
WHAT ROLE FOR CIVIC AND SOCIAL STUDIES?

United States society exhibits wide variations in voter turnout and civic capacity, altering the odds of experiencing the breadth and depth of democracy for different individuals. Over many years, studies in political science have documented the connections between socioeconomic status and political participation; higher levels of income and especially education are directly connected to higher participation rates. Not surprisingly, political participation gaps between Latino and non-Latino populations are partly explained by socioeconomic status (SES). Using the Latino National Political Survey (LNPS), Montoya (2002) compared political activity by income and ethnicity. While Anglos scored 1.5 out of a possible eight political acts, (such as contacting an official, signing a petition, attending a public meeting and/or rallies, campaigning, among others), all Latinos (citizens and noncitizens) scored 0.9, and Latino citizens scored 1.2. In the category of Latino income earners above $75,000, (i.e., higher SES), the gap was smaller (1.9 v. 2.1) but still reflected limited participation. Montoya's analysis, however, showed that organizational membership could compensate for low SES, contributing to higher participation rates for lower-income populations and thus minimizing the usual high SES advantage. Findings like these lead to the question of whether schools build social capital, skills and strengthened capacity for organizational participation.

Our schools can encourage civic capacity through education and exposure to various organizational and institutional means of participation. While "civic education" does not exist per se in Texas (Tolo, 1999), social studies standards are taught and tested in eighth grade through the TAAS (Texas Assessment of Academic Skills) accountability tests, based on Texas Essential Knowledge and Skills (TEKS) curriculum, which established learning expectations by grade level and by content area. The TAAS social studies multiple-choice tests focus on facts and details from the 28 pages of middle-school TEKS standards found on the TEA Web site (in 2003, after this study had been completed, the Texas Assessment of

Knowledge and Skills [TAKS] replaced the TAAS and in 2011, the STAAR [State of Texas Academic Assessment of Readiness] end-of-course examinations will be put into place for grades 7 and up).

Civic education involves a combination of knowledge, skills, motivation, and practice (Hochschild & Scovronick, 2003; Macedo, Assenshoh, Berry, Brintnall, Campbell, Fraga, & Fung, 2005; NAEP, 1999). Civic education is not the same as social studies education, though overlap could occur, depending on teaching methods and assessments. Social studies standardized test regimes emphasize the memorization of decontextualized facts and dates. In Texas, knowledge transfer mostly involves mainstream Anglo history rather than border or Mexican/Mexican-American history (Noboa, 2006). While all students should be expected to acquire knowledge pertaining to mainstream history and government, local and nonmainstream history should not be ignored. The public must understand who prepares the test questions and why. In 2010, the 15-member Texas State Board of Education (SBOE) stirred national controversy when its conservative majority sought to reduce "liberal bias" in the TEKS. For example, the SBOE diminished emphasis on Thomas Jefferson (for his remarks on separating church and state) and on Dolores Huerta (for being a socialist, although she and César Chávez built the United Farm Workers organization). The Center for History Teaching & Learning hosts TEKS Watch (http://tekswatch.utep.edu) to keep the community informed about the process, the proposed changes, and the national media reporting on testing procedures in Texas. As such, Texas social studies education addresses a limited version of knowledge—one of the four measured factors of civic education—while neglecting the motivation, skills, and practice criteria.

Service-learning, involving active experience and reflection, addresses skills, motivation, and practice. The service-learning instructional strategy connects students with real community issues and incorporates writing, reflection, critical thinking, and discussion. Teachers who attempt to enrich the learning process by incorporating other material risk low test scores—despite the potential advantage of long-term, in-depth learning about their own communities that the students co-construct themselves, remember as experience, and become skills in their everyday lives. And in high-stakes standardized test regimes, teachers often resort to teaching to the test, because the risks of test failure involve penalties for both students' and teachers' evaluations.

EDUCATIONAL REFORM EFFORTS IN TEXAS

Texas educational reform began in earnest in the 1980s, resulting in changes regarding teacher certification, "no-pass, no-play" rules for student athletes, and a standardized testing system that evolved into the TAAS test in the early 1990s (Shirley, 1997, pp. 53–56). The first TAAS test produced dismal results statewide and showed glaring achievement gaps between ethnic, language, and economic groups. Latinos and African-American students had lower passing rates than white students, and economically disadvantaged students failed more often than their wealthier peers. Along the U.S.-Mexico border, with its majority Latino population, scores lagged but gradually improved over the years as the accountability system allowed educators "no more excuses" for low achievement and as educators learned and taught ways to prepare for the test. *All* students were expected to pass, and when they did not, teachers, principals, and superintendents shared responsibility in a high-stakes system that penalized all participants with low evaluations.

At the same time, Texas funding formulas also underwent a dramatic change in an educational finance system once overly dependent on local property taxes, burdening property-poor districts (Rocha & Webking, 1993). The combination of accountability testing and more equitable funding narrowed, but did not eliminate, TAAS test gaps between border and nonborder residents (Sharp, 1998). The rapid rise in test scores was unmatched, even counter-indicated, in SAT/ACT scores.

THE STANDARDIZED TESTING CONTROVERSY

The widespread adoption of standardized tests has been a contentious political choice with implications for a wide range of educational issues including civic education. Proponents seek to raise academic expectations through establishing standards of knowledge and then measuring the extent to which students understand those standards. With millions of students to assess, the testing instrument has tended to consist of machine-graded multiple-choice questions. Opponents challenge the standardization of students, education, teaching methods, and outcome measurement. Few researchers have examined assessments in social studies and civics for their connection with declining social capital and civic disengagement in U.S. society, as I do in this chapter with a nuanced comparison of three middle schools.

The rise of standardized testing is coupled with the decline of social capital. *Social capital*, defined as *relationships of trust to accomplish public goals*, is built when people know and trust one another well enough to work toward agreed-upon solutions, such as getting local government to build a park, and/or policy change. The decline of social capital is associated with many changes in U.S. society, including parents' full-time work (reducing volunteer time) and preoccupation with television and computer entertainment. Social scientists like Bellah, Madsen, Sullivan, Swidler, and Tipton (1985), Bellah, Madsen, Tipton, and Sullivan (1992), and especially Robert Putnam (2000) worry about the rise of radical individualism (by which they refer to the extreme focus on self and autonomy, as opposed to community or a balance between individual and community [Bellah et al., 1985]) and the decline of both voter turnout and organizational participation in neighborhood groups, Parent Teacher Associations, and other civic organizations. Relationships of trust, especially organized relations, can build and reflect civic capacity. In *Democracy at Risk*, Macedo et al. (2005) analyzed U.S. political structures and electoral institutions. Although they mention schools only in passing, they call attention to how "place matters" and the importance of nonprofit organizations and local civic engagement, for in U.S. politics, 96% of elected officials serve at the local level (Macedo et al., 2005). And of course, the U.S. constitution delegates many publicly-funded activities that affect people's everyday lives to state and local government, including schools and public safety among others.

Required State Tests v. National Voluntary Tests

By the late 1990s, some parents and teachers grew weary of the ways in which the testing system drove the curriculum and classroom experiences. Except for the written exams in grades 4, 8, and 10, most TAAS tests are multiple-choice exams. The best of multiple-choice exams can tap higher-order thinking and reasoning skills, but a review of sample TAAS questions suggests that they prioritize 1. lower-order skills amenable to drill and memorization, and 2. complex English vocabulary that taps language sophistication more than social studies. "Multiple choice" may be a misnomer for what are multiple-guess questions. As teachers warn students in preparation workshops, two of four responses are obviously incorrect; context clues can then help students guess between the remaining choices.

Unlike state tests, such as the TAAS and TAKS in Texas, the federal government offers voluntary tests with multiple-choice AND short-answer questions. The National Assessment of Educational Progress (NAEP) produces a Civics Report Card each decade. NAEP defines and measures civic education in three parts: knowledge, skills, and motivation.

The *1998 Civics Report Card* (NAEP, 1999) documents alarming civic education test results at the 4th, 8th, and 12th grade levels: one-third of the students score below the basic level and only one-fifth score at the advanced and proficient levels. The gap between Latino and white students is large, comparable to gaps between economically disadvantaged and advantaged students. Unfortunately, flaws in the presentation of NAEP data confound interpretation and findings. For example, the NAEP civics test is administered only in English, and the "minority" group and economically disadvantaged groups overlap (i.e., the NAEP monograph does not control for these issues). In addition, experience and practice are missing from the NAEP's three-part definition of civic education. Although difficult to measure and test, these elements may explain participation gaps in adulthood, given the importance of organizational memberships. Participation gaps during adulthood draw, in part, on roots planted during children's school years.

Illustrations: TAAS v. NAEP questions

Consider examples of the fact and detail orientation of the different testing instruments discussed above: the state TAAS and the national NAEP. The TAAS expects students to demonstrate a high level of knowledge in history. One TEKS social studies standard states, "The student understands traditional historical points of reference in U.S. history through 1877" including "the significance of the following dates: 1607, 1776, 1787, 1803, and 1861–1865" (TEA, 2004, p. 12) implying that one correct event for each date serves to prove proficiency. In the civics section of the TEKS, students are expected to learn about patriotism (including to the state of Texas to which students must pledge allegiance since the 2001 legislature passed such a law), functioning in a free enterprise system, and appreciating the values of Texas and the nation.

Some questions seek "right" answers for complex processes and thereby distort knowledge. For example, political scientists might answer "none of the above," if it were an option, for the following question (Staudt, 2001, p. 53, downloaded from question lists in the TEA Web site):

> In the Declaration of Independence the phrase "all men are created equal" means that:
>   a. Slavery should be abolished.
>   b. Men have more rights than women or children.
>   c. All people have the same talents and abilities.
>   d. Everyone should be treated equally according to the law.

Compared with the TAAS, the NAEP test, reported in the 1998 *Civics Report Card* (NAEP, 1999), offers several redeeming features. Forty percent of NAEP's questions require short responses, and questions are carefully developed from the basic, proficient, and advanced standards. State standards do not necessarily coincide with the implied national standards in the NAEP, which pays more attention to cabinet departments, comparative government, and international issues. Ravitch (1995) discusses the folly of inconsistent state (all 50 of them) standards in social studies, math, and language arts.

One drawback of NAEP questions involves potentially over-complex questions and the potential for linguistic racism. NAEP's 1998 *Civics Report Card*, which reported dismal findings for Latino students, did not disaggregate students on the basis of English proficiency. For eighth-grade

LEP students, questions like the one below would prove to be extremely challenging:

> When two [people] come into [the Supreme] Court, one may say: "an act of Congress means this." The other may say it means the opposite. We [the Court] then say it means one of the two or something else in between. In that way we are making the law, aren't we?" (Earl Warren, Chief Justice of the Supreme Court)

> Some people are troubled by the role of the Court described by Chief Justice Warren. Which argument could they effectively use against it? (This question is followed with four answer options.)

Constant Testing

Multiple benchmark and actual tests frame the school year and students' lifetimes, taking considerable time away from teaching. TAAS tests begin in the third grade, but first and second graders are exposed to what teachers call "baby TAAS" tests to prepare students. Elementary and middle school students take the tests in April, although preparation begins in earnest much earlier. In fall, students sit for a "mock TAAS" in order to identify those likely to fail, who then receive special tutoring with TAAS booklets before the April exam. In classrooms, teachers weave together their study of old TAAS questions and link them to the TEKS to anticipate and prepare for the annual round of tests.

Student Success: Examining Pathways to College

Students' performance in many subjects is affected by many factors in their homes and communities. Research over the last two decades shows that parental engagement and spiritual networks provide support for student learning (Sanders, 1998; Zellman & Waterman, 1998). In Texas, Shirley (1997) showed a positive relationship between parental engagement and TAAS scores in comparative case analyses of Alliance Schools, organized by the faith-based social justice parental engagement strategies of organizations affiliated with the Industrial Areas Foundation (IAF). Technology has also been promoted as a way to provide hands-on learning so that students help construct and retain knowledge. The NAEP civic scores, in fact, show improvement with the occasional and routine use of technology in the classroom, although the amount of improvement is not striking. Finally, experiential and service learning offer the opportunity for students to experience and to construct knowledge in social and meaningful ways, as discussed earlier. Although service-learning workshops and grant opportunities exist in Texas schools, only one among 200 sample TAAS questions that teachers used in classroom planning mentions service learning (see Rippberger & Staudt, 2003).

CASE STUDY: EL PASO

El Paso is home to nearly 800,000 people; the 80% of census-defined Hispanics generally call themselves Mexican American. El Paso's per capita income, 102% of national per capita income in 1950, dropped to 59% by 1990 (Staudt, 1998), remaining constant through the 2000 census. In 1999 dollars, El Paso's median per capita income was $13,421, compared with $19,617 for Texas as a whole and $21,587 nationally (2000 Census, cited in Romero & Yellen, 2004).

Civic capacity in El Paso has been relatively weak over its lengthy history, for many reasons outlined elsewhere (Staudt & Coronado, 2002; Staudt & Stone, 2007). Although a series of registration campaigns in the 1980s added more voters to the rolls, turnout is low: 15% in the 2005 local government elections, 1% in some school board elections, and approximately 35% in state and national elections. El Paso's largest community-based organization, known as the El Paso Inter-religious Sponsoring Organization (EPISO), is affiliated with the Texas Industrial Areas Foundation (IAF), the second oldest such group in the state. Only in the 1970s did the political establishment change from an exclusively wealthy, Anglo, male system to include Mexican-American and female representatives.

As in other places, El Paso's middle schools represent a crucial transition period when students leave the supportive atmosphere of elementary school and prepare for the potentially alienating experience of large high schools. In 2000, data from the El Paso Collaborative for Academic Excellence (EPCAE) indicated that ninth grade is the year when many students get "stuck." They fail to earn credits and often must repeat courses, which may lead them to disengage from learning, putting graduation at risk. Latino students are at greatest risk; over a third of students do not complete their high school degrees (IDRA, 2008; McNeil, Coppola, Radigan, & Vásquez Heilig, 2008). Although TEA indicators report a mere 1% to 3% annual high school dropout rate, EPCAE reports that nearly 33% of the students in the region have not completed high school 6 years after ninth grade.

Middle schools offer a high-priority period to examine civic knowledge. Eighth grade students take TAAS accountability tests in social studies, which have some similarity to the NAEP Civics Assessment test, with its basic, advanced, and proficient standards developed for three grade levels.

A study was conducted to analyze social studies standardized testing material, including the degree to which it can build and enhance civic capacity. In addition, this study assessed teacher instructional strategies at three different campuses, each with its own special climate. Campus climates reflected leadership strategies such as the investment of resources (i.e., money for technology), principals' collaboration with teachers and parent leaders, and emphasis on "teaching to the test." One might expect that certain campus climates, for example those where parents were emphatically engaged and where classrooms were infused with technology, might mitigate an instructional strategy that relies heavily on drilling techniques, which are generally considered to be less enduring than other teaching strategies.

Community-based research is itself an active learning strategy. During the 2000 spring semester, a faculty-led team of three University of Texas at El Paso (UTEP) students assisted three middle schools during February and March (prior to the April TAAS test) and after the completion of the TAAS tests. For the research, students administered a survey (grade-level appropriate) consisting of seven NAEP questions based on sample questions available on the web, 4 local civic knowledge NAEP-like questions, 10 student self-assessment items (on academic confidence, school efficacy, and parental involvement), and 1 open-ended question on important social studies learning. The survey, which also contained demographic questions, was given to 213 students (180 are included in the final analysis). Preliminary results were available to campus leaders. The individual campuses will be referred to as schools X, Y, and Z.

The demographic profiles for the schools were similar in terms of ethnic, economic, and linguistic composition. Each school had admirable physical facilities and student-centered leadership. The schools differed in key characteristics that presumably affected campus climate. School X had extensive state-of-the-art technology available for classroom instruction, including laptops for each student. School Y was an Alliance School, affiliated with the El Paso IAF (EPISO) and its engaged parents. School Z was more typical, without technology or parental leadership components. All schools had computer laboratories for student use.

Qualitative, engaged community-based research enhanced the case study. Each school had one UTEP student available to assist social studies classrooms for up to 20 hours weekly in whatever ways the schools themselves desired. The three students brought social studies expertise, high university GPAs, and enthusiasm to the experience. One student was a political science graduate student and two were prelaw interns who had completed a rigorous summer law institute. Decision makers on each of the middle school campuses decided whether UTEP students could assist in pre-Advanced Placement (pre-AP) classes or not.

The teachers agreed to work with these interns, although they used very different instructional strategies with them, itself indicative of the extent to which test-driven missions engulfed the campuses. Schools X and Z involved students in one or more classrooms as assistants who could enrich learning experiences. For example, eighth-grade students worked on research and performance projects for Black History Month using Internet sources, mock trials, election process materials, and survey construction and analysis.

Curiously, although School Y was affiliated with the IAF as an Alliance School, the campus was more oriented to teaching the test. The university student's assignment was more limited, lacking enriching instructional strategies. He did one-on-one TAAS tutoring after school with students who did not pass the mock TAAS social studies test in fall. One teacher's classroom was devoted to a fully developed knowledge retention process based on lecture, note taking, flashcard development, and interactive flashcard strategies. A former "special education" teacher, she hoped flashcards would increase recall on TEKS/TAAS content.

Many schools separate students into ability groups, segregating students within schools. In the classic study *Keeping Track*, Jeannie Oakes (1985), analyzed a national sample of middle schools with pervasive tracking systems (see Texas schools in Romo & Falbo, 1996). Although the benefits and drawbacks of tracking by ability are hotly contested, each of these campuses allows students to choose whether they wanted pre-AP courses or not. The pre-AP and regular classrooms are quite different, particularly in terms of engaging activities that may lead to success in higher education and political efficacy in adult civic life.

We noticed two important patterns in our student sample with regard to pre-AP placement on campuses. First, few English Language Learner students (known as Limited English Proficient in the Texas Education Agency, or LEP) take advantage of, or are guided into, pre-AP classes. This pattern might mean that LEP students are not learning to their fullest potential. Second, in conversations with teachers, we found (not surprisingly) different expectations about what pre-AP and regular students could or would do in a given semester timeframe. Those expectations resulted in different classroom climates that in all likelihood were less enriching and engaging for the vast majority: regular social studies students.

In the study, relatively more students correctly answered the NAEP civic standard questions in the multiple-choice format, just as TAAS uses. Students do far less well on other multiple-guess questions, perhaps because they are not well covered in the textbook or the packet of over 200 past TAAS questions available for review. Students do less well on short-answer questions, which cannot be memorized or guessed as easily and require more evaluation and knowledge applications to civic action. Because the NAEP Civics Report does not report results by question, comparisons with national results must be interpreted with caution. The study shows that the preparation of these middle school students for the Texas TAAS does not help them reach what approaches a national standard. Two thirds have not achieved at or above the basic national levels, although nearly one fifth achieved proficient and advanced levels.

With local-content oriented, NAEP-like questions, students demonstrated higher proficiency levels than with nationally oriented questions. Many students have an impressive knowledge of the border and Mexico that few U.S. mainstream students likely know. These responses on local and regional knowledge raise questions about who designs test questions and why they are given a national focus, given the grounding and potential civic engagement experiences at the local level—ostensibly an important feature of U.S. federalism. It is useful to recall earlier discussions about the grounding of potential civic engagement experiences at local levels.

Students' knowledge of local community-based organizations is extremely low. The only organizations students could name were MADD, SADD, Tiguas (El Paso's Native American community), church groups, and nonprofit service agencies like the YWCA and YMCA. One student named the KKK, which no longer operates locally. Far more students named government institutions than nongovernment organizations, such as the police, the army, the border patrol, the city council, or agreements like NAFTA. Some named elected officials ("Jorge" [George] Bush, Mayor Carlos Ramírez). One response, a clear outlier, was Windows 95! Students' self-reported responses indicated that they do not read newspapers at high rates, and perhaps little is said or read in social studies classrooms about community organizations in the region. Even in School Y, which included a strong parental engagement agenda, no students named the IAF affiliate. Such responses do not bode well for building social capital and developing capacity to engage in organizations that can override the effects of low SES on reduced political participation.

A comparison of pre-AP and regular student responses is worthwhile, although caution must be used because only 29 of 180 X and Y school students (16%) are in the pre-AP group. Pre-AP students scored an average of 15 points or higher on the NAEP questions. Pre-AP students scored higher on all of the NAEP-like local questions. At the border, youth do not learn much about local and state public affairs; the history and heroes (or anti-heroes) of Texas provide the only avenue to learn about local issues unless teachers are willing to develop non-test-driven instructional strategies.

As for gender differences, girls scored higher on more NAEP questions than did boys, probably because the girls are overrepresented in pre-AP classes. On self-assessment questions, girls demonstrated higher rates on most success indicators, probably pursuing pathways to higher education and sustaining the female-majority figures currently present in U.S. higher education.

Finally, the survey asked an open-end question, adapted from *Keeping Track*: "What was the most important thing you have learned or done so far in your social studies class?" In general, pre-AP students most often expressed content-related answers, while those in regular classes also mentioned study skills and discipline rather than content alone or in addition to content.

In that open-ended question, most students remember and report important social studies topics in three generic content areas: history, wars, and the Constitution. Most are quite succinct, explaining what they've learned with not much more than a single word. Only one student wrote an evaluation rather than simply describing various wars, adding "and what we should do to stop them." Others mentioned individual rights, principles like freedom and equality, and Constitutional amendments. Some responses, such as "mock trials" and "Black History Month," suggested that student engagement projects entered their deeper memories. Only four students (in School X, with its classroom technology) mentioned active civic involvement ("how to vote and how candidates get people to vote for them").

Study skills appeared in some of the regular, non–pre-AP student responses: "turn in work," "get better grades," "to fill out my probe book," "learn and work, nothing else." Several said "I don't know," and 29 (about 19%) left the lines blank. Blank spaces provide testimony to the blank curriculum in students' memories.

CONCLUSIONS

Standardized tests, such as the Texas TAAS and TAKS, may appropriately assess factual knowledge, but they have little to do with other components of civic engagement such as skills, experience, and motivation. These testing strategies put students "at risk" for participation during adulthood, with large gaps between the Latino and Anglo populations, except where mitigated by high SES and organizational membership. Nothing in the Texas high-stakes accountability system addresses these risks, values them, or creates incentives to change them.

Students learn from textbooks. Past test questions, increasingly woven with the TEKS, drive classroom environments in ways that lead to decontextualized and disengaged learning. With this strategy, test scores improve, but not necessarily skills, motivation, and experience. As a visit to the Texas Education Agency (TEA) Web site will show, in an effort to cover a little bit of everything to meet the vast quantity of Texas Essential Knowledge and Skills (TEKS) standards, teachers risk pursuing a "mile-wide, inch-deep" approach to instruction—what international critiques suggest is wrong about U.S. instructional strategies as reflected in student performance, especially in math (on international comparisons, see Ravitch, 1995). Superficial coverage of extensive material, targeted for memorization, represents lower- rather than high-order thinking skills. Nuanced knowledge uncovered in the comparative case studies show the subtle linguistic racism that occurs in tracking students by ability groups.

In contrast, multiple and alternative instructional strategies have the potential to prepare students for advanced social studies knowledge and civic learning. These strategies draw on more than TAAS/TAKS tests, including computer technology, engaged teacher-student interaction, and active learning such as service learning and community-based research (as adopted in this comparative case analysis). In a high-stakes accountability regime, can teachers and principals afford to take classroom time away from test preparation to pursue better and more comprehensive instructional strategies? If not, future civic engagement may be weak and put democracy further at risk.

Technology in the classroom and engaging projects create opportunities for deeper learning that students remember, evaluate with critical thinking skills, and apply to practice. Instructional strategies that produce memorable, co-constructed knowledge (rather than focusing on memorizing details that are likely forgotten soon after taking the tests) would facilitate the development of the social-capital skills necessary for civic engagement, the analytical skills needed to examine local policy and problem solving, and action-oriented learning that provide students and their parents a stake in meaningful civic engagement.

Local civic knowledge could become deeper if schools would prioritize learning that prepares students for active citizenship, including motivation, skills, and experience components with a strong infusion of the local, community, and regional contexts. Instructional strategies in regular social studies for the majority should parallel those in pre-AP or AP classes; "drill and kill" teaching is not conducive to engaged citizenship for all students. Students who absorb social studies in a broader context than wars and constitutions will be better prepared for critical reflection and engagement in adulthood. Texas and national politicians' obsessions with standardized test results should be tempered by multiple means of assessment that embrace short answer and essay writing, communication, and application skills. In social studies and civic engagement matters, multiple-choice and multiple-guess tests do more harm than good in restoring the social capital and civic capacity that the United States needs in order to spread and deepen democracy among all people, including Latinos and Latinas.

Social studies classes and civics lessons generally could do far more to advance deeper knowledge, higher-order thinking skills, and engagement with democracy. Civic educational quality does not mesh well with standardized multiple-guess tests, so central to the Texas educational system. The results of studies like this should help to focus the eyes of the nation on Texas and the danger that standardized testing poses to inclusive democracy.

REFERENCES

Bellah, R. N., Madsen, R., Sullivan, W. M., Swidler, A., & Tipton, S. M. (1985). *Habits of the heart*. Berkeley, CA: University of California Press.

Bellah, R. N., Madsen, R., Tipton, S. M., & Sullivan, W. M. (1992). *The good society*. New York: Vintage.

Hochschild, J., & Scovronick, N. (2003). *The American dream and the public schools*. New York: Oxford University Press.

Intercultural Development Research Association. (2008). *High school attrition rates across Texas education service center regions, 2006–2007*. Retrieved July 31, 2008, from www.idra.org

Kohn, A. (2000). *The case against standardized testing: Raising the scores, ruining the schools*. New York: Heinemann.

Macedo, S., Alex-Assensoh, Y., Berry, J. M., Brintnall, M., Campbell, D. E., Fraga, F. R., Fung, A., et al. (2005). *Democracy at risk: How political choices undermine citizen participation, and what we can do about it*. Washington, DC: Brookings Institution Press.

McNeil, L., Coppola, E., Radigan, J., & Vásquez Heilig, J. (2008, January 31). Avoidable losses: High-stakes accountability and the dropout crisis. *Education Policy Analysis Archives, 16*(3), 1–45.

Montoya, L. (2002). Gender and citizenship in Latino political participation. In M. M. Suárez-Orozco, & M. M. Paez (Eds.), *Latinos: Remaking America* (pp. 411–429). Berkeley, CA: University of California Press.

National Assessment of Educational Progress. (1999). *1998 Civics Report Card*. Retrieved November 1, 2002, from http://nced.ed.gov/nationsreportcard/civics

Noboa, J. (2006). *Leaving Latinos out of history: Teaching U.S. history in Texas*. New York: Routledge.

Oakes, J. (1985). *Keeping track: How schools structure inequality*. Berkeley, CA: University of California Press.

Putnam, R. (2000). *Bowling alone: The collapse and revival of American community*. New York: Simon & Schuster.

Ravitch, D. (1995). *National standards in American education*. Washington, DC: Brookings Institution.

Ravitch, D. (2010). *The death and life of the great America school system: How testing and choice are undermining education*. NY: Basic Books.

Rippberger, S., & Staudt, K. (2003). *Pledging allegiance: Learning Nationalism at the El Paso-Juárez Border*. New York: Routledge Falmer.

Rocha, G., & Webking, R. (1993). *Politics and public education: Edgewood v. Kirby and the reform of public school financing in Texas*. Minneapolis, MN: West Publishing.

Romero, M., & Yellen, T. (2004). *El Paso portraits: Women's lives, potential & opportunities*. El Paso, TX: YWCA and University of Texas El-Paso (UTEP) Center for Civic Engagement.

Romo, H., & Falbo, T. (1996). *Latino high school graduation*. Austin, TX: University of Texas Press.

Sanders, M. G. (1998). The effects of school, family, and community support on the academic achievement of African American adolescents. *Urban Education, 33*(3), 385–409.

Sharp, J. (1998). *Bordering the future: Challenge and opportunity in the Texas border regions.* Austin, TX: Texas Comptroller of Public Accounts. Retrieved November 1, 2001, from www.cpa.state.texas.us

Shirley, D. (1997). *Community organizing for urban school reform.* Austin, TX: University of Texas Press.

Staudt, K. (1998). *Free trade? Informal economies at the U.S-Mexico border.* Philadelphia: Temple University Press.

Staudt, K. (2001). *Democracy education for more than the few.* In R. Soder, J. Goodlad, & T. McMannon (Eds.). *Developing democratic character in the young* (pp. 45–68). San Francisco: Jossey-Bass.

Staudt, K., & Coronado, I. (2002). *Fronteras no más: Toward social justice at the U.S.-Mexico border.* New York: Palgrave.

Staudt, K., & Stone, C. (2007). Division and fragmentation: The El Paso experience in global-local perspective. In M. Orr (Ed.), *Community organizing and political change in the city* (pp. 84–108). Lawrence, KS: University Press of Kansas.

Texas Education Agency. (2004). *Texas assessment of knowledge and skills information booklet: Social studies exit level.* Retrieved June 23, 2010, from http://ritter.tea.state.tx.us/student.assessment/taks/booklets/ss/g11.pdf

Tolo, K. W. (1999). *The civic education of American youth: From state policies to school district practices.* Policy Research Project on Civic Education Policies and Practices Report (no. 133). Austin, TX: LBJ School of Public Affairs, University of Texas at Austin.

Valenzuela, A. (Ed.). (2005). *Leaving children behind: How "Texas-style" accountability fails Latino youth.* Albany, NY: SUNY Press.

Zellman, G., & Waterman, J. (1998). Understanding the impact of parent-school involvement on children's educational outcomes. *Journal of Educational Research, 91*(6), 370–379.

CHAPTER 3

Florida's Program to End Social Promotion

Jay P. Greene and Marcus A. Winters

School systems across the nation have recently enacted substantial new programs to stop schools from promoting students from grade to grade regardless of academic proficiency. To end this practice, known as *social promotion*, several large school systems now require students in particular grades to demonstrate a benchmark level of mastery in basic skills by passing a standardized test before they can be promoted. These controversial mandates have been adopted statewide by Florida and Texas, and citywide by New York City and Chicago.

Proponents of test-based promotion argue that schools do students no favor by promoting them to later grades if they do not possess the skills necessary to succeed at a higher level. They suggest that if a student lacks basic proficiency in reading concepts at the third-grade level, he or she will certainly fail to grasp concepts intended for fourth graders. This view posits that promoting students beyond their skills will only cause them to fall further behind as material becomes more difficult in later years.

Those opposed to ending social promotion, conversely, point to a wide body of research suggesting that students who are retained in a grade for an extra year are academically and emotionally harmed by the experience. Several studies have indicated that students who are held back score lower on subsequent tests and are more likely to drop out than are counterparts who are not held back.

There have been particular concerns about how ending social promotion might disproportionately affect Latino students. For example, Valencía and Villarreal (2003) wrote that ending social promotion in Texas

> will likely have an enormous adverse impact on Mexican American/other Latino and African-American students. Given that our projections are based on data from the easier TAAS test, it is reasonable to suggest that the more difficult

TAKS may result in even higher failure rates across racial and ethnic groups than we have projected here, and in said impact hitting African-American and Mexican American/other Latino students particularly hard. (p. 615)

Discussing efforts to end social promotion in California, Mora (2002) concluded that "ostensibly well-meaning and clearly directed policies operate to aggravate the inequities encountered by students in Latino communities" (p. 30).

However, prior research on grade retention is severely limited by methodological problems that are unavoidable in evaluating retention policies based on subjective criteria (i.e., teacher evaluations that students should be retained). Furthermore, it is questionable whether research on students who were retained based on the professional judgment of their teachers is even relevant to retention policies based primarily on the results of standardized tests. For example, it is possible that the potentially harmful stigma currently associated with retention might not apply to the same extent under the new system, which holds back much larger numbers of students. It is certainly possible that retaining thousands of students according to their standardized test scores might influence student outcomes in ways far different from previous retention practices that singled out a very small number of students for retention based upon the professional judgment of teachers. New research looking directly at the effectiveness of test-score mandates intended to end social promotion is therefore necessary for policy makers and the public to make informed decisions about the effects of ending social promotion, both generally and for Latinos in particular.

This chapter seeks to inform that debate by discussing research on Florida's early experience with ending social promotion through standardized testing. We analyzed the test scores of third-grade students who failed to reach the minimum benchmark on the Florida Comprehensive Assessment Test (FCAT) reading test. We also examined the test score gains made by students one year after they failed to reach the benchmark. We included third graders who missed the benchmark in 2002–2003, the year in which the new policy first took effect, as well as third graders who missed the benchmark in the previous year, when the policy was not yet in effect.

Under a law passed by the state legislature, third graders in Florida must score at the Level 2 benchmark or above on the reading portion of the FCAT, the state's high-stakes test, in order to be promoted to the fourth grade. Students who fail to reach this benchmark are given supplemental instruction and, unless they acquire an exemption, must repeat the third grade. The third-grade class of 2002–2003 was the first affected by the mandate. The introduction of a requirement that had not applied to previous cohorts creates a natural experiment that we utilized to analyze the program's effectiveness.

We performed two analyses using calculations based on data provided by the Florida Department of Education. Our first analysis measures the effect that being subject to the new program has on student achievement. It compares low-scoring third graders in 2002–2003, who were subject to the program, with low-scoring third graders from the previous year, who were not. However, some of the students who were subject to the program received special exemptions that allowed them to advance to fourth grade in spite of their test scores. Thus, not all students who were subject to the new program were actually retained. We therefore performed a second analysis in order to measure the effect of actual retention—whether under the new program or under the old retention policy—on low-performing students. We used an instrumental analysis method to compare students in both years who were actually retained with students in both years who were not actually retained in both years. In addition, we examined these affects based on race (Anglo, African American, and Latino) to examine potentially disproportionate impacts on minority students.

We found that the early stage of Florida's policy to end social promotion has improved academic proficiency. Our first analysis showed that low-performing students subject to the program made modest improvements in reading and substantial improvements in math compared to those made by low-performing students in the previous year's cohort who were not subject to the program because it had not yet taken effect. Our second analysis finds that the effect of actually being retained is even stronger: Low-performing students who were retained make relatively large improvements in reading and exceptional improvements in math compared to similarly low-performing students who were promoted.

These findings are encouraging for the use of standardized testing policies to end social promotion, but they are also limited because we are only able to evaluate the effects of the program's first year. It is certainly possible that students affected by the program made gains that might not hold up later in their academic careers, as proponents of the policy expect. On the other hand, it is also possible that the gap between students who were socially promoted and those who were retained might widen further as they enter later grades and the material becomes even more challenging. Further research following these same groups of students will be necessary to track the effectiveness of Florida's retention program over time.

PREVIOUS RESEARCH ON SOCIAL PROMOTION

Over the last several decades, many studies have examined the effect of grade retention on future student achievement. Of particular note, scholars at the Consortium on Chicago School Research performed a series of evaluations of that city's objective program to end social promotion through testing (Nagoaka & Roderick, 2004). In Chicago, students in the third, sixth, and eighth grades must exceed benchmarks on the Iowa Test of Basic Skills (ITBS), a nationally respected and widely administered standardized test, in order to be promoted to the next grade. This study compared the performance of third- and sixth-grade students who scored just below the benchmark on the ITBS, most of whom were retained because of the mandate, to the performance of students who scored just above the benchmark, most of whom were promoted. They were able to measure test score performance for 2 years after the implementation of the program. Their mixed results show that the policy did not affect the performance of the third-grade students on the ITBS reading test, but it negatively affected the test performance of the sixth-grade students.

In his oft-cited meta-analysis of grade retention research, Holmes (1989) included 63 studies on grade retention with a total of 861 findings. Of the 63 studies he evaluated, 54 reported overall negative effects of grade retention on students. Of the studies that directly measured academic achievement, Holmes determined that their cumulative finding was that retained students performed 0.19 standard deviation units below promoted students. He concluded, "the weight of empirical evidence argues against grade retention" (p. 28).

While Holmes' meta-analysis is often treated as definitive, some researchers have pointed out serious flaws with his finding (Alexander, Entwisle, & Dauber, 2003; Reynolds, 1992). They argue that the studies in Holmes' meta-analysis are not of high enough quality to support definitive conclusions.

The most serious limitation of previous research on retention is the lack of an adequate control group. Finding an adequate control group that can be compared to retained students has not been easy to solve in previous studies. Despite researchers' great efforts to develop adequate comparison groups, the subjectivity of grade retention decisions rendered these efforts futile. In the past, the retention of a student has largely been the result of a teacher's subjective assessment of the student's ability to succeed at the next level. Therefore, we can expect that students who were retained are fundamentally different from students who were promoted, even if they are similar in all measurable factors such as race, socioeconomic status, or gender, because their teachers evaluated them as being fundamentally different. To further complicate matters, student assessments are likely to differ greatly not only between teachers but also among a single teacher's evaluations of various children. In previous studies, the students who were retained are simply not comparable to the promoted students to whom they are compared. The existence of an objective retention policy in Florida provides an adequate comparison group not available in previous evaluations. Unlike previous studies, this study compares students who were subject to retention to other students who we know would have been subject to retention had they only been born a year later.

Reynolds (1992) points out that most of the previous studies included in Holmes' meta-analysis evaluated the effect of retention on white, middle-class students in suburban or rural schools. Such studies might tell us very little about the effects of retention on urban minority students, for whom the new retention policies are most often aimed at helping and who are in fact the most likely to be retained under them. The study we conducted and are discussing here utilized data from the entire student population in the state, thereby mediating this concern.

FLORIDA LAWMAKERS ADDRESS SOCIAL PROMOTION

In May, 2002, the legislature decided to focus its attention on the problem of social promotion—the practice of promoting students to the next grade level independent of their academic proficiency—at the end of the third-grade year. Florida revised its school code to require third-grade students to score at the Level 2 benchmark or above (which is the second lowest of five levels for test results) on the reading portion of the FCAT—the state's already high-stakes standardized test—in order to be promoted to the fourth grade. By requiring that all students possess at least the basic proficiency necessary to succeed in the next grade level, reformers hoped that ending social promotion would lead to great academic gains. The third-grade class of 2002–2003 was the first to be affected by the law.

The law allowed for some exceptions to the retention policy. A child who misses the FCAT benchmark can be exempted from the policy and promoted to fourth grade if he or she meets any one of the following criteria:

1. is a Limited English Proficient (LEP) student who has received less than 2 years of instruction in an English for Speakers of Other Languages program
2. has a disability sufficiently severe that it is deemed inappropriate for him or her to take the test
3. demonstrates proficiency on another standardized test
4. demonstrates proficiency through a performance portfolio
5. has a disability (the law does not specify type) and has received remediation for more than 2 years, or
6. has already been held back for 2 years.
   (Florida Department of Education Fact Sheet, n.d.)

Of third grade students in 2002–2003 who scored below the Level 2 threshold and were thus subject to retention under the new policy, 41.3% received an exemption and were promoted.

Florida's policy is similar to those recently enacted by other large school systems. As in Florida, all third-grade students in Texas must pass the reading portion of that state's standardized test to be promoted to fourth grade. New York City has a similar reading mandate for third graders and has recently expanded its mandate to require fifth-grade students to pass a standardized test to earn promotion. Chicago requires that students pass the reading and math sections of the Iowa Test of Basic Skills (ITBS) in the third, sixth, and eighth grades. These four school systems alone enroll nearly 17% of the nation's third-grade students.

DESCRIPTION OF OUR RESEARCH

Our data include low-scoring students from 2 school years. First, we include all Florida students who entered the third grade for the first time in 2002–2003 and scored below the Level 2 threshold on the FCAT reading test in that year. This was the first cohort of students in the state subject to the policy requiring them to pass the FCAT reading test in order to be promoted. Our dataset includes all students who did not pass the FCAT reading test; however, because exemptions from the new policy were available, nearly 40% of the students we include were not actually retained. We also include all students who entered third grade for the first time during the 2001–2002 school year and scored below Level 2 on the FCAT reading test. These students' test scores would have made them subject to the new policy's retention mandate had it been in effect in that year. Of third graders in 2001–2002 examined here, 8.7% were retained. The students from both school years are very similar in all respects except for the year in which they happened to have been born, making comparisons between their improvements particularly meaningful.

We analyzed the 1-year test score gains students made on state-mandated math and reading tests. The existence of developmental scale scores on each of the tests allows us to compare the test score gains of all the students in our study even though they took different tests designed for different grade levels. Developmental scale scores are designed to measure academic proficiency on a single scale for students of any grade and in any year. For example, a third grader with a developmental scale score of 1000 and a fourth grader with a developmental scale score of 1000 have the same level of academic achievement; if a student gets a developmental scale score of 1000 in 2001–2002 and then gets the same score of 1000 in 2002–2003, this indicates that the student has not made any academic progress in the intervening year.

We analyzed the improvements made by students over 1 year in math and reading scores on both the criterion-referenced and norm-referenced versions of the FCAT. Both of these are standardized tests that Florida students are required to take. For purposes of clarity, throughout the rest of this study we will follow widespread practice and refer to the criterion-referenced version of the test as *the FCAT* and the norm-referenced version as *the Stanford-9*.

The existence of the Stanford-9 is particularly helpful for our analysis. Several researchers argue that the results of high-stakes tests like the FCAT are routinely distorted because they create adverse incentives for teachers and school systems to manufacture high scores either by "teaching to the test"—changing curriculum and teaching practices in such a way as to raise test scores without increasing real learning—or by outright cheating. The absence of any substantial consequences attached to the results of the Stanford-9 helps to remove these concerns for our analysis. Because no meaningful stakes are tied to it, teachers or school systems have no particular incentive to attempt to manipulate its results. Thus, if we find similar results on both the high-stakes FCAT and the low-stakes Stanford-9, we can be confident that our findings indicate improvements in real learning and are not distorted by adverse incentives created by high-stakes testing. Such concerns remain widespread, though prior research indicates that the results of high-stakes tests, particularly the FCAT, are reliable (see Greene, Winters, & Forster, 2003) precisely because their results correlate highly with those of low-stakes tests.

With the cooperation of the Florida Department of Education, we obtained individual student-level test scores on the math and reading sections of the FCAT and Stanford-9 for the entire population of students in the state of Florida who met the necessary criteria to be part of our study. We obtained test-score data for all students in the state of Florida who first entered third grade in 2001–2002 and scored below the Level 2 threshold on the FCAT reading test in that year, as well as for all Florida students who entered the third grade in 2002–2003 and scored below Level 2 on the FCAT reading test in that year. The developmental scale scores required to reach Level 2 on the FCAT reading test were consistent for each year's cohort. For each student in our analysis, we also collected data on race, free or reduced-price lunch status, and whether the student was considered LEP.

We calculated the developmental scale score gains on the FCAT and Stanford-9 made in each student's first third-grade year and the following year. For the students affected by the retention policy, we measured the test-score gains they made between the 2002–2003 and 2003–2004 administrations of the tests. For students who were not affected by the program, we measured their test-score gains between the 2001–2002 and 2002–2003 administrations of the tests. For students in each group, our calculations of test-score gains were independent of whether the student was administered the third-grade test (indicating the student was retained) or the fourth-grade test (indicating the student was promoted). Because developmental scale scores are consistent between year and grade, the gains we calculated are equivalent for all students.

Our first analysis measured the effect of Florida's retention policy. For this, we were not concerned with whether students who were subject to the retention policy were actually retained or received an exemption and were promoted to the next grade, although the availability of exemptions is a meaningful part of the retention policy and thus should be included in its evaluation. The state's policy is intended as a treatment for every third-grade student who scored below the necessary benchmark on the FCAT, even those students who earned an exemption.

To measure the effect of the program, we performed a linear regression comparing the developmental scale score gains made by our treatment group (students who first entered third grade in 2002–2003 and scored below the FCAT benchmark in that year) to our control group (students who first entered third grade in 2001–2002 and scored below the FCAT benchmark in that year). In this regression we controlled for dummy demographic variables indicating race, free or reduced-price school lunch program status, and LEP status. We also controlled for each student's test score during his/her first third-grade year, providing a control for the baseline test performance for each student.

For our second analysis, we evaluated the effect of actually retaining low-performing students. Here we compared low-scoring students from either year who were actually retained with low-scoring students from either year who were not actually retained. To do so, we performed a two-stage least squares regression analysis, where the variable of interest was whether a student was retained or promoted. This model uses student demographics and an exogenous variable—the cohort to which a student belongs, which for all intents and purposes is determined by the year in which a student was born—to predict whether each student will be retained. It then uses that prediction to measure the relationship between retention and test score improvements. We again controlled for student race, free or reduced-price lunch status, LEP status, and baseline test scores.

In addition to performing these two analyses for the general student population, we also performed each analysis for racial subgroups. This allows us to examine whether the retention policy, or actually retaining students, is having a different effect on students of different races.

STUDENT OUTCOMES

After the first year of the program, we found that retention makes a significant improvement in student test scores. Examining the difference between the 2002–2003 and the 2001–2002 cohorts, the performance of students who were subject to the retention policy exceeded the performance of students who were not subject to the retention policy. Likewise, the performance of low-scoring students who were actually retained showed significant improvements over those who were promoted in both years. Our results are also remarkably consistent between the high-stakes FCAT and the low-stakes Stanford-9, indicating that they have not been tainted by manipulations of the high-stakes testing system.

Tables 3.1 and 3.2 summarize our findings (full regression models are available from the authors upon request). Table 3.1 reports the number of standard deviation units this difference represents in order to facilitate comparisons between results on the different subjects and tests. Standard deviation units are equivalent between the subjects and tests, and allow for more meaningful comparisons across subjects and between the FCAT and Stanford-9. Given that some readers may be unfamiliar with standard deviation units, we also convert all results into the equivalent gain in national percentile points in Table 3.2.

These tables show that students subject to the retention policy make gains of .06 standard deviation units in reading and between .14 and .15 standard deviation units in math relative to students not subject to that policy. Those benefits translate into about 2 national percentile points on reading and 5 percentile points on math over a 1-year period for the average student in our study. Students actually retained made between .11 and .13 standard deviation unit gains on reading and .28 to .30 standard deviation unit gains on math relative to students who were promoted. Those benefits translate into a benefit of about 3 or 4 percentile points in reading and about 9 or 10 percentile points in math over a 1-year period for the average student in our study.

Table 3.1. Gains Made by Students Translated into Standard Deviation Units

	Standard Deviation Unit Gain for Students Subject to Policy (2002–03 Cohort) Relative to Students Not Subject to Policy (2001–02 Cohort)	Standard Deviation Unit Gain for Low-Scoring Retained Students (both years) Relative to Low-Scoring Promoted Students (both years)
FCAT Reading	0.06	0.13
Stanford-9 Reading	0.06	0.11
FCAT Math	0.15	0.30
Stanford-9 Math	0.14	0.28

Table 3.2. Gains Made by Students Translated into Percentile Scores

	Percentile Gain for Students Subject to Policy (2002–03 Cohort) Relative to Students Not Subject to Policy (2001–02 Cohort)	Percentile Gain for Low-Scoring Retained Students (both years) Relative to Low-Scoring Promoted Students (both years)
FCAT Reading	1.85	4.10
Stanford-9 Reading	1.85	3.45
FCAT Math	4.76	9.98
Stanford-9 Math	4.43	9.26

Note: Percentile gain calculated for student with average baseline Stanford-9 reading score among all students in our analysis (23rd percentile).

We also performed both types of analyses disaggregating for whether the student is white, black, or Hispanic. Table 3.3 reports the results of the analyses of the effect of being subject to Florida's retention policy disaggregated by race, and Table 3.4 reports the results of our analyses of the effect of actually being retained disaggregated by race. The results in each table are translated into standard deviation units to facilitate comparisons. The results show that there are only modest differences in the effects across race/ethnicity on both math and reading assessments when students are subject to the retention policy and when they are actually retained.

The lone exception in our findings is that white students fail to make gains relative to the control groups on the FCAT reading test in both analyses, even though the Stanford-9 reading test results indicate that they do in fact benefit. Given the large number of analyses in our study, it is possible that this is an anomalous finding produced by chance. If it is not the product of chance, it is not clear why white students would fail to benefit from the

Table 3.3. Effect of Being Subject to Retention Policy by Race (in Standard Deviation Units)

Race	FCAT Reading	Stanford-9 Reading	FCAT Math	Stanford-9 Math
White	0.01	0.04*	0.14*	0.12*
Black	0.07*	0.07*	0.15*	0.17*
Hispanic	0.12*	0.06*	0.17*	0.14*

* Indicates result is statistically significant at .001 level.
Note: Complete regression results available upon request.

Table 3.4. Effect of Retention by Race (in Standard Deviation Units)

Race	FCAT Reading	Stanford-9 Reading	FCAT Math	Stanford-9 Math
White	0.02	0.09[**]	0.31[**]	0.26[**]
Black	0.13[**]	0.12[**]	0.28[**]	0.31[**]
Hispanic	0.23[**]	0.12[**]	0.33[**]	0.26[**]

[**] Indicates result is statistically significant at .001 level
Note: Complete regression results available upon request.

retention policy and actually being retained as measured by the FCAT reading test but would be shown to benefit as measured by the Stanford-9 reading test. This issue should be examined further in future research efforts.

IMPLICATIONS OF STUDENT OUTCOMES RESEARCH

The results of our analyses offer support for the use of objective retention policies based on standardized test scores. With the one exception noted above, each of our analyses found consistently positive results for the use of such retention policies. And we found no evidence to support concerns that ending social promotion would be harmful for Latino students or other racial or ethnic subgroups.

The gains made both by students subject to retention and those who were actually held back are substantial in comparison to gains we would expect from other popular education reforms. For example, the Tennessee Star Project's widely cited study of class-size reduction found that reducing class sizes from about 24 students per teacher to about 15 students per teacher led to a statistically significant increase of about .2 standard deviations (Hanushek, 2003). The highest quality research on school vouchers has found that the use of such scholarships to attend private schools leads to a gain of 2 to 11 percentile points (for example, see Greene, 2002, and Howell & Peterson, 2002). We similarly find that subjecting students to a retention policy improves scores by about .06 standard deviation units (about 1.85 percentile points) in reading and about .15 standard deviation units (about 4.76 percentile points) in math. We also find that actually retaining students leads to about a .12 standard deviation unit point gain in reading (about 4 percentile points) and about a .3 standard deviation point gain in math (or about 9 percentile points). This indicates that Florida's retention policy is likely at least as effective at increasing student test scores as these other popular reforms.

That the results of our study are largely uniform between the FCAT and the Stanford-9 indicates that they are not distorted by perverse incentives for schools and teachers to manipulate their test results. Many argue that teachers and schools will respond to the new retention policy by manipulating test scores, either directly by cheating or indirectly by teaching students skills that will help them to improve their test scores but will not provide real academic proficiency. This argument would only have merit if we found strong gains on the high-stakes FCAT and no similar gains on the low-stakes Stanford-9, on which there is no incentive to manipulate scores. If teachers are in fact changing their curricula with the intent to "teach to" the FCAT, they are doing so in ways that also contribute to gains on the highly respected Stanford-9. This indicates that whatever changes teachers have made have resulted in real increases in student proficiency.

Some might be surprised that we found much greater gains in math than in reading in both analyses. This might seem particularly odd given that students must pass the reading portion of the FCAT to earn promotion, and that the rhetoric supporting Florida's retention program emphasizes that it will improve student literacy.

It is important to remember we do find modest improvements in reading for students who were subject to the policy, and relatively large improvements for students who were actually retained. The larger test score gains in math do not in any way imply the program is failing to live up to expectations in reading.

Furthermore, there are strong theoretical reasons to believe that retained students would make greater improvements in math than in reading. It is reasonable to assume that most students whose reading skills are deficient are likely to be deficient in math as well. If retention were beneficial for students with low proficiency, we would expect them to make gains in both subjects. In addition, the cumulative nature of the skills required in math may be more pronounced than that of reading. For example, a student who cannot add properly is very unlikely to adequately learn multiplication because the latter requires knowledge of the former. Reading instruction is also cumulative, but it is less so than math. Thus, reviewing the material they failed to master in the previous year before advancing to more difficult material might improve the performance of low-performing students more dramatically in math than in reading. School systems that implement objective retention policies might consider using both reading and math tests as determinants of whether a student should be promoted.

One important implication of our results is that students who are given an exemption and promoted despite their failure to demonstrate reading proficiency apparently would have been likely to benefit from another year in the third grade. While students who were subject to the retention program outperformed those who were not regardless of whether they were actually retained, our second analysis shows that low-performing students who were retained significantly outperformed those who were promoted.

This does not mean that it would be wise to eliminate all exemptions to the testing requirement. There are certainly students for whom testing is either inappropriate or whose performance on other academic measures could reasonably indicate that they would be better served by moving on to the next grade. Our findings indicate, however, that teachers and school systems should be cautious when granting exemptions and that many of the students who were promoted during the first year of Florida's program would have made greater gains if they had been retained.

Our study has provided important information about the effects of Florida's retention policy in the year after students are retained, but it cannot answer the more important question of the policy's effects over time. Further evaluations of the program are needed to follow these same cohorts of students throughout their academic careers to find whether the gains made by students subject to Florida's retention policy grow through accumulation, recede, or remain constant over time. It will also be possible to evaluate whether this retention policy for third-grade students has any substantial effect on other outcomes, including the probability that they will graduate from high school. Further research on similar programs throughout the nation would also prove useful. However, it is reasonable to assume that our results in Florida have strong implications for other school systems that have implemented similar programs, such as Texas, Chicago, and New York.

It is clear that Florida's retention policy has significantly improved the academic proficiency of low-performing third-grade students after 1 year. Although further research on this and other programs will add vital information to the debate over educational reform through objective retention policies, the early results are quite encouraging for the use of retention based on standardized tests to improve academic proficiency.

REFERENCES

Alexander, K. L., Entwisle, D. R., & Dauber, S. L. (2003). *On the success of failure: A reassessment of the effects of retention in the primary school grades* (2nd ed.). Cambridge, UK: Cambridge University Press.

Florida Department of Education's Fact Sheet for School Districts (Reading Expectations for Grade Three). (n.d.). Retrieved May 18, 2009, from http://info.fldoe. org/dscgi/ds.py/Get/File-434/grade_3_reading_.pdf

Greene, J. P. (2002). *The effect of school choice: An evaluation of Charlotte's children's scholarship fund.* New York: Manhattan Institute.

Greene, J. P., Winters, M. A., & Forster, G. (2003). Testing high stakes tests: Can we believe the results of accountability tests? *Teachers College Record, 106,* 1124–1145.

Hanushek, E. A. (2003). The failure of input-based schooling policies. *Economic Journal, 113,* 64–98.

Holmes, C. T. (1989). Grade level retention effects: A meta-analysis of research studies. In L. A. Shepard, & M. L. Smith (Eds.), *Flunking grades: Research and policies on retention* (pp. 16–34). New York: The Falmer Press.

Howell, W., & Peterson, P. E. (2002). *The education gap: Vouchers and urban schools.* Washington, DC: Brookings Institution Press.

Mora, J. K. (2002). Caught in a policy web: The impact of education reform on Latino education. *Journal of Latinos and Education, 1*(1), 29–45.

Nagoaka, J., & Roderick, M. (2004). *Ending social promotion: The effects of retention.* Chicago: Consortium on Chicago School Research.

Reynolds, A. J. (1992). Grade retention and school adjustment: An explanatory analysis. *Educational Evaluation and Policy Analysis, 14,* 101–121.

Valencia, R. R., & Villarreal, B. J. (2003). Improving students' reading performance via standards-based school reform: A critique. *The Reading Teacher, 56*(7), 612–621.

CHAPTER 4

Problem or Solution? Charter Schools, Latino Students, and Traditional Texas Public Schools

John Bohte, David L. Leal, Jerry L. Polinard,
James P. Wenzel, and Robert D. Wrinkle

The emergence and growth of charter schooling is among the most note-worthy public policy developments in education in recent years. In an era where a significant percentage of the public believes that public education is experiencing a crisis, charter schooling rapidly emerged in the 1990s. While there were no charter schools in 1991, the next 7 years saw charter legislation passed in 34 states and the District of Columbia. The first state to enact a charter school law was Minnesota, and federal legislation passed in 1994 (Leal, 1999). By 1998, the result was 1,100 charter schools and a quarter million enrolled students (Hassel, 1999). Ten years later, there were about 4,600 schools with 1.5 million students (Center for Education Reform 2009).

Although often confused with private schools, charter schools are nontraditional public schools that are organized under state authority and publicly funded. They "have been freed of many state restrictions, are independent of traditional local school districts, and actually compete for students with traditional public schools" (Maranto, Millman, Hess, & Gresham, 1999, p. 2). They can be started by individuals, which is the most common method, but also by organizations, such as a university. They are mostly small and consist of both new schools and some converted public schools. Contrary to some expectations, charter schools do not generally serve a disproportionately wealthy or white student body, and in Texas they disproportionately serve minority students (RPP International, 1998). As is sometimes the case in education reform, the charter movement attracts strange bedfellows; it is not unusual to find support ranging from free market conservatives to African-American community leaders. According to Finn, Manno, and

Vanourek (2000), "A charter school is a new species, a hybrid, with important similarities to traditional public schools, some of the prized attributes of private schools—and crucial differences from both" (p. 14).

Charters begin with a state law that authorizes their creation. An individual, group, or organization (the *operators*) can then apply to the state or local board (the *sponsors*) and receive permission to open the school. As with a private school, students and parents must choose to apply. Unlike a private school, if there are more applicants than spaces, assignment is by random selection. As with private schools, charter schools can choose their faculty, administrators, and curriculum, and are largely free from day-to-day oversight from local and state educational authorities. Unlike a private school, the charter does not charge tuition; the funding comes from the school district and follows the students.

Charters do not have carte blanche to operate in any manner they choose. The contract between the operator and the sponsor often includes stated achievement goals, and a school can be closed if it fails to meet these goals or otherwise does not abide by regulations (such as fire safety and health laws). However, it is not entirely clear to what degree such schools are consistently held accountable for student academic achievement.

It is difficult to speak in generalities about charters because there is much variation within the category. Because the regulatory environment for charter schools varies by state, the schools themselves are not uniform in terms of how they are allowed to form and operate. Some state laws allow a great deal of flexibility to the schools and those who want to start them. Other state laws contain a variety of restrictions, such as allowing school boards to veto the creation of charter schools or limiting the fiscal independence of charter schools. Advocates often refer to state charter laws as "strong" or "weak," while opponents will have a different perspective. In Texas, Hassel (1999) found that the law is "strong,"[1] which means charters are relatively easy to form and have a good degree of independence.

Unlike more controversial reform options, such as school vouchers, there is less opposition to charter schools among the general public and politicians alike. While supporters may in fact have different reasons for supporting vouchers, this is masked by apparent agreement. As Wells, Grutzik, Carnochen, Slayton, and Vasudeva (1999), observed, "charter school legislation is less a clear consensus on views of education than it is a fragile compromise between policy makers and local activists with different intended outcomes and goals" (p. 532). Nevertheless, charter schooling is a reform that can offer something for everyone: some supporters see charters as necessary because the public school system is broken and a market approach is needed; others think the system can be fixed and want to avoid more systematic reforms; and some see it as just another useful, but not radical, reform tool.

While many liberals would prefer to simply increase school expenditures and are generally suspicious of market metaphors in education, some see charters as attenuating demand for more dramatic reform. They also appreciate that charter schools cannot be religious, are filled by application and lottery, are still part of the public school system, and in some states are subject to significant regulation by state and local educational authorities. Charters therefore allow choice in a way that is not uncomfortable for many traditional public school advocates.

For conservatives, charters inject an element of competition into the public schools. By allowing for greater parental choice, they see charter schools as potentially benefiting all students. The argument is that not only will charters benefit enrolled students, but all public school students will benefit by the systemic reform caused by competitive pressure. While some conservative reformers might favor vouchers, these are more politically difficult to enact than charters. And successful charter experiments might lead to future interest in additional market-oriented reforms.

Opponents have raised a number of concerns about charter schools. Some worry that charters will "cream" the best students from traditional public schools, thereby providing escape hatches for a few while leaving traditional public schools with less funding and fewer positive peer role models. Others are concerned that charters are the first step in a movement toward market-based reforms like school vouchers. Such opponents may oppose charters not because of the nature of charter schooling itself, but because of a fear that charters are the first step in the demise of the common school.

While most critics are on the left, a few are on the right. They argue that charters may satiate a demand for reform while not going far enough to fundamentally change schools. Charters may also prove too similar to public schools, despite the deregulated environment, and there may not prove to be enough charter schools to unleash significant competitive dynamics.[2] Supporters respond that innovation is difficult in the sclerotic public schools, as described in Chubb and Moe (1990). Because charters free schools from much regulation, they allow a rare opportunity for greater educational experimentation, innovation, and efficiency. Others point to the many school reform efforts that have come and gone throughout the 20th century, typically with little to show (see Hess, 1998, and Tyack & Cuban, 1995), which suggests that more fundamental change is necessary.

If some see increased funding as the solution for schools, others see the free market. Backers of choice-based reforms, like vouchers and charters, believe that education can be usefully envisioned as a marketplace. As with other markets, regulation is the problem and competition the solution. By offering an alternative to traditional public schools, charters allow consumers (students and their families) the opportunity to leave underperforming public schools and enter schools more to their liking. While charter school competition may be viewed as a threat by the public school establishment, including teacher unions, the possibility of losing students (and therefore funding) might force public schools to compete for students in the education marketplace. This, it is argued, may then stimulate the traditional schools to reform and upgrade their performance level—although it is unclear whether this is how public schools in fact respond in the face of competition (Hess, 2002). Our geographic focus of inquiry is Texas. The state has more charter schools than any state other than Arizona. With over 1,000 school districts and considerable ethnic, racial, population, economic, and urban/rural diversity, Texas has proved a fertile ground for charter schools. The relative success enjoyed by charter schools in Texas may be, in part, due to the receptive audience found among Texas' political leaders. Despite their growth, charter schools continue to be outnumbered by Texas' public schools. Starting in 1996 with 17 operating charter schools serving 2,498 students, charter schools increased to more than 190 by 2005 and served over 46,000 students. By 2008, there were 354 schools and almost 130,000 students. However, Texas public schools enrolled over 4.5 million total students in 2008.

THE CHARTER SCHOOL DEBATE

Charter Schools in Theory

Supporters of charter schools typically point to three potential benefits. Such claims are disputed by opponents, of course, but it is important to understand the claims made on their behalf. First, charter schools have the potential to serve as minilaboratories for the development of innovative instructional tools and techniques. Freed from the shackles of intrusive regulation spawned by large and bureaucratic public school districts (PSDs), charter schools are able to try new approaches. Those approaches that work can then be incorporated in other locations (traditional public schools, for instance), thereby benefiting education as a whole.

Second, supporters contend the existence of charter schools serves to improve the performance of PSDs. In principle, a competitive charter school alternative will draw students away from existing public schools. This, in combination with the student enrollment-based funding arrangements used by most states, will put local public schools in the position of needing to compete for students with the charter school(s). This leaves local public school districts to choose between the alternatives of reforming or losing students (and, by extension, funding).

Third, charter schools offer the promise of both improved student achievement and enhanced public accountability. Achievement should improve as charter schools are able to shed the restrictions imposed by bureaucratic PSDs and develop innovative approaches to instruction. By empowering parents with both information and choice, the competitive forces of the marketplace may hold all schools, both charter and traditional public, more accountable for the quality of the service they provide.

Evidence of Effectiveness

The $64,000 question is, of course, whether any of this works. To date, the answer is "maybe" or "depending"—and in only some cases and some places. On the question of charter school contributions to educational innovation, the data are ambiguous. In a study of the impact of charter schools in Michigan, Mintrom (2001) found charter school practices seldom deviate from those in the established public school sector. As Mintrom and Plank (2001) noted, "Some charter schools are using old policies and practices in new ways, but many are using old approaches in old ways" (p. 52).

The degree to which competitive pressures applied by charter school programs alter the behavior of local public school districts depends in large part on contextual variables. It seems reasonable to expect PSDs to respond to the existence of one or more charter schools only to the extent that: 1. charters find a sympathetic audience among school officials, 2. the charter schools demonstrate the efficacy of an alternative pedagogy or, more likely, 3. charter schools pose a threat to the funding or existence of the public schools.

Research to date has found that under certain conditions public schools do, indeed, respond to the threat posed by charter schools (Hess, Maranto, & Milliman, 2001a; Hess, Maranto, & Milliman, 2001b; Teske, Schneider, Buckley, & Clark, 2001). Public school response, however, was mediated by a series of contextual variables. For example, a receptive school culture led to a positive response, as principals in these schools worked to establish a cooperative relationship with their charter school counterparts. Conversely, when public school administrators resisted the establishment of charter schools, public schools were less likely to respond by altering their practices (Hess et al., 2001a; Hess et al., 2001b; Teske et al., 2001).

On the other side of the ledger, growing district student populations leading to expanding enrollments has the effect of limiting the financial impact of student departures from the traditional public schools, thereby muting to some extent the incentive for PSDs to alter their behavior in response to charter schools. Indeed, in public school districts plagued by overcrowding, some administrators seem to welcome the presence of charter schools as a means of addressing an otherwise intractable problem (Hess et al., 2001a). Statutory environments limiting the extent to which funding follows defecting students to charter schools further insulate PSDs from competitive pressure, diminishing their incentive to change practices (Hess et al., 2001a; Teske et al., 2001).

There is also evidence that, in some situations, the market metaphor itself breaks down. Charter schools sometimes seek to do more (and less) than compete with their public school competitors in the area of service delivery. Rather than focusing strictly on the provision of more and better educational services, some charters have chosen to expend some of their energies lobbying local officials in an effort to alter the political landscape in which they operate. They may seek governmental support in acquiring facilities, expanded per pupil compensation, and exemptions from account-ability requirements (Henig, Holyke, Lacireno-Paquet, & Moser, 2003).

Perhaps the most contentious claim made by charter school proponents is that they lead to improved educational outcomes relative to their tradi-tional public school counterparts. One meta-analysis of research on charter school performance found the one area in which charter schools met expec-tations was in student achievement (Lin, 2001). Other research has been less encouraging. In 2003, the U.S. Department of Education used the National Assessment of Educational Progress (NAEP) to conduct an assessment of reading and mathematics skills of fourth-grade students in samples of both charter and public schools across the nation. Initial analyses of the data suggested that, contrary to the claim of charter school supporters, charter schools were not outperforming their public school counterparts. Indeed, on some dimensions, charter schools appeared outclassed by traditional public schools (Carnoy, Jacobson, Mishel, & Rothstein, 2005).

In 2004, the American Federation of Teachers (AFT) published a report focusing on the failure of charter schools to fulfill their promise of enhanced achievement. Among the claims in the AFT report was that disadvantaged and minority students in charter schools underperformed similar students in public schools. Charter school proponents responded that the AFT analysis failed to take into account a series of contextual variables that, if controlled for, would eliminate or reverse the difference (Carnoy et al., 2005). Not to be outdone, supporters of traditional public schools countered that if the same controls were applied to the assessment of public schools, the achieve-ment deficits in those institutions would in all likelihood be erased, along with the rationale for charter schools.

In the summer of 2006, NAEP published a more comprehensive analy-sis of the 2003 data (Braun, Jenkins, & Grigg, 2006). Using Hierarchical Linear Modeling (HLM), the NAEP study controlled for a number of the contextual, student- and school-level factors that fueled the debate between charter school supporters and opponents. The results did not bode well for charter schools. On no measure did charter school students outperform stu-dents in public schools. In those analyses yielding statistically significant dif-ferences, public schools consistently outperformed their charter competitors.

Thus, to date, charter schools may not have lived up to their initial billing. Nevertheless, additional research is clearly needed, and our chapter will examine the effect of charter schools on public schools in Texas.

A QUANTITATIVE ANALYSIS OF TEXAS CHARTER SCHOOLS

Our study of charter schools in Texas schooling covered the period 1998–2001. We focused on two primary hypotheses. We first examined the effect of the presence of charter schools on public school student enrollment. To the extent that the presence of a charter school alternative presents a real threat to traditional public schools, we might see overall public school enrollments decline in the presence of charter schools. Further, if charter schools are disproportionately serving non-minority students, we ought to find a positive relationship between the presence of charter schools and Latino enrollment in traditional public schools.

Our second hypothesis examined the effect on student achievement from competition between charter schools and traditional public schools. There are several reasons to anticipate that competition might foster change in public school behavior. Texas charter laws specify that funding follows the student. If students move into charter schools, the dollar amount that otherwise would go to the traditional public schools will follow the students into the new setting. The potential loss of students (and funds) may provide an incentive for educational leaders to innovate their programs to maintain enrollment figures and funding. In addition, public school leaders may respond to the competition (real or perceived) from charter schools in the interest of job preservation. Hess et al., (2001b) documented the loss of jobs by superintendents and principals who did not effectively respond to competition from charter schools.

As we lack direct measures of public school innovation, we assume that innovation translates into improvement (a potentially optimistic assumption; see Hess, 1998) and we therefore use improvement as a proxy for innovation. Therefore, to the extent that public school administrators see charter schools as a threat, and to the degree they are able to foster improvements, we expect to see student performance in traditional public schools improve. On the other hand, it is possible that public schools will undertake largely symbolic reforms in the face of competition, not attempt any reforms, or not be able to find effective solutions to difficult educational problems.

We are particularly interested in the effect of charter schools on Latino (primarily Mexican-American) students, and thus limited our analysis to school districts with at least 1,000 students and a minimum of 10% Latino student enrollment. Our analysis is a pooled time series of data from 1998–2001. We control for serial correlation by including a series of dummy variables. Our first dependent variables include both total public school enrollment as well as total Latino public school enrollment. We also examined student performance on the Texas standardized exams (TAAS), which were a major part of the school accountability and ranking system. In addition, we use a series of high-end performance measures that are meant to account for performance of the better students in the district. These include the number of students in Advanced Placement (AP) courses, the number of students taking either the ACT or SAT (indicators of students planning on attending college), the percentage of students taking advanced courses, and the number of students scoring at or above criterion on AP exams.

Our independent variables include several measures that influence educational performance. These measures typically are found in educational production functions (see Burtless, 1996).

- State aid to the district, which varies greatly in Texas.
- Two measures of teacher quality: percentage of teacher turnover, because turnover tends to reduce the effectiveness of instruction and depress student performance; and the number of teachers with advanced degrees, which is an indicator of teacher quality.
- Class size and Latino student attendance rates. Larger class sizes tend to depress student performance, and students cannot learn if they are not attending classes.
- A measure of bureaucracy—the percent of district staff in the bureaucracy. Chubb and Moe (1990) argued that a greater degree of bureaucracy leads to poor performance. On the other hand, Meier and Smith (1994) and Meier, Polinard, and Wrinkle (2000) suggest greater levels of bureaucracy may be a response to the difficult environment of public schools. Poorly performing public schools may therefore produce additional bureaucracy in an effort to solve problems.
- The percentage of Latino and African-American students. Meier, Polinard, and Wrinkle (2000) have suggested that public school districts with a large percentage of Latino students respond to poor performance by Latino students. In Anglo dominated districts, poor Latino student performance has no such effect.

CHARTERS SCHOOLS AND PUBLIC SCHOOLING

The study results suggest that charter school enrollments do not reduce student enrollment or academic performance in the traditional public schools.

Table 4.1 shows the regression analysis on total public school enrollment and Latino public school enrollment.

In this first model, our independent variables are simply lagged (1 year) charter enrollment and lagged (1 year) public school enrollment. The table therefore ascertains whether charter schools raise or decrease overall and Latino student enrollment while taking into account (*controlling for*, to use the statistical term) the common sense fact that contemporary enrollment is likely related to the enrollment of the past year.

As Table 4.1 indicates, the charter enrollment variable is statistically significant and positive in both models. This means that charter enrollments do not reduce either total public school enrollment or the Latino public school enrollment. However, this positive effect is quite minimal; a 100% increase in charter school enrollment would increase total enrollment by about 3% and Latino student enrollment by about 5%. The explanation is possibly that as charter schools grow in enrollment, so do the public schools, which reflects expanding school enrollment in Texas in both public and charter schools.

Table 4.2 models the Latino student pass rate on the TAAS exam. As Bohte (2004) notes, Texas charter schools are designated as county-level schools. While charter enrollment is small in some areas, the presence of charter schools in any given area might stimulate a response from traditional school districts. Thus, following Bohte (2001), we introduce the dummy variable for the presence of charter schools in the county.

The results show that the number of enrolled students in charter schools leads to a higher Latino student pass rate in the traditional public school

Table 4.1. The Effect of Charter School Enrollment on Texas Public School Enrollment

	Dependent Variable			
	Total Public School Enrollment		Latino Public School Enrollment	
Independent Variable	*Slope*	*t*	*Slope*	*t*
Lag charter enrollment	.026	4.837	.048	12.183
Lag public school enrollment	1.011	1949.269	—	—
Lag Latino student enrollment	—	—	1.027	1423.737
Adjusted R^2	.99		.99	
F (significance)	6010 (.000)		6010 (.000)	
N	2716		2178	

Table 4.2. Latino Student Pass Rates in Traditional Texas Public Schools

Variables	Model 1		Model 2	
	Slope	*SE*	*Slope*	*SE*
Lag charter enrollment	.0003**	.0001	—	—
Lag charter dummy	—	—	2.09***	.44
Class size	.005	.12	-.058	.125
Teacher with advanced degree	-.036	.022	-.044*	.022
Teacher turnover	-.347***	.037	-.346***	.036
Percent bureaucracy	-.575	.290	-.517	.285
State aid	-.030**	.009	.030**	.009
Percent Latino students	-.055***	.007	-.062***	.007
Percent African-American students	-.094***	.015	-.099***	.015
Latino student attendance rate	2.12***	0.20	2.07***	.20
N	2038		2039	
Adjusted R²	.55		.56	
F	178.16		180.9	

* Indicates result is significant at .05 level.

** Indicates result is significant at .01 level.

*** Indicates result is significant at .001 level.

Note: Dummy variables of individual years not reported.

system, although once again, the effect is quite small. We might therefore conclude that charter school enrollment has little effect on the performance of Latino students. We also see that the effects of the other variables in the model on Latino student achievement are as hypothesized above. For instance, as we might expect, higher teacher turnover leads to lower student achievement.

On the other hand, we might imagine that the public school might respond if a charter school operates nearby, but not worry about the size of its enrollment. In other words, maybe the very presence of even a small charter school may spur a response. The regression model in the second column of the table indicates exactly this. The charter school dummy variable is strongly associated with Latino student achievement.

Why and how might this happen? One possibility is that competition from charter schools might cause traditional public schools to respond by focusing on their better students, as their achievements might send a signal to parents that the traditional public school system is effective. Table 4.3 therefore examines whether the above-noted series of high-end performance measures are increased by the presence of a charter school or the number of student in such schools.

The regression results show that the percentage of students taking the college boards, as well as the percentage scoring at or above the criterion on AP classes, are not apparently affected by charter school enrollments. There are, however, some visible but minor effects of charter school enrollments on advanced placement classes and the percentage of students taking advanced classes.

Table 4.4 uses the same models, but with the dummy variable substituted for the enrollment variable. These new models show that all four high-end achievement measures are higher when there is a charter school in the county. These findings are consistent with the hypothesis that charter schools will trigger a competitive response from traditional public schools, and that having charter schools in the neighborhood will benefit the higher-achieving students in the traditional public schools.

CONCLUSIONS

The results in this chapter indicate that charter school enrollments do not have a significant effect on either overall enrollment or the academic performance of Latino students in traditional Texas public schools. On the other hand, the very presence of a charter school in a district—not the number of students enrolled in it—may spur public schools to improve student achievement in traditional public schools.

Table 4.3. The Effect of Charter School Enrollment on Latino Students' High End Performance Measures

Measure	Coefficient	Standard Error	R^2
Students in AP courses	.00029**	.000094	.14
Students taking SAT/ACT (%)	.0003	.00016	.13
Students taking advanced courses (%)	.00018*	.00009	.076
Students scoring at or above criterion on AP	.00017	.00027	.37

* Indicates result is significant at .05 level.

** Indicates result is significant at .01 level.

Note: Independent variable = Lag Charter School enrollments.
Control variables are the same as in Tables 4.1 and 4.2 (not reported).

Table 4.4. The Impact of Charter School Dummy on Latino Students High End
Performance Measures

Measure	Coefficient	Standard Error	R^2
Students in AP courses	2.620[***]	.362	.173
Students taking SAT/ACT (%)	5.558[***]	.955	.103
Students taking advanced courses (%)	2.763[***]	.398	.086
Students scoring at or above criterion on AP	4.573[***]	1.875	.606

*** Indicates result is significant at .001 level.

Note: Independent variable = Lag Charter School dummy variable.
Control variables are the same as in Tables 4.1 and 4.2 (not reported).

Why do charter school enrollments not have much effect on Latino students? First, there is the question of size. At this stage of their development, charter schools enroll only a fraction of the total public school student population in Texas. As the number of charter schools grows and their enrollments expand, this might change. If charter school enrollments grew larger relative to the overall student enrollment, then we might see additional competitive dynamics.

Second, the fact that the mere presence of charter schools has such an effect on enrollment and achievement suggests that school districts are reacting to and anticipating the possibility of competition from the charters. This appears to be most evident when one looks at overall student performance as well as high-end student performance. That is, leaders in traditional public schools appear to be looking over their shoulders at the (not quite yet) looming presence of charter schools and upgrading the performance of their schools (although what measures they may be undertaking is a different question). While some funding losses due to charter schools have likely occurred, given the nature of school funding, it is doubtful if the amounts, at their current levels, significantly affect the districts. A trickle may turn into a torrent, however, and districts may be cautiously preparing for a flood.

NOTES

This chapter draws on a paper presented at the 2003 annual national meeting of the Midwest Political Science Association (Bohte, Wrinkle, & Polinard, 2003).

1. Strong because the law allows entities other than school boards to create charter schools; a wide range of people and organizations can start charter schools; charters schools may be legal and fiscally independent of the local school board; and

charter schools receive automatic exemptions from a broad range of state and local policies. However, the Texas law had restrictions on the number of charter schools.

2. As Hess (2004) noted, "Those who suggest that a smattering of charter schools, that a handful of school vouchers, or that the public choice provisions of No Child Left Behind are sufficient to force systematic improvement are allowing their enthusiasm to get the best of them" (p. 249).

REFERENCES

Bohte, J. (2001). School bureaucracy and student performance at the local level. *Public Administration Review, 61*(January/February), 92–99.

Bohte, J. (2004). Examining the impact of charter schools on performance in traditional public schools. *Policy Studies Journal, 32,* 501–520.

Bohte, J., Wrinkle, R. D., & Polinard, J. L. (2003). *Examining the impact of charter schools on public school performance.* Paper delivered at the annual national meeting of the Midwest Political Science Association, Chicago.

Braun, H., Jenkins, F., & Grigg, W. (2006). *A closer look at charter schools using hierarchical linear modeling.* Washington, DC: National Assessment of Educational Progress, National Center for Education Statistics. U.S. Department of Education.

Burtless, G. (1996). *Does money matter? The effect of school resources on student achievement and adult success.* Washington, DC: Brookings Institution Press.

Carnoy, M., Jacobson, R., Mishel, L., & Rothstein, R. (2005). *The charter school dust-up: Examining the evidence on enrollment and achievement.* Washington, DC: Economic Policy Institute; New York: Teachers College Press.

Center for Education Reform. (2009). *National charter school & enrollment statistics 2009.* Washington, DC: Author. Retrieved June 17, 2010, from http://www.edreform.com/_upload/CER_charter_numbers.pdf

Chubb, J., & Moe, T. M. (1990). *Politics, markets and America's schools.* Washington, DC: Brookings Institution Press.

Finn, C., Manno, B. V., & Vanourek, G. (2000). *Charter schools in action.* Princeton, NJ: Princeton University Press.

Hassel, B. C. (1999). *The charter school challenge: Avoiding the pitfalls, fulfilling the promise.* Washington, DC: Brookings Institution Press.

Henig, J., Holyoke, T. T., Lacireno-Paquet, N., & Moser, M. (2003). Privatization, politics, and urban services: The political behavior of charter schools. *Journal of Urban Affairs, 25,* 37–54.

Hess, F. (1998). *Spinning wheels: The politics of urban school reform.* Washington, DC: Brookings Institution Press.

Hess, F. (2002). *Revolution at the margins: The impact of competition on urban school systems.* Washington, DC: Brookings Institution Press.

Hess, F. (2004). Markets and urban schooling: What choice-drive competition is doing and how to make it do more. In C. Lartique, & D. Salisbury (Eds.), *Educational freedom in urban America: Brown v. Brown after a half a century* (pp. 247–264). Washington, DC: Cato Institute.

Hess, F., Maranto, R., & Milliman, S. (2001a). Responding to competition: School leaders and school culture. In P. Peterson, & D. E. Campbell (Eds.), *Charters, vouchers, and public education*. Washington, DC: Brookings Institution Press.

Hess, F., Maranto, R., & Milliman, S. (2001b). Small districts in big trouble: How four Arizona school systems responded to charter competition. *Teachers College Record, 103*, 1102–1124.

Leal, D. L. (1999). Congress and Charter Schools. In R. Maranto, S. Milliman, F. Hess, & A. Gresham (Eds.), *School choice in the real world: Lessons from Arizona charter schools*. Boulder, CO: Westview Press.

Lin, Q. (2001). An evaluation of charter school effectiveness. *Education, 122*, 166–177.

Maranto R., Milliman, S., Hess, F., & Gresham, A. (Eds.). (1999). *School choice in the real world: Lessons from Arizona charter schools*. Boulder, CO: Westview.

Meier, K. J., Polinard, J. L., & Wrinkle, R. D. (2000). Bureaucracy and organizational performance: Causality arguments about public schools. *American Journal of Political Science, 44*, 590–602.

Meier, K. J., & Smith, K. B. (1994). Politics, bureaucrats and schools. *Public Administration Review, 54*, 551–558.

Mintrom, M. (2001). Policy design for local innovation: The effects of competition in public schooling. *State Politics and Policy Quarterly, 1*, 343–63.

Mintrom, M., & Plank, D. N. (2001). School choice in Michigan. In P. Peterson, & D. E. Campbell (Eds.), *Charters, vouchers, and public education*. Washington, DC: The Brookings Institution.

RPP International. (1998). *A national study of charter schools: Second-year report*. Washington, DC: U.S. Office of Educational Research and Improvement.

Teske, P., Schneider, M., Buckley, J., & Clark, S. (2001). Can charter schools change traditional public schools? In P. Peterson, & D. E. Campbell (Eds.), *Charters, vouchers, and public education*. Washington, DC: Brookings Institution Press.

Tyack, D., & Cuban, L. (1995). *Tinkering toward utopia: A century of public school reform*. Cambridge, MA: Harvard University Press.

Wells, A. S., Grutzik, C., Carnochen, S., Slayton, J., & Vasudeva, A. (1999). Underlying policy assumptions of charter school reform: The multiple meanings of a movement. *Teachers College Record, 100*, 513–535.

CHAPTER 5

The Latino Student–Teacher Gap in Immigrant Gateways: Constraints and Policy Solutions

Paru Shah and Melissa Marschall

Between 1990 and 2000, the Latino population in the United States increased by approximately 10 million, accounting for 38% of the nation's overall population growth during the decade. This new demographic pressure has meant that an influx of diverse and relatively young migrants and families is seeking services from public institutions not accustomed to serving them, among them, the public school system.

Currently, Latino children account for about one in six school-aged children (NCES, 2002), and one in four immigrant children (Fix, Passel, & Ruiz de Velasco, 2004). This rapid influx of Latino students has not been met with a concurrent increase in the numbers of Latino teachers, however. Indeed, while American students are becoming more racially, linguistically and ethnically diverse, diversity among the teaching force is decreasing. Teachers continue to be predominantly Anglo, female, monolingual and middle class (Kirby, Berends, & Naftel, 1999; Rong & Preissle, 1998; Urban Teacher Challenge, 2000). Moreover, despite targeted recruitment efforts, minority teachers constituted less than 10% of the teaching force in 2008 (National Center for Education Statistics, 2009), down from roughly 15% in 1994 (Goodwin, Genishi, Asher, & Woo, 1997).

This gap between Latino students and Latino teachers is significant for a number of reasons. First, most studies report that the presence of racial and ethnic minorities positively affects school policies and institutional practices with implications for minority students (National Collaborative on Diversity in the Teaching Force, 2004; Urban Teacher Challenge, 2000). Second, research finds that Latino and other minority teachers and administrators serve as cultural brokers between the school and home environments, and thereby foster more supportive relations and stronger ties (Goodwin, 2002;

Lomotey, 1989). Finally, evidence suggests that the smaller the gap between Latino teachers and students, the greater the likelihood of student academic success (Polinard, Wrinkle, & Meier, 1995).

Given the importance of Latino teachers for the schooling and educational outcomes of Latino students, we feel it is important to identify where the problem is most severe while also developing a better understanding of how various institutional and contextual factors influence the gap between these students and teachers. Thus, this chapter considers two questions. First, how big is the Latino student-teacher gap and does it vary according to the social and political characteristics of the local context? Second, are the governance and organizational structures within districts tied to Latino teacher recruitment and retention efforts, and if so, which structures and recruitment practices are the most effective?

LATINO TEACHER SUPPLY AND DEMAND: IMMIGRANT GATEWAYS

The national call to address the minority teacher shortage came onto the public agenda as early as 1996 following concerns of a more general shortage of teachers across the United States (Kirby, Berends, & Naftel, 1999; Urban Teacher Challenge, 2000). Studies cite numerous culprits, including the age of the population, educational attainment, and resources (Jorgenson, 2001; National Collaborative on Diversity in Teaching, 2004). Ironically, in an era where more minorities are enrolled in college, fewer are pursuing a degree in education because access to more resources provides multiple new job opportunities (Darling-Hammond, Pittman, & Ottinger, 1987; Kirby, Darling-Hammond, & Hudson, 1993).

Latinos seeking teaching jobs are further constrained by language, nativity, and citizenship issues; thus, while a substantial adult population is part of the answer to the teaching shortage, it masks the larger issue of generating a pool of eligible and able Latinos who are interested in teaching careers. We posit that structural constraints, which affect levels of social and political incorporation, influence the probability of Latinos entering the teaching force and thus the supply of Latino teachers. We also believe that regional differences in immigration and the distribution of social services and political structure mean that this gap between Latino teachers and students manifests itself differently according to location.

Relying partly on Singer's (2004) conceptualization of immigrant "gateways," we categorize major metropolitan areas into four types of destinations in order to explore how regional differences in immigration patterns, experiences with Latino native and foreign-born populations, and the impact of these factors on social structures, political institutions, and minority representation contribute to the Latino teacher-student gap.

Continuous Gateways have been the entry point for immigrants since the beginning of the 20th century, and continue to be the first destination for many immigrants. They are predominantly racially heterogeneous cities in the Northeast and Midwest, and include sizeable immigrant populations from Latin America, Eastern Europe, and Asia (U.S. Census, 2001). While these cities have struggled to accommodate new immigrants, their long history with immigrant populations place continuous gateways at an advantage for providing social services to new immigrants and assimilating them into American life (Judd & Swanstrom, 2006). In addition, Continuous Gateway cities are characterized by governing arrangements, namely district elections, the mayor-council form of government, and larger council sizes, that are associated with greater participation and representation among minority groups. As relatively recent immigrants in these cities, Latinos have benefited from these arrangements and gained political representation through the actions of previous generations (NALEO, 2001).

Post-World War II Gateways became attractive immigrant destinations after the passage of the Immigration and Nationality Act of 1965, and include cities in California, Florida, and Texas. The rapid influx of immigrants from predominantly Latin American and Asian countries caught many Post-WWII Gateway cities without sufficient infrastructure to provide social services to this new population (Judd & Swanstrom, 2006). In addition, the implementation of a number of federal anti-immigration policies, such as the 1996 Personal Responsibility and Work Opportunity Reconciliation Act, and the Illegal Immigration Reform and Immigrant Responsibility Act, scaled back the rights of legal and unauthorized immigrants, made it easier to deport, remove, or bar immigrants from the United States, and paved the way for additional state-level anti-immigration policies that affect Latinos in these gateway cities.

Finally, unlike the Continuous Gateways, Post-WWII Gateways have reform-style governments, which are characterized by nonpartisan, at-large electoral structures, council-manager or commission forms of government, and smaller city councils, which tend to weaken minority voting blocs and discourage minority and immigrant participation (Banfield & Wilson, 1963; Karnig & Welch, 1982). In sum, compared to the Continuous Gateways, Latinos in Post-WWII Gateways have found themselves in cities unaccustomed to immigration, ill equipped to deal with a large influx of new, foreign-born residents, and less likely to accommodate minority interests in local politics.

New Destinations experienced tremendous growth only in the last decade or two; the majority of the new foreign-born population has come from Mexico (Chapa & de la Rosa, 2004). These metropolitan areas are not only unaccustomed to immigration, but the influx of mainly young, primarily Spanish-speaking Latinos has also created a shift in the traditional black/white racial dynamics of many of these cities. Many New Destination cities have reformed governments that make Latino political incorporation more arduous. Finally, anti-immigration sentiments originally espoused in Post-WWII Gateways are finding themselves on the policy agenda in New Destinations in North Carolina, Georgia, and Arkansas (Southern Poverty Law Center, 2005). Thus, compared to Continuous and Post-WWII Gateways, Latinos in New Destinations are perhaps the most disadvantaged in terms of social services and political incorporation.

In addition to immigrant gateways, we also consider how settlement patterns and the social and institutional context of *Historical Destinations* influence the Latino student-teacher gap. These areas predominantly include border areas with traditionally large Latino populations but low levels of foreign–born Mexicans. Because Latinos (Mexicans) lived in Arizona, California, Colorado, New Mexico, and Texas prior to annexation by the United States, they cannot be considered immigrants. And, unlike other destinations and gateways, these locales comprise the heartland of second- and third-generation Latinos, most equipped to handle Latino issues socially and politically. Indeed, of the 4,050 Latino elected officials in the United States in 2001, 3,623 (89.5%) are in the five states listed above (NALEO, 2001).

In sum, demographic shifts and differential immigration patterns have resulted in very different levels of Latino social and political incorporation across regions and immigrant gateway cities. In general, we expect that, compared to Historical Destinations, all immigrant gateways will have more difficulty addressing the Latino teacher-student gap. Moreover, as we discuss below, we expect variation within gateway types due to differences in migration patterns, social structures, political institutions, and minority representation that pose greater structural constraints in some gateway types than others.

REMEDYING THE GAP: POLITICAL AND POLICY SOLUTIONS

The proportion of Latino teachers in the United States is declining. This is explained, in part, by demographic features of the Latino population (age, nativity, citizenship, educational attainment). However, generating a pool of eligible Latino teachers requires more than a large adult population base. It must also involve overcoming the structural constraints that affect levels of social and political incorporation. Political and governing arrangements and policy changes represent two means by which districts can begin remedying the Latino teacher-student gap.

Political and Governing Arrangements

Research on minority politics suggests that the composition of governing bodies plays an important role in both the agenda setting and implementation stages of the policy process. One area where minority representation has been found to have an especially large impact is on public sector hiring policies (Mladenka, 1989; Stein, 1986). In the domain of schools, extant research has demonstrated that increases in the representation of Latinos on school boards are associated with greater Latino representation in teaching and administrative positions (Leal, Martinez-Ebers, & Meier, 2004; Polinard et al., 1995). Not only are school boards responsible for hiring superintendents, but they also have the capacity to enact formal policies and exert informal pressure on higher-level school administrators when it comes to hiring decisions at lower administrative levels (Stewart, England, & Meier, 1989). School administrators, in turn, play an important role in hiring teachers and so can influence the extent to which Latinos are represented in these positions in the school district (Leal et al., 2004). School districts with Latino representation at the board level therefore have a greater capacity to enact policies to address Latino teacher shortages and, more generally, are expected to be more proactive in their efforts to recruit Latino teachers.

Another means by which educational stakeholders can increase their influence on school policy in general, and hiring practices more specifically, is by creating charter schools. Because charter schools are granted autonomy over their operation and are freed from certain traditional public school regulations, they have considerably greater flexibility with many institutional aspects of schooling, including teacher recruitment and retention policies, and often hire teachers from "nontraditional" backgrounds (Burian-Fitzgerald & Harris, 2004). State laws regarding teacher certification requirements for charter schools vary considerably. Some states require charter school operators to hire only certified personnel while others are allowed to hire a specified percentage of uncertified teachers. This may have implications for charter schools' capacity to hire Latino teachers.

That charter schools in many states are not covered by collective bargaining agreements raises the more general question of how teacher's unions influence school governance and decision making in the area of teacher hiring and recruitment. Because unions typically impose greater barriers to entry and reduce the schools' and districts' flexibility to hire new teachers or teachers from nontraditional backgrounds, it is commonly believed that they play a role in reducing the incidence of minority teachers, particularly in urban districts (Levin & Quinn, 2003). For example, union transfer requirements that give existing teachers the first choice of openings before any new teacher can be hired are especially likely to disadvantage prospective Latino teachers in areas where they are new arrivals. Likewise, union contracts that allow transferring teachers to displace less-senior teachers from their positions are also likely to adversely affect Latino teachers in many districts.

Policy Tools

While certain political and governing arrangements increase the likelihood that policies seeking to address the Latino teacher-student gap get on the agenda and receive adequate support, these arrangements tell us little about what kinds of policies have actually been pursued or how effective these policies are in addressing that gap. In our review of the literature we found two broad policies—certification requirements and state and district incentives—that were most strongly associated with changes in the supply of Latino teachers.

ALTERNATIVE CERTIFICATION. Beginning in the early 1990s most states instituted stronger requirements for teacher certification, including the use of standardized tests (Kirby, Darling-Hammond, & Hudson, 1993). The initiation of these more stringent requirements resulted in a decline in minority teachers, especially African-American and Latino teacher candidates. Coupled with the overall decline in persons entering the teaching force (NCES, 2002), many states opted for some form of alternative certification. In its broadest sense, alternative certification programs refer to programs that bring new teachers into the system without a bachelor's degree *in education*. The majority of these programs still require a bachelor's degree in some field and in addition, intensive mentoring programs for 1 to 2 years (National Center for Education Information, 2005).

Many districts began implementing alternative certification programs in the early 1980s with success. For example, approximately 18% of new hires in California enter teaching through one of the state's 63 alternative routes and almost half of these teachers were from underrepresented minority groups (National Center for Education Information, 2005). In Texas, which implemented its first alternative teacher certification program in 1985, 48% of new hires now come through its 75 alternative teacher certification programs (National Center for Education Information, 2005). During roughly this same period, the Latino teaching force in Texas increased from 12% to 18% (Kirby, Berends, & Naftel, 1999).

In recent years, many districts have adopted alternative certification programs across the country. According to a 2005 poll conducted by the National Center for Education Information, 619 providers of individual programs in 47 states as well as the District of Columbia had implemented 122 alternative routes to teacher certification. Given these programs' objectives, we would expect that districts actively using alternative certification options would have larger numbers of Latino teachers and potentially a smaller Latino teacher-student gap.

STATE AND DISTRICT INCENTIVE POLICIES. The demand for more teachers in general and more diversity in the teaching force is not uniform across the country. Urban school districts tend to suffer from large teacher shortages due to high teacher turnover rates and the reluctance of certified teachers to accept jobs in these settings (National Commission on Teaching and America's Future, 1996; Clewell & Villegas, 1999). In order to address these concerns, many states have implemented geographic shortage incentives. These typically involve legislation that provides financial incentives for teachers to relocate to high-need areas, like urban and rural school districts. Included in these financial incentives are salary increases, bonuses, or tax credits (Education Commission of the States, 2002).

In addition to the disproportionate need for teachers in general in certain geographic locations, specific fields have become severely underrepresented, such as English as a Second Language (ESL) and bilingual education (Urban Teacher Challenge, 2000). Attempts to address these shortages include monetary incentives as well as offering additional training and support for teachers. In their analysis of the effectiveness of incentives in Texas, Hanushek, Kain, and Rivkin (2002) found that salary plays only a modest role in teacher retention, whereas effective training and a supportive teaching environment are more important. Unfortunately, although many states have implemented these shortage area incentive programs, few have evaluated their effectiveness (National Association of State Boards of Education, 2002). While these incentive programs are not always targeted specifically at Latino teacher recruitment, we expect that their implementation could signal a district's willingness to address the need for a more diverse teaching force to Latino candidates.

VARIATION ACROSS THE GATEWAYS

Understanding the different immigration and migration patterns of Latinos across the United States provides a unique context in which to both assess the demographic, social, and institutional characteristics of our four gateway/destination types and evaluate policy incentives and political structures. Table 5.1 provides an overview of each of these factors by gateway type. Although the gap between Latino students and teachers hovers consistently around 25%, Historical Destinations have the largest number of Latino teachers and students. Given the history of large Latino settlements in these areas, this is not unexpected. Historical Destinations, as expected, also include fewer foreign-born and noncitizen Latinos, and their Latino populations tend to have more resources than the other immigrant gateway

Table 5.1. Demographic, Social, and Institutional Characteristics of School Districts by Gateway/Destination Type, 1999–2000 (in Percentages)

	Historical Destinations (n = 139)	Continuous Gateways (n = 61)	Post-WWII Gateways (n = 83)	New Destination Gateways (n = 104)
Latino students	48.8	27.4	38.8	29.8
Latino teachers	22.8	4.9	10.2	7.5
Latino population 25 years and older	31.2	20.0	27.8	17.2
Latinos foreign born	26.4	50.2	39.0	39.1
Latinos non-citizens	19.3	35.4	27.5	31.1
Latinos with a bachelor's degree, 2000	6.1	11.8	5.6	7.0
Latino homeowners	59.6	39.4	55.1	50.9
Latino school board representation	43.8	4.9	28.9	19.2
Charter schools	15.1	11.4	24.1	15.3
Teacher's unions	56.8	100.0	80.7	62.5
Alternative certification programs	85.6	78.6	93.9	86.5
Relocation incentives	10.7	6.5	9.6	10.5
Shortage incentives	40.2	16.3	38.5	35.5
Free ESL training	46.0	34.4	57.8	52.8
Average district entry salary (with BA)	$27,879	$31,987	$31,088	$28,360

Source: National Association of Latino Elected Officials, 1999; National Center for Education Statistics, 2001; U.S. Census Bureau, 2000.

cities. Latino political incorporation is also strongest in the Historical Destinations, where 43.8% of school boards have at least one Latino school board member. On the other hand, Post-WWII Gateways are most likely to have charter schools, and teachers' unions are most prevalent in Continuous and Post-WWII Gateways.

With regard to policy tools, we find that alternative certification programs are common everywhere, but are most prevalent in Post-WWII Gateway districts. On the other hand, stringent certification requirements are more common in the Continuous Gateways, which perhaps have spent the most time addressing teacher quantity and quality issues. Incentive programs are also common across all gateway types, although New Destinations are more likely to have multiple incentive programs, including relocation, shortage and ESL training, whereas Continuous Gateways are distinguished by having the highest entry-level salaries.

In sum, while a general Latino teacher shortage exists across the United States, this framework helps explain the various ways in which this shortage is manifest. Keeping in mind the structural constraints that underlie the Latino teacher shortage, including citizenship issues, educational attainment, and resources, in the next section we analyze the roles that these institutional, contextual, and policy factors play in terms of the number of Latino teachers within a given district.

EMPIRICALLY ANALYZING THE RELATIONSHIP BETWEEN LATINO STUDENTS AND TEACHERS

To examine the set of relationships articulated in the preceding section, we used the 1999–2000 National Center for Educational Statistics, Schools and Staffing Survey district sample. We selected districts with at least 10% Latino students located either in a central city or in a suburban or county district situated in a metropolitan area. With 387 districts in four immigrant gateways/destinations, our sample includes the districts where the majority of Latino students attend school and captures the regional variation in district organization and Latino ethnic origin, migration patterns, and political incorporation.

Modeling the "Gap" between Latino Teachers and Students

Arguments decrying the need for more Latino teachers often point to the difference in the proportion of Latino students and Latino teachers. Simply creating a difference measure misrepresents the extent of the gap, however, since the proportion of Latino students almost exclusively drives this measure. To circumvent this issue, we utilized both a proportion and an incident rate to assess the Latino teacher shortage. Our first analysis investigated the factors that explain the proportion of Latino teachers (relative to all teachers) within a school district, whereas the second examined more directly the Latino teacher-student gap by looking at the rate of Latino teachers per 100 Latino students. This standardized measure of the student-teacher gap allowed comparisons across districts with different proportions of Latino students and teachers. We hypothesize that the size of the gap will be a function of political and governance structures, district policies, sociodemographic constraints, and immigrant destination.

POLITICAL/GOVERNANCE STRUCTURES. We operationalized Latino political incorporation as the number of *Latino School Board Members* in 1999 and expected that as the number of Latino school board members increased, the proportion and incidence of Latino teachers would also increase. We also included a binary variable for districts that allow *Charter* schools (1 = yes, 0 = no), with the expectation that districts with more schooling options and more alternative staffing programs would have more Latino teachers. Lastly, we controlled for whether or not the teachers within the district had an agreement with the teacher's *Union* for collective bargaining (1 = yes, 0 = no), with the expectation that this agreement would diminish the ability of the district to implement alternative solutions for the teacher shortage.

DISTRICT POLICIES. We also included three district-level variables that measure policies aimed at remedying the gap: 1. providing teachers with free *Training* in ESL or bilingual education (1 = yes, 0 = no); 2. using *Emergency Certification* to fill shortages (1 = yes, 0 = no); and 3. providing incentives for teachers to *Relocate* to shortage areas or for *Shortage* areas to recruit teachers (1 = yes, 0 = no). We expected districts with these policies to have greater proportions and rates of Latino teachers. Because the *Stringency* of the district's certification standards was also likely to affect the proportion and incidence of Latino teachers, we tested for this as well. This variable measured the extent to which a district had incorporated the NCLB teacher requirements of 1. having a bachelor's degree, 2. being fully state-certified, and 3. demonstrating competence in each subject area taught (each counted for one point, so the measure ranged from 0–3). Given these mandates, as well as the evidence suggesting that Latino teachers may have more difficulty meeting all of these requirements, we expected a lower proportion and incidence of Latino teachers in districts that attempted to meet these requirements. Last, we included *Entry Level Salary* for teachers with a bachelor's degree and no teaching experience as a control for desirability of teaching versus other careers. Districts with higher salaries should attract more candidates, regardless of race, thereby increasing competition and potentially reducing Latino candidates' chances of securing a teaching position.

SOCIO-DEMOGRAPHIC CONSTRAINTS. The supply of potential Latino teacher candidates is a critical variable that must also be considered. We expected the pool of available and/or eligible Latino teachers would be smaller in districts with higher proportions of new immigrants and where the Latino adult population was smaller, less assimilated, and less educated. In order to test these effects, we included variables that measure the district percentage of: 1. Latinos *25 and Older*, 2. Latino *NonCitizens*, 3. Latinos with a *Bachelor's Degree*, and 4. Latino *Homeowners* in the district. Last, we controlled for the total enrollment of students in the district (*District Size*, logged), and those districts within *Central Cities*.

IMMIGRANT GATEWAYS. Lastly, we included variables for each of the three immigrant gateway types: *Continuous*, *Post-WWII*, and *New Destination*.

The excluded category or reference group here is the Historical Destinations. Given the impact of the contextual and institutional differences on the social and political incorporation of Latino immigrants discussed above, we expected immigrant gateways—in comparison to Historical Destinations—to have smaller proportions of Latino teachers, and lower Latino teacher incidence rates. Further, the supply problem was likely to be worse in immigrant gateways where Latinos were less established.

STUDY FINDINGS

Table 5.2 provides the results from our Ordinary Least Squares (OLS) regression models. Beginning with model 1, which tested for the proportion of the total teacher population within the district, we find that governance and organizational arrangements have a significant effect on the proportion of Latino teachers. First, Latino representation on the school board increases the proportion of Latino teachers by .034 per elected board member. In other words, school districts with two Latino school board members have almost 7% more Latino teachers on their teaching force than schools with no Latino representation in governance. This finding supports previous research and our hypothesis regarding the positive impact Latino representation can have on the supply of Latino teachers. Translating the substantive effect of school-board membership on the proportion of Latino teachers by immigrant gateway/destination, we find, as expected, more Latino teachers in Historical Destinations than in either Post-WWII Gateways or Destinations.

Districts that provide charter school options also have a higher proportion of Latino teachers, although this can be offset by the presence of teachers' unions, which decreases the proportion. In sum, districts with greater Latino representation at the school-board level and more flexibility in personnel and other policies provided by charter schools have larger proportions of Latino teachers.

In terms of district-implemented policies, we find that programs aimed specifically at the Latino teacher shortage—alternative certification and ESL training—increase the proportion of Latino teachers within the district. On the other hand, more general incentive programs (relocation and shortage incentives) were not significant. We speculate that while the provision of these incentives signals that a district is perhaps open to alternative methods of attracting more Latino teachers, the incentives themselves are not race- or ethnicity-specific, and thus may also reward non-Latino teachers.

Greater stringency in certification requirements does not appear to affect the supply of Latino teachers. Given our cross-sectional design, it is

Table 5.2. OLS Estimates of the Latino Teacher Supply/Student–Teacher Gap

	Model 1: Proportion of Latino Teachers	Model 2: Latino Teacher Incidence Rate
Latino school board member	.034*** (.004)	.198*** (.046)
Charter schools	.024* (.014)	.403*** (.152)
Teacher's union	-.028** (.012)	-.358*** (.129)
ESL training	.017* (.010)	.117 (.109)
Alternative certification	.061** (.026)	.639** (.274)
Relocation incentives	.0002 (.017)	.032 (.179)
Shortage area incentives	.004 (.011)	-.095 (.120)
Stringency of certification requirements	.006 (.004)	.079 (.051)
Entry level salary	-.000 (.000)	.000 (.000)
Latinos 25+	.574*** (.046)	2.95*** (.484)
Noncitizen Latinos	-.024 (.052)	-1.78*** (.544)
Latinos with bachelor's degree	.379*** (.113)	5.29*** (1.18)
Latino homeowners	.113*** (.041)	.967** (.431)
District size, logged	.006 (.004)	.062 (.048)
Central city	.011 (.012)	.088 (.127)
Continuous gateways	-.017 (.021)	-.304 (.219)
Post-WWII gateways	-.064*** (.016)	-.848*** (.167)
New destinations	-.047*** (.014)	-.334** (.151)
Constant	-.160** (.077)	-.652 (.803)
F (18, 366)	45.27 (.000)	20.34 (.000)
R^2	.6901	.5000

$^*p < .10,$ $^{**}p < .0,$ $^{***}p < .001$

not possible for us to analyze how the initiation of these more stringent requirements impacts the Latino teacher population over time; however, our findings suggest that these requirements are not having adverse effects on the Latino student-teacher gap, as we expected they would. Finally, entry-level district salaries have no effect on the proportion of Latino teachers in a district. Again, because our analysis is restricted to one point in time, we cannot assess how increases or decreases impact the number of Latino teachers. Moreover, without information on starting salaries in other professions, it is not easy to tease out how starting teacher salaries compare or whether competition between teaching and other professions exists.

In addition, the results support our hypotheses regarding the eligibility and availability of Latino residents within the district. Specifically, the proportion of Latinos 25 years and older, as well as the proportion with a bachelor's degree and homeowners, are positively related to the proportion of Latino teachers within the district. While not the sole factors related to the Latino teacher shortage, our analysis demonstrates the importance of having a population of eligible Latino adults with the resources necessary to become teachers.

While many of the socio-demographic measures we employ capture the constraints districts face in developing a sufficient pool of potential Latino teacher candidates, other unmeasured factors are captured by the dummy variables representing the different types of immigrant gateways. For example, compared to districts in Historical Destinations, significantly fewer Latinos teach in the Post-WWII Gateways and New Destinations. Given their more recent experience with immigration in general, the tendency for cities in these locations to be characterized by reformed governments, and the absence of institutionalized arrangements to foster immigrant political incorporation, these types of immigrant gateways face greater supply problems than do Historical Destinations. Further, Continuous Gateways, which have a longer history of immigration, a higher incidence of unreformed governments, and a greater tradition of immigrant political incorporation, do not appear to have significantly greater supply problems than Historical Destinations.

Model 2 investigates these same relationships with a different operationalization of the Latino teacher shortage as an incidence rate per 100 Latino students. It takes into account the number of Latino teachers per 100 Latino students in the districts. Thus, the analysis here is not simply of the size of the Latino teacher force, but also of how well the Latino teacher force meets the demand posed by the size of the Latino student body.

In general, we find very similar results to model 1. Governance and organizational arrangements prove to be significantly related to the Latino teacher incidence rate, with gains in Latino school board seats increasing the rate by .198 points. Substantively, we can interpret this in the following way: increasing Latino school-board representation from one to five members translates into an increase of one additional Latino teacher per 100 Latino students. Charter school provisions are more strongly tied to an increase in Latino teachers, whereas again we find a negative relationship between teacher's unions and the incidence rate.

District-level policies also follow a similar pattern in model 2; the only district policy that substantially decreases the gap between students and teachers is alternative certification programs, however. That is, districts with an alternative certification program have 0.639 more teachers per 100 Latino students than districts without certification. Unlike model 1, English as a Second Language (ESL) training is not significant in this model. As the incidence rate specifically takes into account the number of Latino students, we speculate that districts with large numbers of Latino students may be more likely to already have a large Latino teacher population, and thus not need ESL training, or may employ para-educators to supplement the ESL classes, again restricting the likelihood of offering ESL training (Genzuk, Lavadenz, & Krashen, 1994; Ng, 2003). Thus, results from the Latino teacher incidence rate model again point to the importance of policies directed specifically at diversifying the teaching force.

Finally, our hypotheses regarding the role socio-demographic constraints and immigrant gateway/destination cities are confirmed in model 2 as well. The effect of education is particularly noteworthy here, with a 0.20 increase in the proportion of the Latino population with a bachelor's degree resulting in approximately one additional Latino teacher per 100 Latino students. Again, compared to Historical Destinations, both Post-WWII Gateways and New Destinations have fewer Latino teachers per Latino students.

CONCLUSIONS

Our analysis of the Latino student-teacher gap within the framework of Latino immigration and migration patterns provides a unique understanding of the ways in which institutional and contextual variables impact the supply of Latino teachers. Our findings demonstrate that districts with a larger eligible Latino teacher pool are characterized by a particular set of socio-demographic features, as well as by important district-level political structures and policies. Importantly, the Latino teacher shortage is intrinsically related to the proportion of "eligible" Latinos within the district; that is, those 25 and older who hold a bachelor's degree. In addition, citizenship status matters, as does the extent to which Latinos are attached to their local community, as measured by the percentage of Latino homeowners. These findings suggest that the gap found in newly settled areas will continue to be large, since in these communities Latino populations tend to be younger, less educated, less likely to own a home, and are comprised of a greater percentage of noncitizens. Thus, they face greater constraints in increasing the pool of eligible Latino teachers from which their local school districts draw.

Our analyses also provide some evidence of the effectiveness of alternative hiring practices, incentive structures, and political arrangements. Our findings echo those of previous researchers as to the inadequacy of incentive programs to demonstrably change the supply of teachers. Moreover, we find that general policies aimed at the overall teacher shortage are not particularly well suited to address the Latino teacher-student gap. Demonstrating an interest in specifically recruiting Latino teachers and providing Latinos with a representative voice in school governance and the educational process more generally are important ways districts can increase the supply of Latino teachers and reduce the Latino student-teacher gap. This holds especially in Post-WWII Gateways and New Destinations, where the immigrant population is less incorporated both politically and socioeconomically.

REFERENCES

Banfield, E. C., & Wilson, J. Q. (1963). *City politics.* New York: Vintage Books.

Burian-Fitzgerald, M., & Harris, D. (2004). *Teacher recruitment and teacher quality? Are charter schools different?* Education Policy Center, Michigan State University. Available at: www.epc.msu.edu

Chapa, J., & De la Rosa, B. (2004). Latino population growth, socioeconomic and demographic characteristics, and implications for educational attainment. *Education and Urban Society, 36*(2), 130–149.

Clewell, B. C., & Villegas, A. M. (1999). Creating a nontraditional pipeline for urban teachers: The pathways to teaching careers model. *Journal of Negro Education, 68*(3), 306–317.

Darling-Hammond, L., Pittman, K., & Ottinger, C. (1987). *Career choices for minorities: Who will teach?* Unpublished manuscript. Washington, DC: National Education Association/Council of Chief State School Officers' Task Force on Minorities in Teaching.

Education Commission of the States. (2002). *State incentive policies for recruiting and retaining effective new teachers in hard to staff schools.* Denver, CO: Author.

Fix, M., Passel, J., & Ruiz De Velasco, J. (2004, July). *School reform: The demographic imperative and challenge.* Paper presented at the 2004 Institute for the Study of Labor Conference, Bonn, Germany.

Genzuk, M., Lavandenz, M., & Krashen, S. (1994). Para-educators: A source for remedying the shortage of teachers for Limited English-Proficient students. *The Journal of Educational Issues of Language Minority Students, 14*, 211–222.

Goodwin, A. L. (2002). Teacher preparation and the education of immigrant children. *Education and Urban Society, 34*(2), 156–172.

Goodwin, A. L., Genishi, C. S., Asher, N., & Woo, K. (1997). Voices from the margins: Asian American teachers' experiences in the profession. In D. M. Byrne & J. McIntyre (Eds.), *Research on the education of our nation's teachers: Teacher education yearbook V* (pp. 219–241). Thousand Oaks, CA: Corwin Press.

Hanushek, E., Kain, J., & Rivkin, S. (2002). *Why public schools lose teachers.* (Working Paper 8599). Cambridge, MA: National Bureau of Economic Research.

Joint Center for Policy Studies. (2000). *Black elected officials roster 2000*. Washington, DC: Author.

Jorgenson, O. (2001). Supporting a diverse teacher corps. *Educational Leadership*, (5), 64–67.

Judd, D., & Swanstrom, T. (2006). *City politics: The political economy of urban America* (5th ed.). New York: Pearson Longman.

Karnig, A., & Welch, S. (1982). Electoral structure and black representation on city councils. *Social Science Quarterly*, 63(3), 99–114.

Kirby, S., Berends, M., & Naftel, S. (1999). Supply and demand of minority teachers in Texas: Problems and prospects. *Educational Evaluation and Policy Analysis*, 21(1), 47–66.

Kirby, S., Darling-Hammond, L., & Hudson, L. (1993). Nontraditional recruits to mathematics and science teaching. *Educational Evaluation and Policy Analysis*, 11(3), 301–323.

Leal, D., Martinez-Ebers, V., & Meier, K. (2004). The politics of Latino education: The biases of at-large elections. *Journal of Politics*, 66(4), 1224–1244.

Levin, J., & Quinn, M. (2003). *Missed opportunities: How we keep high quality teachers out of urban classrooms*. New Teacher Project. Retrieved July 7, 2008, from http://www.tntp.org/report.html

Lomotey, K. (1989). Cultural diversity in the school: Implications for principals. *NASSP Bulletin*, 73(521), 81–88.

Mladenka, K. R. (1989). Blacks and Hispanics in urban America. *American Political Science Review*, 83(1), 165–191.

National Association of Latino Elected Officials. (1999). *Directory of Latino elected officials, 1999*. Washington, DC: Author.

National Association of Latino Elected Officials. (2001). *National directory of Latino elected officials*. Los Angeles, CA: Author.

National Association of State Boards of Education. (2002). *State incentive programs for recruiting teachers: Are they effective in reducing shortages? Issues in brief*. Alexandria, VA: Author.

National Center for Education Information. (2005). *Alternative routes to teacher certification: An overview*. Washington, DC: Author.

National Center for Education Statistics. (2001). *School and staffing survey, 1999–2000*. Washington, DC: Author.

National Center for Education Statistics. (2002). *Status and trends in the education of Hispanics*. Washington, DC: Author.

National Center for Education Statistics. (2009). *Digest of education statistics, 2009*. Washington, DC: Author.

National Collaborative on Diversity in the Teaching Force. (2004). *Assessment of diversity in America's teaching force*. Washington, DC: Author.

National Commission on Teaching and America's Future. (1996). *What matters most: Teaching for America's future*. New York: Author.

Ng, J. (2003). Teacher shortages in urban schools. *Education and Urban Society*, 35(4), 380–398.

Polinard, J. L., Wrinkle, R. D., & Meier, K. J. (1995, Autumn). The influence of educational and political resources on minority students' success. *Journal of Negro Education*, 64, 463–474.

Rong, X. L., & Preissle, J. (1998). *Educating immigrant students*. Thousand Oaks, CA: Corwin Press.

Singer, A. (2004). *The Rise of new immigrant gateways*. Washington, DC: The Brookings Institution.

Southern Poverty Law Center. (2005). *Anti-immigration intelligence report*. Montgomery, AL: Author.

Stein, L. (1986). Representative local government: Minorities in the municipal work force. *Journal of Politics, 48*(8), 694–713.

Stewart, J. Jr., England, R. E., & Meier, K. J. (1989, June). Black representation in urban school districts: From school board to office to classroom. *Western Political Quarterly, 42*, 287–305.

Urban Teacher Challenge. (2000). *Teacher demand and supply in the Great City Schools*. Belmont, MA: Recruiting New Teachers, Inc.

U.S. Census Bureau. (2000). *2000 census: Summary file 4*. Washington, DC: Author. Retrieved June 25, 2008, from http://factfinder.census.gov/

CHAPTER 6

The Anglo Politics of Latino Education: The Role of Immigration Scripts

Edmund T. Hamann

In the 41 states without a substantial historic Latino population, large-scale schooling of Latinos is a comparatively new issue and the nature of that schooling is fundamentally shaped by how the more established (usually Anglo) populations understand this task. This chapter describes the understandings that led to, but also limited, one particularly comprehensive attempt in Georgia to respond to Latino newcomers. In that sense, this is a study of the cosmologies that can undergird the politics of schooling of Latinos. This chapter utilizes the concept of the *script*, or broadly shared storylines about how things are or should be, to illustrate how two such competing scripts were employed in Dalton, Georgia.

Script is a term used by Marcelo Suárez-Orozco (1998) in a chapter referenced extensively here. Depending on the research tradition, script, as used here, is synonymous with trope, meta-narrative, and cultural model. The core premise of script is that there are foundational storylines—like "rooting for the underdog" or "hero as a rebel victim"—that can be and are retold in myriad ways, but that resonate because of a simple and familiar core message. Moreover, those scripts, because of their familiarity and ubiquity, steer us away from more nuanced or less expected interpretations. In this chapter, the emphasis is on two intertwined scripts—the pro-immigration script and the anti-immigration script—that, though superficially quite different, preclude other ways of understanding local demographic change. These scripts, in turn, manifest themselves in political arguments about schooling and other institutional arenas where the presence of Latino newcomers is being negotiated.

THE GEORGIA PROJECT AS RESPONSE TO CHANGE

In March 1997, two Georgia school districts, a committee of leading citizens, and a private Mexican university formally began a novel binational partnership called the Georgia Project. At that time, Dalton, Georgia, was negotiating an unprecedented demographic change—that city's school district would become Georgia's first majority Latino district in 2001, even though the Latino enrollment was just 4% as recently as 1989. The larger surrounding Whitfield County district was also enrolling larger numbers of Latinos, but the proportional change was slower. Not surprisingly, such a dramatic and sudden demographic transformation was often disorienting to newcomers and long-established residents alike (Súarez-Orozco, 2003).

The Georgia Project was the most tangible local educational response to this demographic transformation; it became a reflection of, as well as a template through which, this disorientation was negotiated and definitions of community and responsibility to newcomers were contested. As such, considering the economic, social, political, and ideological dynamics that surrounded the Georgia Project's creation—including how it informed other issues from workplace organization to housing—sheds insight more generally into the politics of Latino education, particularly as negotiated in the "new Latino diaspora" in areas outside traditional Latino enclaves in the Southwest, California, and metro Chicago and New York (Hamann & Harklau, 2009; Wortham, Murillo, & Hamann, 2002).

By 2008, 11 years after it began, the Georgia Project had largely withered away, although the Latino presence in northwest Georgia had become both permanent and substantial. Latino students were graduating from high schools in record numbers, but unprecedented numbers were also dropping out and scoring much lower on state mandated tests than their non-Latino peers. At 70.9%, the official Hispanic graduation rate was also lower than any other group (Georgia Public Education Report Card, 2007–2008), although it exceeded Georgia's statewide average Hispanic graduation rate of 65.5%. To use the phrasing of Gitlin, Buendía, Crosland, and Doumbia (2003), Latinos continued to be both "welcome" and "unwelcome."

To explore the ways that the Anglo population made sense of the newcomers as the demographic transition was at its swiftest 11 years earlier, when the binational partnership was launched, helps to explain why Dalton and surrounding Whitfield County have unevenly supported the school success and acculturation of Latino newcomers. Perhaps it will also help explain why the unorthodox Georgia Project was largely gone by 2008, although its legacy of teacher training, Latino scholarship recipients, and even marriages between visiting Mexican instructors and Anglo locals continues.

This chapter examines the *imagining* (Anderson, 1991; Chavez, 1994) of Latino immigrant newcomers by local Anglos in Dalton in the mid-1990s, as manifest in the editorials and letters to the editor in the local newspaper, in the advocacy efforts of the Georgia Project's initiators, and in patterns of employment and social organization that marked Dalton at that time. Imagining in this instance literally references the mental constructs or models that community members deployed to think about Latino newcomers. It was this imagining that shaped how the Georgia Project was constructed, launched, adapted, and ultimately limited. It was also this imagining that linked understandings from one sphere (the economic) to another (the educational). Finally, this imagining set up Latinos to be, as Foucault (1977) would have put it, "objects of information, but [almost] never subjects of communication" (p. 200).

In Dalton, as elsewhere, Anglos' conceptualizations of Latinos were the product of existing and sometimes discrepant and unreconciled assumptions about self, place, community, and fairness. Those abstractions formed the lenses through which Anglos tried to make sense of encounters with Latinos in the workplace, at school, and in a few other public settings. Anglo conceptualizations also were the product of their vicarious experiences with Latinos through representations in the media and in the daily talk of their fellow Anglo community members. See Santa Ana (2002) for a particularly compelling explanation regarding media representations of Latinos that shape how they are conceptualized in the public sphere and how, in turn, those conceptualizations become salient to what Latinos must navigate/encounter. See Pollock (2004) for a powerful analysis of the dilemmas Americans encounter when they do (and do not) talk about race, particularly as pertaining to schooling and educational advancement.

Reflecting the tension that is embedded in schooling in a capitalist society—where the private good of having schooling make one more qualified than a peer coexists with the public good of all doing well (Labaree, 1997)—the Georgia Project was supposed to remedy and *not remedy* an unequal social order that imperiled social cohesion. On the one hand, the ongoing viability or at least prosperity of many local employers depended on a low-wage, largely Latino newcomer labor force. Yet permanent or egregious exploitation risked tearing the already fragile social fabric. The Georgia Project needed to exemplify a fair and compassionate response to newcomers, but practicality dictated that Dalton and Whitfield County still "needed" the social stratification that assured an abundant supply of low-wage workers and the continuation of the traditional community order. The play of immigration scripts enabled this prospect because the paternalism and more subtle racism of Suárez-Orozco's (1998) pro-immigration script was obscured by the overt racism of the anti-immigration script.

THE PRO-IMMIGRATION / ANTI-IMMIGRATION
SCRIPT DUALISM

The pro-immigration script casts immigrants as familial, hard working, religious, loyal, and willing to take jobs that others will not. It derives much of its appeal from its nostalgic reiteration of the important assimilationist storyline that America is a land of opportunity—a land where hard work, even in trying circumstances, can lead to success—and thus, that America is essentially fair. In a time of anxiety and dislocation, such a familiar script is comforting. Immigration validates and rejuvenates America, but per the script's understanding, it only imagines America within preexisting terms of what it means to be a good American.

Given the appeal of this script, those who espouse it do not easily tolerate deviations from it. Any newcomer resisting language loss or characterizing employment conditions as less than fair violates the script. The pro-immigration script may seem pro-immigrant, but it is colonialist in dismissing the value of anything newcomers might want to retain that is not "American." It actually offers only a confining range of possible immigrant actions and little support for immigrants who contest what Spener (1988) calls the "ambiguous social contract" actually available in this stratified society:

> The United States offers immigrants an ambiguous social contract. It reads, more or less, as follows: "In order to participate in a non-marginal way in the U.S. economy, you must become an American by giving up your loyalty to your home country and language, and you must learn the language of the American elite. In order to become an American, you must meet certain standards. This country is in the process of raising its standards because, unfortunately, there are already too many Americans. If you aren't allowed to become an American, there's still plenty of room for you in this country—at the bottom. (pp. 145–146)

Although the pro-immigration script's nostalgic appeal is broad, as is its gloss of inclusiveness, those who gain directly from the presence of newcomer laborers are those who most willingly embrace it. If the employment hierarchy can be equated to a pyramid, a proposition supported by segmented labor market theory (Griffith, 1995), anyone in a position above those that are occupied by newcomer laborers benefits from the expansion of the employment base below them. This means that most people in management, as well as others in the same class, gain from and articulate this script. For example, a carpet company CEO who crucially linked Dalton leaders with business and university partners in Mexico on repeated occasions (thereby helping originate the Georgia Project), emphasized that Dalton's growing Latino presence was "an opportunity, not a problem."

In contrast, Suárez-Orozco's (1998) "anti-immigration script" views the same demographic change as threat. In this script, immigrants are illegal aliens, welfare cheats, criminals, and job stealers. Notably, the contradiction between alleged government dependency and stealing jobs is unexplored. The anti-immigration script closely matched the virulently anti-immigrant content of the 1995 letters to the editor that led Dalton's daily newspaper to declare a temporary moratorium on publishing letters about immigration and Latinos. It also describes arguments made by the protesters outside a 1997 city council meeting who complained about a $750,000 municipal allocation for the Georgia Project.

Because the two scripts vehemently contradict each other, even as both ignore the actual voices of newcomers, those who espouse the different scripts tend to talk past each other, often heatedly. This miscommunication leaves the anxiety untouched, but enables each side to dismiss opposing viewpoints and rationales. Because the more powerful community members typically champion the pro-immigration script, while the less powerful community members generally promote the anti-immigration script, the rejection of the anti-immigrant script and its espousers becomes conflated with the play of hegemonic reproduction. This was the case in Dalton.

According to Suárez-Orozco's (1998) model, when their script is dismissed, those articulating anti-immigrant views feel more disempowered, more anxious, and, as a result, even more anti-immigrant. Thus, the likelihood of articulating the anti-immigrant script in a still more unacceptable fashion only increases. Plaut (1983) notes a longstanding dynamic in Appalachia where communitarian voices of marginal locals are first ignored and then, as the expressions of disenchantment take on less appropriate forms, their hostility increasingly becomes a rationale for their exclusion.

Natives use both scripts for formal and informal debates about how new immigrants should be treated and what social station they should be offered by the host society. Necessarily tied to such debates is the social construction of the class-related meanings of being native and being Anglo, or white (Gibson, 1996). These class-related meanings are the product of the economic and cultural-historical dynamics in play in the community. To understand those meanings and how they related to the use of the immigration scripts merits a brief description of Dalton's intertwined transformations.

DEMOGRAPHIC TRANSFORMATION

Dalton and Whitfield's school enrollment changes in the 1990s and early 2000s were partially based on white flight to private schools and less demographically changing nearby districts, but it reflected more the enrollment of 3,000 Latino newcomers in the schools and the arrival of 20,000 or more

Latinos into the larger community. In 1995, when the pro-immigration and anti-immigration scripts first became broadly visible in local newspaper accounts, Dalton's school enrollment of Latinos had grown by a multiple of seven from 1989 and constituted more than a quarter of enrollment. In turn, Latinos, mainly of Mexican descent, made up nearly all of the newcomer population, so reaction to newcomers and reaction to Latinos were nearly synonymous.

The business and civic elite shaped much of the imagining of the Latino *other* in this community; this elite class was responsible for the hiring practices at local carpet and poultry facilities that brought thousands of Latino workers and their families to Dalton and surrounding Whitfield County. They also instigated the novel Georgia Project, which formally partnered the local schools with researchers at a private university in Mexico for the purposes of:

1. bringing bilingual teachers from Mexico to Dalton
2. sending Dalton teachers for summer training in Mexico
3. revising the district's version of Georgia's Quality Core Curriculum to accommodate bilingual instruction, and
4. initiating a series of community studies and Latino leadership development seminars
   (Hamann, 1999a, 1999b, 2002, 2003, 2004).

Mexican university partners created about three fourths of this design, however. Therefore, while the Georgia Project became a key template for Anglo thinking about the school and community *accommodations* required by Dalton's and Whitfield County's new demography, its most powerful champions were not necessarily willing or capable of defending all of its design elements. In the public sphere, the Mexican project partners' "third way" of more respectful inclusion was not as compelling as the pro-immigration script to Dalton's leaders.

The use of the pro- and anti-immigration scripts dominated the public sphere and private sense-making of long-time community stakeholders, but concerns about how to negotiate demographic change in schools did not mainly drive the use of these scripts. Rather, the scripts were used for talking about community and economic change more generally. Thus, understanding the scripts requires the understanding of other co-existing dynamics that generated the need for the scripts' deployment.

Local manifestations of three dynamics—reducing labor costs by expanding the labor supply, corporate externalizing indirect costs, and creating/maintaining labor market segmentation—triggered the arrival of newcomers into Dalton, assignment of their social location, and the related need for public scripts to make sense of them. In the 1990s Dalton's major employers were carpet factories and a poultry processing plant; in both instances, these were mature industries (i.e., industries that were not growing quickly), so increased profitability depended on cutting costs. One way to do this was to expand the potential labor supply and thereby put downward pressure on wages. Latinos, whose local presence had been slowly growing since a Texas dam construction company had first brought Latino laborers to the area in the 1970s, were a key target population for such expansion, in part because their extensive familial ties could be tapped to recruit more workers. Also, a successful dropout prevention consent decree in the late 1980s, through which local employers agreed not to hire those under 18 who lacked a high school diploma during school hours, meant that other (largely non-Latino) sources of prospective low-wage labor were declining.

Still, recruiting a new laborer population needs to be cheaper than not doing so. Recruiting businesses have to avoid indirect costs related to the recruitment and retention of this new labor supply. Businesses that externalize costs do not pay for new or changed costs of housing, health care, language instruction, skills training, and other human services (Hackenberg, 1995). From a profit standpoint, companies that externalize costs gain if others carry their indirect costs (Griffith, 1993). Of course, others (e.g., taxpayers) can resent extra costs that they have to bear; in order to reduce community resentment, the creator of these costs may explain that the costs are worthwhile, are preferable to other options (like relocating the business away from the area), and/or are mitigated by other actions that the cost creator has undertaken. The Georgia Project, championed by local employers, could be (and was) framed as proof of mitigating the social consequences of their employment strategies.

It is important to note that the externalization of indirect costs is only one source of resentment. The community can also resent the downward pressure on wages caused by expanding the labor supply, as well as the disorienting sense that one's home and community are changing. As Suárez-Orozco (1998) summarizes: "Anti-immigrant sentiment—including the jealous rage that 'illegals are getting benefits instead of citizens like my friend'—is intertwined with an unsettling sense of panic in witnessing the metamorphosis of 'home' into a world dominated by sinister aliens" (pp. 296–297). One way this tension is relieved is through the emergence of workplace segmentation and segmentation in other social domains.

In segmented labor markets, laborers, managers, and others internalize ideas regarding job-status hierarchies and corresponding wage differentials, and workers seek to protect the relative advantage of their position and avoid questioning the larger organization altogether. For these to be stable, there need to be palatable ideological rationalizations for differing compensation and deflections of challenges to the unequal social structure. Differences in race, ethnicity, language, gender, and school experience often become grounds for such differentiation (Griffith, 1995). But this differentiation needs to feel natural, inevitable, or impermanent, or it violates the American concern with fairness. The task of the scripts is to rationalize the status quo while relieving pressure related to the unfairness of that status quo by 1. promising how existing problems will be remedied or 2. explaining why a complaining party's complaint deserves to be ignored or dismissed.

In 1997, Dalton's local newspaper, *The Daily Citizen-News* (1997a), acknowledged the public complaints about externalization of costs:

> [The] former superintendent of Dalton Public Schools said more than once to our reporters that business and industry here must get more involved with solving community problems related to the rapid growth of the Hispanic community . . . After all, our Hispanic neighbors are here because local businesses gave them jobs . . . Business leaders here must accept some responsibility beyond handing out a regular paycheck. (p. 4A)

But the newspaper raised this issue to praise local businesses for organizing the new Georgia Project and, indirectly, to counter the former superintendent's claim. According to the newspaper's editorial board, the Georgia Project's existence refuted the criticism that businesses were not meeting their community responsibilities.

CONNECTING THE SCRIPTS TO LOCAL POLITICS

According to a school district contact, the influx of Latinos in the 1990s was displacing low-income whites and blacks from Dalton's East Side, where the bulk of the city's lower-cost housing was located. According to the same source, Latinos were gaining a reputation among local landlords for being more prompt with rent payments and better at keeping up properties than other types of tenants. A local landlord subsequently confirmed this sentiment.

The dynamic described by the school district informant and the landlord depicts physical ramifications of the pro-immigration script—newcomers were better than or preferable to others in their class (a stance that surely stoked the anti-immigration script). This script helped structure the local social order along ethnic/racial lines, and it helped shape the related ideational lenses through which members of different ethnic/racial groups viewed one another.

Echoing the landlords, other leading Anglo voices in Dalton also cast local Latinos in preferable terms in comparison to low-income portions of the more established population. Repeating Suárez-Orozco's (1998) impossibly virtuous pro-immigration script, a December 1996 editorial that endorsed the Georgia Project in *The Daily Citizen-News* (1996), claimed, "For too long Dalton and Whitfield County have walked by the growing Latino community, rarely offering substantial help" (p. 4A). They seemed unaware that they had differentiated Latinos from the named city and county population. The editorial writers identified Latinos as "hardworking," "filling some of the toughest manual labor jobs around," and "an example of intensive familial ties" (p. 4A). Having praised local Latinos, the editorial writers thus exempted themselves from the following charge that was aimed at articulators of the anti-immigration script and was also in the editorial: "Meanwhile [Latinos] have been virtually ignored—even hated by some—simply because of their presence" (p. 4A).

If Latinos were the primary group referred to in the editorial, a shadow referent, an unnamed group or people were therefore *not* hardworking, *not* willing to take on the tough manual labor jobs available, and *not* exemplars of intensive familial loyalty. If local Latinos were meritorious because of their family and work habits, as per the pro-immigration script, those without those virtues were not deserving of support or sympathy. The closest the editorial came to mentioning the shadow referent was with the vague pronoun "some" in the phrase "even hated by some."

A brief retelling of local history, particularly as it involves the local newspaper, clarifies to whom "some" referred. In 1995, before anyone had conceived of the Georgia Project, several citizens began a stream of letters to the editor questioning Dalton's changing demographic face. The author of one early letter (Letters to the Editor, 1995) sarcastically wrote:

> Am I to understand that people in our community are upset Dalton has become a haven for uninvited guests? . . . Just because the crime rate in Dalton has risen considerably in the past couple of years. Just because the local law enforcement is overburdened by a whole new (to them) criminal subculture. Just because native Daltonians prefer to retain their own language—poor English or not—is no reason to be uncivil to guests. (p. 4A)

Several components of this letter merit highlighting: Latinos were labeled as a criminal subculture, Latinos were characterized as guests, and Latinos were labeled as uninvited, hinting at a distinction among long-time Dalton residents between those who "invited" Latinos (by employing them) and those who did not. With a leap of logic, the author implied that the presence of Latinos had imperiled the retention of English by English speakers. Finally, the author made claims about her own socioeconomic status and group membership with the self-denigrating reference to "poor English." Though, as the letter itself shows, the author's English was fine, she distinguished herself from the presumably more educated speakers of English who perhaps were not threatened by the Latino influx. Her loyalty was with native-born Daltonians, who might not be so scholastically accomplished, but who maintained a right to express their concerns about changes in their community.

In contrast, in 1998, a carpet industry executive mentioned the same rise in Whitfield County's crime rate mentioned in the above quoted anti-immigrant letter, but he rationalized its increase as related to a disproportionate Latino citation and arrest rate for DUIs (Driving Under the Influence). He went on to explain that this was the simple product of newcomer Latinos lacking awareness of local rules regarding alcohol use. The same executive also claimed that, because of Latinos' relative poverty, they lacked sufficient private space in which to be festive without running afoul of the law. Neither the defender of "poor English" nor the carpet executive suggested that the changing arrest rate could be a product of an entirely non-Latino police force targeting the newcomers for closer scrutiny or an inchoate complaint by some Latinos about their "welcome."

By the autumn of 1995, a year before the Georgia Project was first proposed, the trickle of anti-immigrant letters-to-the-editor had become a torrent. Claims like "We're losing control of our borders" from a letter in May became increasingly common. In October, shortly after an Immigration and Naturalization Service (INS) raid at a local carpet mill had led to the arrest of several hundred undocumented workers (Rehyansky, 1995a, 1995b), the letters became especially virulent. *The Daily Citizen-News* responded by declaring a temporary moratorium on anti-immigrant and anti-Latino letters to the editor. Though the local paper has long been identified with advocating local business leaders' points of view (Kelley, 1996) and for rebuffing the more nativist or reactionary perspectives, the letter-to-the-editor moratorium blocked access to one of the few public forums through which populist doubt about immigration could be expressed.

The point here is not to defend a racist discourse, which is what the letters to the editor often were. Rather, what needs highlighting are the divergent responses that actions like the newspaper's moratorium and the INS raids precipitated. As noted above, the less educated, predominantly white, working class had serious doubts about how immigration was changing their community, but these residents' resistant voices were formally silenced. In the meantime, many of the civic-minded elite were concerned about the increasingly obvious fracture in their community and the social ferment that might become directed at their businesses. The implicit priorities of the civic-minded elite included repairing the social fabric and thus, indirectly, reiterating the rationale for a social order that benefited them. Repressing the anti-immigration script was an incomplete gesture. They needed to proactively demonstrate their responsiveness to immigration-related community concerns. The Georgia Project did this dramatically.

LOCATING THE GEORGIA PROJECT IN PUBLIC DIALOGUES

In the public discourse, neither the anti-immigration nor the pro-immigration scripts provided a rationale for community transformation, for the ready acceptance of immigrants as they were, or for the rearticulation of school goals to prepare transnational students to negotiate the multiple social and economic environments that they might encounter as children and later as adults. The Georgia Project's original compact—authored mainly by Mexican partners—promised such changes, but the pro-immigration script, the anti-immigration script, and their shared de facto silencing of Latino newcomer voices together created a simplified ideological landscape in which the transformative prospect of the project was emasculated.

In late 1996 and early 1997, concurrent with visits by Dalton leaders to Mexico and by Mexican project partners to Georgia, the pro-business local newspaper, *The Daily Citizen-News*, published several articles favorably describing the promise of the Georgia Project (e.g., Hamilton 1996a, 1996b, 1997a, 1997b). These articles were organized to lay a favorable foundation for popular acceptance of the project. As they were published, the most important Dalton instigator of the Georgia Project was busily sending descriptions of the project and bids for its support to several of the state's most powerful political and educational leaders.

Both the articles and the instigator's letters contrasted markedly with the anti-immigration sentiment noted in the last section, but they, too, conveyed a simplified, overly homogenized rendering of the growing local Latino population and, in particular, of the Latino newcomer students who were to be main targets of the Georgia Project's programs. While this portrayal was expedient for the purpose of gathering support from the Anglo community, it did not actually convey a sense of what the project needed to accomplish if it was to accomplish more than what was promised by the pro-immigration script (i.e., the welcome of the uncomplaining to menial jobs).

The first newspaper article (Hamilton, 1996a) was published the day local project leaders left for their first visit to Mexico for the first face-to-face contact with prospective Mexican partners. The article began with the question, "How do you teach someone you cannot communicate with?" and the answer: "You can't." Titled "Educators seek ways to reach Hispanics," the article identified the problem of Latinos in Dalton schools as a communication problem and presented the project as a solution to the problem. The article described the project one-dimensionally (referring only to the prospect of bilingual Mexican teachers coming to Dalton), and for the first time, published the Georgia Project's "creation story," a rationale for why the project was initiated.

The creation story (Hamilton, 1996a) went as follows: One day, the project's founding attorney listened to his exasperated daughter describe the great difficulty she and her colleagues faced as *parapros* (paraprofessionals) at a pre-K through grade two elementary school on the poorer and more Latino side of town. She and her colleagues were all monolingual English speakers, while many of their students and their students' parents were monolingual Spanish speakers. According to the daughter, the two sides could not communicate. Feeling compelled to try to remedy this mismatch, but not immediately sure how to proceed, the attorney visited the school where his daughter worked. Disconcerted by what he observed, he mentioned his daughter's complaint to the CEO of one of Dalton's largest carpet manufacturers. That CEO then contacted the head of one of his company's Mexican trading partners. That contact, who was also a lead supporter of a private Mexican university, telephoned that university's rector. Within a short time, a parapro's complaint was transformed into a binational discussion about how a Mexican university might help the public schools in Georgia.

This creation story was repeated frequently and was central to selling the Georgia Project to both skeptical and enthusiastic local Anglos. While the creation story was readily intelligible to its target audience and effective in gaining their support, it simplified the challenge facing the school and community and, in the security of its problem diagnosis, it precluded any need to consult with any of Dalton's Latino newcomers. During the planning for the first year of the project's enactment, only one local Latino was even intermittently involved with its coordination. Apart from this limited exception, the project was fully the product of local Anglo business leaders, Anglo school district leaders, and Mexican university officials.

The second December 1996 newspaper article (Hamilton, 1996b) promoting the proposed Georgia Project was also a front-page piece. It was printed shortly after the Dalton contingent returned from their visit to the Mexican university, and was crucially different from the first. The second article outlined four proposed components of the project (expanding on the original conception of recruiting Mexican teachers for Dalton schools). At the request of the Mexico-based partners, summer training in Mexico for Dalton educators, a bilingual education-oriented curriculum overhaul, and a community research component were added to the project's action plan. Despite the increase in the number of proposed components, the second article did not change its straightforward depiction of Dalton's challenge as the remedy for the communication gap between newcomers and teachers at the public schools.

Within a week, a third article, an editorial, celebrated the Georgia Project's initiator as "Citizen of the Week" ("Mitchell Leads Effort to Help Educate Hispanic Students," 1996, p. 4A). Perhaps seeking a metaphor that would be broadly appealing at Christmastime, the article compared him to the Good Samaritan described by Jesus in the New Testament. The initiator was lending a helping hand while other locals remained silent. The moral of the Bible story is that those who lend a helping hand are blessed and holy, while the silent—those who do not offer a helping hand—are not so virtuous. It is worth remembering that the man helped by the Samaritan in the Bible had been robbed and beaten and was a stranger to the Samaritan. Per the analogy, Latinos in Dalton were abused, suffering, and needy strangers.

The day after Christmas 1996, the project's instigator penned a letter describing the proposed Georgia Project to the newly appointed Chairman of the State Board of Education. This letter emphasized how he and the new chairman were personally connected (i.e., college fraternity ties, shared friends, and acquaintances). It conveyed his enthusiasm for the nascent project and it suggested the need to account for Dalton's changing demography. It did not mention the project's proposed four-component structure, however. Rather, it reduced the project again to a program to remedy the communication gap, and suggested that recruiting Mexican instructors for Dalton classrooms would help solve the problem.

The daily newspaper printed another flurry of favorable articles at the end of January 1997 during the 4-day visit of the Mexican university representatives. Headlines for those articles include: "Communication revolution arrives in Dalton today" (Hamilton, 1997a), "Visiting professors shocked by size of communication problem" (Hamilton, 1997b), and "Business involvement aids binational partnership" (*The Daily Citizen-News*, 1997, p. 4A). Reiterating that Latino students and Anglo teachers in Dalton faced a communication gap and that the Georgia Project would bridge that gap, thus solving Latino students' problems, the "Visiting Professors Shocked" story began with a description of a lengthy conversation (presumably in Spanish) between one of the Mexican visitors and a young Latino student. The student's local teacher was reportedly shocked by the exchange because she had never seen the girl particularly expressive. According to the article, the teacher had previously worried that the girl had a speech or learning problem. The article's intended conclusions were easy to draw. If only somebody could communicate with these Spanish-speaking students, their talents could be cultivated.

These articles did not note obstacles to Latino students' achievement such as their parents' economic vulnerability, the unfamiliarity of the curriculum, or their families' uncertain ties to Dalton. Nor did the articles critically consider how the macrodynamics of businesses' externalization of indirect costs, the segmentation of labor markets, the ethnic typing of jobs, or the national and local constructions of Latino newcomers in the media might also have been impediments to Dalton Latino students' achievement. Absent a public discourse describing the intertwined factors that can inhibit Latino newcomers' school success, the intentional complexity of the project's four-component design lacked public rationale. Still, the project was officially inaugurated in March 1997 as a four-component effort. Major municipal funding ostensibly to support all four components was obtained a month later,[1] although the Dalton school district's willingness to spend funds and to develop programs in each of the areas for which funding had been obtained later proved problematic.

By 1999, the Georgia Project was a significant and sometimes celebrated local presence that had gained national attention from the *Washington Post*, *Time*, the *San Jose Mercury-News*, Scripps-Howard News Service, National Public Radio, and more. The Director of the U.S. Department of Education's Office for Bilingual Education and Minority Language Affairs (OBEMLA) spoke favorably at length about Dalton in her congressional address supporting the reauthorization of Title VII funding.

Yet within Dalton, the Georgia Project was on the brink of disappearing, with most of its accomplishments more ephemeral than transformative. With the exception of a self-sustaining Latino community leadership initiative, most portions of the three components initiated at the request of the Mexican partners (the bilingual curriculum adjustment, the summer institute in Mexico, and the community research initiative), were frozen or withering (and soon to end). Only the component originally proposed by Dalton leaders (the effort to bring Mexican instructors into Dalton classrooms) was thriving, and even it was vulnerable to the pending end of various funding allocations. In fact, the next superintendent terminated local funding for the program, although one component continued operating using federal funds for a few more years.

MAKING SENSE OF THE GEORGIA PROJECT'S RAPID RISE AND FALL

Figuring out why so much of the Georgia Project's promise was not realized requires looking back at two crucial 1997 partnership-related events and, more generally, considering the role of culture in framing the politics of Latino education, in this case, shaping the persistent Anglo conceptualizations of local Latino roles, needs, and entitlements.

In March 1997, the Georgia Project was formally inaugurated at a ceremony at Dalton High School (Hamilton, 1997c). The ceremony was attended by several Dalton carpet executives, the project's initiating attorney, Dalton and Whitfield County school district officials, the rector of the Mexican university, the Mexican industrialist who had facilitated the binational link, the Mexican Consul General from Atlanta, and several scholars from the Mexican university. Despite the large official contingent, however, the high school auditorium was largely empty. No students, no parents, no high school administrators, and no teachers were present. The start of the

Georgia Project was not cause to interrupt anyone's school day. The three-page accord signed that day outlined all four proposed components; it alluded to ideals like "globally competitive education for all learners" and "adult biliteracy," and it promised involvement not just of educators, but also work-places, parents, and the University of Georgia System. Few heard this comprehensive vision, however, and fewer proved willing to adhere to it.

One month later, two challenges to the Georgia Project were presented at a City Council meeting that ultimately approved $750,000 for the project. The first challenge was the previously noted angry chorus of protesters assembled outside city hall. One of the protesters held a sign that read, "Would the last person out of [Whitfield] County please bring the flag." Given Whitfield County's fast growing population, the sign's argument, a perfect articulation of the anti-immigration script, was as absurd as it was angry. Not surprisingly, those inside the meeting ignored the protesters. Later the newspaper dismissed the protesters as offensive racists ("Georgia Project's Aim is to Teach English," 1997).

The second challenge superficially seemed even less serious than the first one, but it compelled a public redefinition of the Georgia Project in such narrow terms that, in retrospect, its influence demands recognition. The second challenge was the circulation of a *Reader's Digest* article by Linda Chavez (1995), a conservative critic of bilingual education, to a city councilman (and subsequently to the whole city council). The article in-cluded a strong attack against bilingual education and all who advocate for it. The article further asserted that Latinos needed to be taught English, positing the flawed argument that those promoting bilingual education did not want Latinos to learn English and reducing the broad academic goals of bilingual education to a simplified concern with language acquisition rather than academic achievement in all subject areas. While this article does not review bilingual education research, readers should note that many re-searchers have contradicted Chavez's claims (e.g., Thomas & Collier, 1997; Cummins, 1996; and Ramirez, cited in Cazden, 1992). Because the Georgia Project proposed a bilingual education-tied curricular overhaul, the article encompassed a criticism of at least a portion of the project.

The project's instigator dismissed Chavez' argument in a reply to the councilman. He compared its validity to the pseudo-science claims that blacks were less intelligent than whites. Nonetheless, he and other local leaders of the Georgia Project responded to the Chavez challenge by clarify-ing that the project's primary intent was to teach Latino children English, a story line that was dutifully echoed in an editorial in the local newspaper ("Georgia Project's Aim is to Teach English," 1997). As soon as this argu-ment was put forth, the rationales for enacting the portions of the Georgia Project that could not be directly related to this language education task were diminished.

To understand how such a redefinition of task could occur (and how the redefinition was not recognized as a redefinition) requires returning attention to Dalton Anglos' understanding of Latinos and their needs. With the exception of the project's instigating attorney who, at times, articulated a nuanced understanding of the complexity of Latino community circumstances in Dalton, local proponents of the project saw the challenges before them through the lens of Suárez-Orozco's (1998) pro-immigration script. The simplistic vision of assimilation embedded in this script supported the original rationale for the project—Latino newcomers were deserving people and as such deserved to be able to be communicated with. In the short term, bringing in bilingual educators from Mexico would remedy this communication problem; in the long-term, assimilation would prevail; per Grey (1991), assimilation here is presumed to be unilateral—i.e., Latino newcomers changing to become more "mainstream."

This simplistic vision prevented its adherents from identifying any problem with a language-education-only program and inhibited the project from taking any kind of political stance in relation to ethnic segmentation in the workplace and other issues. Nor did project advocates see that Latino newcomers confronted obstacles that were more complex than simply those associated with language skills. Thus, the pro-immigration script did not require tending to complicated circumstances and realistic needs, nor did it compel its adherents to defend the Georgia Project's full action plan.

Sarason (1990) noted that transformative school reform efforts require both inclusion of the larger community and attention to power issues. At first glance, the Georgia Project attended to both of those dynamics, as it involved the business community and used its power to push for school change. The exercise of the business community's power did not provide a sufficiently coherent and sophisticated problem diagnosis, however; it did not clarify what accommodations local Latinos most needed, nor did it clarify how non-Latinos could redefine community or school tasks. In the absence of a local, Anglo-recognized script that supported the Georgia Project's comprehensive vision, the prevailing, more simplistic, pro-immigration and anti-immigration scripts had free play in the community; this interplay excluded Latino representation and obscured the embedded simplifications in each script.

McQuillan (1998) noted that, while culture is routinely contested, it is also resilient, equivalent to a kind of default setting for expectations. Culture puts parameters on what seems possible and supports the hierarchies that group members agree are normal and appropriate. In the absence of a clear framework to act otherwise, most of the Georgia Project's Dalton-based supporters were limited in imagining its transformative potential, even though on paper they had accepted a transformative four-component plan.

NOTE

1. Full disclosure: my entree to Dalton was as a grant writer hired to draft a $500,000 Title VII Systemwide Bilingual Education federal proposal that focused on the Georgia Project. That grant was funded in July 1997. Nonetheless, both when I was writing that grant and afterward, my role as a researcher studying the Georgia Project was always overt (and formally approved by Dalton Public School's Superintendent).

REFERENCES

Anderson, B. (1991). *Imagined communities: Reflections on the origin and spread of nationalism* (Rev. ed.). London: Verso.

Business Involvement Aids Binational Partnership. (1997, January 23). *The Daily Citizen-News, 34*, pp. 4A.

Cazden, C. B. (1992). *Language minority education in the United States: Implications of the Ramirez report.* Washington, DC: National Center for Research on Cultural Diversity and Second Language Learning.

Chavez, L. R. (1994). The Power of the imagined community: The settlement of undocumented Mexicans and Central Americans in the United States. *American Anthropologist, 96*(1), 52–73.

Chavez, L. (1995). One nation, One common language. *Reader's Digest,* (8), 87–91.

Cummins, J. (1996). *Negotiating identities: Education for empowerment in a diverse society.* Ontario, CA: California Association for Bilingual Education.

Foucault, M. (1977). *Discipline and punish: The birth of the prison* (A. Sheridan, Trans.). New York: Vintage Books.

Georgia Project's Aim is to Teach English. (1997, April 24). *The Daily Citizen-News,* pp. 4A.

Georgia Public Education Report Card. (2007–08). Retrieved June 23, 2010, from http://www.gaosa.org/report.aspx

Gibson, J. W. 1996. The social construction of whiteness in Shellcracker Haven, Florida. *Human Organization, 55*(4), 379–389.

Gitlin, A., Buendía, E., Crosland, K., & Doumbia, F. (2003). The production of margin and center: Welcoming–unwelcoming of immigrant students. *American Educational Research Journal, 40*(1), 91–122.

Grey, M. A. (1991). The context for marginal secondary ESL programs: Contributing factors and the need for further research. *Journal of Educational Issues of Language Minority Students, 9,* 75–89.

Griffith, D. (1993). *Jones's minimal: Low-wage labor in the United States.* Albany, NY: State University of New York Press.

Griffith, D. (1995). *Hay trabajo*: Poultry processing, rural industrialization, and the Latinization of low-wage labor. In D. D. Stull, M. J. Broadway, & D. Griffith (Eds.), *Any way you cut it: Meat-processing and small-town America* (pp. 129–151). Lawrence, KS: University Press of Kansas.

Hackenberg, R. A. (1995). Joe Hill died for your sins. In D. D. Stull, M. J. Broadway, & D. Griffith (Eds.), *Any way you cut it: Meat-processing and small-town America* (pp. 129–151). Lawrence, KS: University Press of Kansas.

Hamann, E. T. (1999a). *The Georgia Project: A binational attempt to reinvent a school district in response to Latino newcomers.* (University Microfilms No. 9926134). Ann Arbor, MI: UMI Dissertation Services.

Hamann, E. T. (1999b). Anglo (mis)understandings of Latino newcomers: A north Georgia case study. In J. G. Lipson, & L. A. McSpadden (Eds.), *Negotiating power and place at the margins: Selected papers on refugees and immigrants, Vol. VII* (pp. 156–197). Arlington, VA: American Anthropology Association.

Hamann, E. T. (2002). ¿Un paso adelante? The politics of bilingual education, Latino student accommodation, and school district management in southern Appalachia. In S. Wortham, E. G. Murillo, & E. T. Hamann (Eds.), *Education in the new Latino diaspora: Policy and the politics of identity* (pp. 67–97). Westport, CT: Ablex.

Hamann, E. T. (2003). *The educational welcome of Latinos in the new south.* Westport, CT: Praeger.

Hamann, E. T. (2004). The local framing of Latino educational policy. *Harvard Journal of Hispanic Policy, 16,* 37–51.

Hamann, E. T., & Harklau, L. (2009). Education in the new Latino diaspora. In E. G. Murillo (Ed.), *Handbook of Latinos and Education* (pp. 157–169). New York: Routledge.

Hamilton, D. W. (1996a, December 12). Educators seek ways to reach Hispanics. *The Daily Citizen-News*, pp. 1, 6A.

Hamilton, D. W. (1996b, December 17). Trip to Mexico may lead to historic deal. *The Daily Citizen-News*, pp. 1, 5A.

Hamilton, D. W. (1997a, January 22). Communication revolution arrives in Dalton today. *The Daily Citizen-News*, p. 1A.

Hamilton, D. W. (1997b, January 25). Visiting professors shocked by size of Communication Problem. *The Daily Citizen-News*, pp. 1, 3A.

Hamilton, D. W. (1997c, March 20). Dalton in historic pact with Mexican university. *The Daily Citizen-News*, pp. 1.

Kelley, K. A. (1996). *On their own: American working class women married to Mexican immigrant men in the rural south.* Unpublished masters thesis, Georgia State University, Atlanta, Georgia.

Labaree, D. (1997). *How to succeed in school without really learning: The credentials race in American education.* New Haven, CT: Yale University Press.

Letters to the editor. (1995, January 17). *The Daily Citizen-News*, pp. 4A.

McQuillan, P. J. (1998). *Educational opportunity in an urban American high school: A cultural analysis.* Albany, NY: State University of New York Press.

Mitchell leads effort to help educate Hispanic students. (1996, December 21). *The Daily Citizen-News*, pp. 4A.

Plaut, T. (1983). Conflict, confrontation, and social change in the regional setting. In A. Batteau (Ed.), *Appalachia and America: Autonomy and regional dependence* (pp. 267–284). Lexington, KY: The University Press of Kentucky.

Pollock, M. (2004). *Colormute: Race talk dilemmas in an American school.* Princeton, NJ: Princeton University Press.

Rehyansky, M. (1995a, September 21). Raid Nets 108 Illegals. *The Daily-Citizen News*, pp. 1.

Rehyansky, M. (1995b, September 26). Operation Southpaw comes to an end. *The Daily-Citizen News*, pp. 1.

Santa Ana, O. (2002). *Brown tide rising: Metaphors of Latinos in contemporary American public discourse*. Austin, TX: University of Texas Press.

Sarason, S. B. (1990). *The predictable failure of educational reform: Can we change course before it is too late?* San Francisco: Jossey-Bass Publishers.

Spener, D. (1988). Transitional bilingual education and the socialization of immigrants. *Harvard Educational Review, 58*(2), 133–153.

Suárez-Orozco, M. M. (1998). State terrors: Immigrants and refugees in the post-national space. In Y. Zou & E. T. Trueba (Eds.), *Ethnic identity and power: Cultural contexts of political action in school and society* (pp. 283–319). Albany, NY: State University of New York Press.

Suárez-Orozco, M. M. (2003). Right moves? Immigration, globalization, utopia, and dystopia. In N. Foner (Ed.), *American arrivals: Anthropology engages the new immigration* (pp. 45–74). Santa Fe, NM: School of American Research Press.

Thomas, W. P., & Collier, V. (1997). *School effectiveness for language minority students*. (NCBE Resource Collection Series, 9). Washington, DC: National Clearinghouse for Bilingual Education.

Wortham, S., Murillo, E. G., Jr., & Hamann E. T. (Eds.). (2002). *Education in the new Latino diaspora: Policy and the politics of identity*. Westport, CT: Ablex.

CHAPTER 7

How Electoral Structure Affects Latino School Board Representation: Comparing 1986 and 2001

Kenneth J. Meier, Eric Gonzalez Juenke, David L. Leal, and Valerie Martinez-Ebers

This chapter compares the representation of Latinos in American school boards across a 15-year period. By examining the results of two national surveys of school boards conducted in 1986 and 2001, we are able to see not only changes in the number of board members in selected districts, whether the electoral systems used in such districts have changed, and whether the effects of the various electoral systems on Latino representation have changed.

It is well known in the political science elections literature that *at-large systems* (where each candidate faces a districtwide electorate) disadvantage minority candidates. By definition, a minority group constitutes less than half of a constituency. Given the tendency of many voters to support candidates of the same race and ethnicity, it is difficult for a minority candidate in an at-large system to assemble a winning coalition when most of the voters are not from that group.

By contrast, *ward systems* (where each candidate runs in a specific electoral district) can provide advantages to candidates who represent populations that constitute a minority of voters. For example, if a district is 20% Latino, one of the school-board districts may include a majority of Latino voters. While a ward system would not guarantee the election of a Latino candidate, it would significantly increase the likelihood.

In order to better understand such dynamics, two similar surveys were conducted in 1986 and 2001. They were based on questionnaires mailed to a wide range of school boards. Districts were asked to fill out these surveys, and the investigators matched the responses with district-level data available from the U.S. Census. Kenneth J. Meier was the lead investigator of both surveys. The study compared the same 130 districts in both time periods—which constitutes a rare opportunity to study representational change—as opposed to a snapshot in a given year.

As the Latino population continues to grow, one key question is whether Latino political influence is growing in a commensurate fashion. If not, what are the obstacles? This chapter addresses such questions by discussing whether Latino school-board representation has increased; whether ward electoral systems have become more common; whether the negative effects of at-large systems have diminished; and whether Latino school-board members are increasingly able to translate a presence on school boards into substantive educational gains for Latinos.

To preview, the study finds that the Latino student population has grown considerably across a decade-and-a-half. In addition, the percentage of boards elected by ward systems has increased and the share elected by at-large systems has decreased. Because of these electoral changes, the percentage of Latinos on school boards has become larger over time.

THE CHANGING DEMOGRAPHICS
OF THE LATINO COMMUNITY

Among the most significant developments of the last 15 years is the changing demography of the U.S. Latino population. These changes have occurred predominantly on six dimensions. First, and most importantly, the Latino population is now much larger and represents a larger share of the national population. The Latino population grew 58% between 1990 and 2000 (U.S. Census, 2000). The 2000 census revealed that Latinos were 12.5% of the U.S. population, surpassing African Americans as the largest minority group (who constituted 12%). More recent data from the Bureau of the Census indicate that the Latino population grew by 2007 to 15.1% (U.S. Census Bureau 2008), and it should reach over a quarter of the U.S. population by 2050 (Passel & Cohn, 2008).

Second, Latino population growth is driven by both continued immigration and native births. Growing employment opportunities is one major explanation for increasing Latino migration, but new immigration policies also contributed. For example, the Immigration Reform and Control Act of 1986 (IRCA) regularized the immigration status of a significant number of people, many of whom were then able to sponsor additional family members to enter the country. Recent immigration restriction and enforcement policies have had the unintended effect of encouraging undocumented migrants to remain in the country, rather than risk apprehension by traveling between a home country and the United States (U.S. Commission on Immigration Reform, 1997). The largest source of population growth is not immigration, however, but native births. From 2000 to 2007, the Latino population grew by 10.2 million people; over half (58.6%) were born in the United States (El Nasser, 2008).

Third, the national origin of the Latino population is increasingly more diverse. In 1990, people of Mexican descent represented 60.3% of Latinos in the United States; Puerto Ricans comprised 12.2%, and Cubans were 4.7%. By 2000, however, substantial immigration from Central America and the Latin Caribbean reduced the percentage of Latinos of Mexican origin to 58.5%, of Puerto Rican origin to 9.6%, and Cuban origin to 3.5%, while Dominicans, Salvadorans, Columbians, Guatemalans, Ecuadorians, and those from unspecified countries now comprise 28.4% of the total U.S. Latino population (Therrien & Ramirez, 2001).

Fourth, a growing share of Latino immigrants is choosing to naturalize. Past research shows that Latino immigrants, especially Mexicans, have lower rates of naturalization relative to other immigrant groups (DeSipio, 1996). Changes in Mexican nationality law, however, as well as the natural progression to citizenship eligibility of those newly documented by IRCA, resulted in a boom in Latino naturalization in the early and mid-1990s. In California, this boom was accelerated further due to the politicization of ethnicity resulting from immigrant-targeted ballot initiatives and by immigrant-unfriendly provisions of the 1996 Personal Responsibility and Work Opportunity Reconciliation Act (the federal welfare reform act). More recently, the number of Latinos applying for citizenship has surged nationwide. Officials attribute the application increase to several factors, including: citizenship campaigns launched across the country, the announcement of a significant increase in application fees beginning July 2007, the politically charged immigration debate, and the presidential election (Chishti & Bergeron, 2008). One result: while Mexicans still have a comparatively lower tendency to become U.S. citizens, the number of naturalized citizens from Mexico rose by 144% from 1995 to 2005—the most of any major sending country (Passel, 2007).

Fifth, Latinos are now geographically dispersed throughout the country. Historically, Latino communities were located primarily in southwestern states, Florida, New York City, and Chicago. The 2000 census shows, however, that Latinos now have a clear national presence. In 1990, Latinos were the largest minority group in only 16 of the 50 states, and their share of the population exceeded 5% in only 15 states. In 2000, Latinos outnumbered all other minorities in 23 states, and their population exceeded 5% in almost half the states.

Finally, and perhaps more dramatic than the population changes noted above, is the growing presence of Latinos in the public schools. Between 1980 and 2000, the Census Bureau estimated that nationally the proportion of Latinos students enrolled in grades K–12 doubled from 8% to 16.6% of the total student population (U.S. Census Bureau, 2000). Latino student enrollment in public schools doubled in the Northeast to 11.4%, grew nearly four times in the Midwest to 5.5%, grew nearly three times in the South to 16%, and doubled in the West to 31.6%. Latinos now comprise the largest subgroup of students enrolled in California public schools at 43%, and they comprise 50% of all students in New Mexico and 41% of all public school students in Texas. Most Latino students attend schools in larger cities, and Latinos represented the largest percentage of ethnic-racial students in the 10 largest school districts in the country in 2000 (National Center for Education Statistics, 2003). The number and magnitude of changes within the Latino population could lead us to reasonably expect significant change in Latino representation with respect to the politics of education.

COMPARING THE 1986 AND 2001 SAMPLES

The 1986 survey (see Meier & Stewart, 1991) included those U.S. school districts with both 5,000 or more total students and at least 5% Latino enrollment. They reported a 67% response rate to their survey, which meant a total of 145 districts took part. The statistical analysis was able to include a maximum of 138 cases; as is often the case with surveys, not all questions were filled out, and not all data were available for all districts.

In 2001, a similar national school-board survey was conducted (for more information, see Leal, Martinez-Ebers, & Meier, 2004). It was mailed to all districts with at least 5,000 students. The investigators used three mail waves, six phone calls, and one e-mail contact, which resulted in a very high response rate of 96%.

The 1986 dataset was then matched with the 2001 dataset. A total of 130 school districts were found to be in both surveys and were thus able to be statistically compared.[1]

Census data aggregated at the school district level supplemented both surveys. For the 1986 survey, the 1980 census was used. For the 2001 survey, the 2000 census was used.

CHANGES IN LATINO SCHOOL BOARD REPRESENTATION

Table 7.1 presents descriptive information on the sample of school districts. As one would expect given the overall changes in the composition of the population, this set of urban school districts has become significantly more Latino over time. The overall Latino population percentage in these districts has increased from 21.1% to 34.6%, and the Latino student percentage

Table 7.1. School Board Comparisons: 1986 and 2001 Data

Variable	1986	2001
Latino population (%)	21.1	34.6
Latino students (%)	29.3	42.5
Latino school board (%)	12.2	20.4
Latino representation x population ratio	.58	.59
Latino administrators (%)	12.3	18.5
Latino teachers (%)	11.5	15.4
Number of pure ward systems	21	34
Number of pure at-large systems	85	74
Number of pure appointed systems	8	4
Number of mixed systems	16	15

increased from 29.3% to 42.5%. By contrast, the percentage of African-American students in these districts remained stable at 16% while the percentage of Anglo students dropped from 48% to 32%. In 1986, 21 of the districts had a Latino student majority; this increased to 45 districts in 2001. The number of Anglo majority districts declined from 66 to 30 during the same time period.

Latinos were underrepresented on the school boards surveyed in 1986; they held 12.2% of all seats, and just 43.1% of districts included at least one Latino representative. By 2001, Latino representation increased to 20.4% of all seats, and 60.6% of districts had at least one Latino representative. On the other hand, Latino population increases meant that their representation ratio (percent seats divided by percent population) changed only slightly from 0.58 to 0.59 during the intervening 15 years.

These static representation ratios are even more surprising when one examines electoral structure changes. The number of pure ward systems (where all board members are elected from single member districts) increased by 13 while the number of at-large systems decreased by 9. Appointive systems declined from eight to four, but appointive systems are also used when states or cities take over control of school systems, so this number is likely to have fluctuated more in recent years (see Henig & Rich, 2004). This change in selection systems presents an interesting puzzle: Given the known relationships between at-large systems and lower levels of Latino representation (Leal et al., 2004), why have these districts not made greater gains in terms of Latino board representation?

Latino representation among school administrators and teachers has also grown in these districts, but at a rate slower than both population and student growth. The share of Latino administrators increased from 12.2% in 1986 to 18.5% in 2001, while the respective percentages for teachers are 11.5% and 15.4%. In fact, the rate of increase for Latino administrators (50.4%) is slightly higher than the rate of increase in Latino students (45.1%), but not as rapid as the population growth (64.0%). The rate of increase in Latino teachers lags behind all these other trends at 33.9%.

THE IMPACT OF ELECTORAL STRUCTURES

The now accepted statistical method to determine the effect of electoral structures on minority representation is to interact the various electoral structures with population percentages to determine how structures affect both the translation of population into representation and whether there are any threshold effects below which population nets no representation at all (see Engstrom & McDonald, 1981).

There are essentially three different selection processes for school boards: at-large elections, ward-based elections, and appointive systems. In at-large elections, all candidates for the school board run in an election where all citizens eligible to vote in the jurisdiction can vote. As an example, assume there are three seats available. All candidates run essentially against each other for these three seats; voters are allowed to vote for three candidates, and the top three vote getters are the winners. In a ward-based election system, the school district is divided up into smaller districts, and one person is elected to the school board from each district. An appointive system is usually adopted for a dependent school district, that is, a district without its own independent taxing authority. In such a case, some other elected body or official (county board members, the mayor, and so forth) appoints the members of the school board.

Table 7.2 provides simultaneous estimates for both years of the impact of structural biases on Latino representation on school boards. Because of space considerations, we cannot explore the statistical results in any detail, but the overall results will be summarized. The model in the first column combined the data from the original 1986 survey, as well as the newer 2001 survey data for these same cities. It indicated that Latinos do not receive any representation until their population exceeds 8.3% of the total district population.[2] After breaching that threshold, a .84 to 1 ratio holds for representation versus population for at-large election systems.

When we estimate the relationship between population and representation in pure ward-based systems, we see that the coefficients for ward and

Table 7.2. Representation and Electoral Structures 1986–2001

Independent Variable	1986 and 2001 sample		2001 sample	
	Slope	t-score	Slope	t-score
Intercept	-7.0082	3.21***	-8.9872	11.22***
Latino population	.8439	11.36***	.8158	32.97***
Ward percentage	1.0370	.23	-.1380	.09
Appointed percentage	7.2717	.80	10.8749	2.41**
Ward x Latino population	.1569	1.00	.0822	1.70*
Appointed x Latino population	-.0470	.08	-.2300	1.76*
2001 x				
Intercept	-6.8284	1.89*		
Latino population	.1339	1.32		
Ward system	-1.2712	.19		
Appointed system	3.2509	.18		
Ward x Latino population	.0810	.65		
Appointed x Latino population	-.1232	.22		
R^2	.69		.66	
Standard error	13.42		12.72	
F	49.56		328.10	
N	256		853	

$^*p < .10; ^{**}p < .05; ^{***}p < .01.$

at-large systems are both statistically insignificant. We might therefore conclude that Latinos did as well in at-large elections as they did in ward-based
systems in 1986. Similarly, the insignificant coefficients for the appointive
systems also imply that appointive systems are no better or worse than at-
large systems for Latino representation. In addition, the various intercepts
with the year dummy variable (2001) indicate no representational differences between 1986 and 2001.

However, one reason to be a bit skeptical of this apparent lack of relationship between structure and representation in 1986 is the small number

of cases (130) used to estimate the relationship. In fact, the effects for ward elections are pointing in the direction we hypothesized, and its coefficient of approximately 1.0 indicates representational outcomes almost equal to population share. Nevertheless, there are too few cases to be confident that a relationship exists.

To illustrate the influence of sample size, the second model in Table 7.2 estimates the exact set of relationships for all 853 school districts with 5% or more Latino enrollment in the 2001 sample. It shows that Latinos do in fact fare better in ward-based systems. Appointive systems also differ from at-large systems. Although a discussion of these differences for 2001 is beyond the scope of this chapter, the relationships show that Latinos fare better in appointive systems until their population numbers exceed 47.3% after which they do much better in at-large electoral systems.

The models also test for changes over time in terms of how electoral systems translate into representation. A comparison of these intercepts shows that Latinos faced a higher threshold for representation in 2001 than they did in 1986. None of the other relationships are statistically significant, which suggests that the relationships (despite the much larger population slope) in 2001 are not significantly different from those in 1986.

One might examine this table, therefore, and conclude that the process of selection in these school districts had little or no impact on Latino representation in either 1986 or in 2001. That conclusion would be premature, however, because of the statistical problem of collinearity caused by the inclusion of the multiple interaction terms (Draper & Smith, 1981).

Such nonfindings should be qualified further in light of recent published work by Leal et al. (2004). Their results show that the relationship between Latino population and Latino school-board members is nonlinear. Table 7.3 provides such a nonlinear estimation, which clearly shows that only two factors affect Latino representation: the variable that squares the Latino population, and the interaction term that multiplies this variable by the variable for Ward elections. There is no difference in coefficients in 1986 compared to 2001. Substituting various population percentages (or working through the calculus) shows that Ward elections improve the level of Latino representation by approximately 12% more than at-large elections at similar population percentages.

To further examine the relationship between electoral structure and school-board representation for Latinos, we examined the 15 school districts that changed their systems from pure at-large systems to pure-ward systems between 1986 and 2001 (this is larger than the change indicated by Table 7.1 because some ward systems changed to at-large, four appointed systems were changed, and some of the mixed systems converted to pure systems). Table 7.4 lists these 15 districts along with their population and

Table 7.3. Nonlinear Estimates of the Population Seats Relationship

Independent Variable	Slope	t-score
Intercept	2.8748	2.03**
Latino population squared	.01092	13.02***
Ward percentage	.05565	.02*
Ward x Latino population squared	.00367	1.91
2001	-.39341	.17
2001 x		
Latino population squared	-.00031	.30
Ward percentage	.07594	.02
Ward x Latino population squared	-.00211	.93
R^2	.74	
Standard error	12.21	
F	100.89	
N	256	

$^*p < .10;\ ^{**}p < .05;\ ^{***}p < .01.$

representation percentages in 1986 and 2001. Given the population gains made by Latinos, we would expect some representation gains even under an at-large system.

Only 5 of the 15 districts in 1986 had Latinos on the school board, compared to 11 of 15 in 2001 after the conversion to ward elections. Two of the districts with Latinos on the board in 1986, Santa Fe and Gadsen, also had Latino population majorities; we would expect this to be an advantage to Latinos (or any majoring group) in an at-large system. Nine of the districts that changed gained Latino representation, five remained constant, and only one lost representation (Farmington). To control for population gains, we calculated representation/population ratios for each of the districts in both years. The Latino representation/population ratio increased from .30 in 1986 to .53 in 2001.

To provide a further check, we also calculated similar figures for those districts that reported changes from pure ward systems to pure at-large systems. Of those districts, the average representation ratio did increase, but this increase could virtually all be accounted for by the huge gains in

Table 7.4. Population and Representation in Districts that Shifted from At-Large to Ward Systems Between 1986 and 2001

District	1986 Latino		2001 Latino	
	Pop.	Rep.	Pop.	Rep.
Dade County, FL	35.7	14.3	57.4	44.4
Wichita, KS	3.3	0	1.8	0
Tyler, TX	4.2	0	15.5	0
Midland, TX	15.2	0	29.5	14.3
Northside, TX	30.7	14.3	48.0	14.3
Northeast, TX	17.4	0	32.5	14.3
Sanger, CA	47.5	0	61.8	42.9
Vallejo City, CA	8.5	0	16.3	20.0
Mesa, CO	7.2	0	10.2	0
Alamagordo, NM	20.5	0	33.5	20.0
Farmington, NM	14.6	20.0	18.4	0
Gadsen, NM	70.8	60.0	86.6	80.0
Santa Fe, NM	54.6	80.0	48.8	80.0
Galveston, TX	17.6	0	25.4	14.3
Lamar, TX	33.1	0	38.9	14.3
Los Angeles, CA	31.1	14.3	49.5	14.3
Orange County, CA	11.9	14.3	28.8	28.6
Jersey City, NJ	18.7	11.1	28.3	11.1
Patterson, NJ	28.7	22.2	50.1	22.2
Brownsville, TX	33.2	0	91.5	85.7
Arlington, TX	5.6	0	18.6	0
Centralia, CA	14.0	0	27.9	40.0
Napa Valley, CA	7.6	0	23.5	0
Thompson, CO	5.2	0	7.6	0
LaPorte, TX	8.9	0	19.7	0

Brownsville (with its now overwhelming Latino majority) and with the district of Centralia electing a second Latino to their board. The results in Table 7.4 are only suggestive, but they generally support the argument that ward-based systems benefit Latinos more than at-large electoral systems.

BUREAUCRATIC REPRESENTATION

While school-board representation is important in and of itself, much of the literature is interested in descriptive representation because of the link to substantive representation (Lublin, 1997; Tate, 2003). Latino representation is associated with increases in Latino representation in administrative and teaching positions, which are in turn associated with improved performances by Latino students (see Hess & Leal, 1997; Meier & Gonzalez Juenke, 2005; Meier & Stewart, 1991).

The first two columns of Table 7.5 model the percentage of Latino administrators as a function of Latino population, Latino board representation, the ratio of Latino to Anglo incomes, and Latino education levels (administrative employment is also a function of the labor pool which includes the level of education for Latinos and how attractive administrative jobs are compared to the private sector). For both Latino population and board representation there are interactions with the year of the survey.

The first three coefficients for administrators show that Latino population was the most important factor in 1986 followed by Latino school-board members. A 1-percentage point increase in Latino population was associated with a .63 percentage point increase in Latino administrators; the respective increase for Latino school board members was .21 percentage points. Neither of the coefficients in the 2001 year interaction was statistically significant, indicating that the process of gaining Latino administrative positions has not changed much between 1986 and 2001. The drop in the size of the population slope, while suggestive and foreshadowing other relationships, does not meet the traditional levels of statistical significance.

The relationships for Latino teachers are more interesting than those for Latino administrators. This equation now includes the percentage of Latino administrators as well as an interaction between Latino administrators and the year 2001 variable. Latino administrators are the most important factor in hiring teachers, regardless of year. For 1986, a 1 percentage point increase in Latino administrators was associated with a .56 percentage point increase in hiring Latino teachers, all other things being equal. When "year = 2001" interacts with Latino administrators, the coefficient is zero, indicating that this relationship remains the same for both years.

The primary finding from this analysis is that, over time, while the effect of Latino population on Latino representation decreased, the importance of

Table 7.5. Administrative and Teacher Representation

	Administrators		Teachers	
	Slope	t-*score*	*Slope*	t-*score*
Intercept	5.44	1.42	-.66	.99
Latino population	.63	8.61**	.25	5.17**
Latino representation	.21	2.82**	-.06	1.46
Latino administrators	—	—	.56	11.97**
2001				
Latino population	-.14	1.49	-.13	2.44*
Latino representation	.01	.13	.14	2.44*
Latino administrators	—	—	.00	.02
Latino-Anglo income (%)	-.20	3.28**	—	—
Latino education	.16	3.06**	—	—
R^2	.72		.86	
Standard error	9.76		5.58	
F	97.89		238.06	
N	238		235	

*$P < .05$; **$p < .01$.

Latino school-board representation increased. The impact of Latino population drops by approximately half in its positive impact on Latino teachers between 1986 and 2001. By contrast, the effect of Latino school board members was negative and insignificant in 1986, but reverses signs and becomes positive in 2001. So while the importance of Latino population has declined, the importance of Latino political resources has increased.

Such a finding makes some sense given the rapid influx of Latinos into these school districts. Because these new arrivals include some immigrants who are not eligible to vote, the value of population size by itself as a political resource declines. At the same time, the mobilized political resource—the school board representatives—comes into play as a significantly more important factor. Latino political representation, as a result, has a more extended reach, influencing hiring patterns lower down in the educational bureaucracy.

There is a growing consensus in the professional education community that minority students gain academically when they are taught by minority teachers (Goodlad, 1990; Riley & Pompa, 1998; and Spring, 2000). This proposition is increasingly supported by the research literature (Dee, 2001; Hess & Leal, 1997; Meier, Wrinkle, & Polinard, 1999; Meier, Eller, Wrinkle, & Polinard, 2001).

We also need to consider this issue from the perspective of representation theory. Considerable evidence suggests that the Latino community wants more Latinos teaching their children (Romo & Falbo, 1996; Garcia, 2001; Reyes, Scribner, & Paredes Scribner, 1999; Valenzuela, 1999). Regardless of whether Latino teachers enhance the achievement of Latino students, their hiring is therefore evidence of political responsiveness.

CONCLUSIONS

This chapter examines Latino representation in the educational policy process at two different time points—1986 and 2001. Despite the substantial change in Latino population in the United States during this time period, the representation process and the translation of population into political positions did not change much. The one exception was the selection of Latino teachers, where the role of political representation has become more important. That difference aside, political representation is a major factor in increasing bureaucratic representation, which in turn has a large influence on the representation of teachers. Because Latino teachers are so essential to the performance of Latino students, these findings reaffirm that many of the educational inequities faced by Latinos have their roots in the inequities of the political process.

NOTES

For additional information about the variables, the methodology of the reported study, and the statistical results, contact the authors at dleal@post.harvard.edu. These could not be fully described in this chapter because of space considerations.

We would like to thank Miner P. Marchbanks, III, and Nick Theobald for their assistance in collecting data and compiling the data set. Financial support was provided in part by the Carlos H. Cantu Hispanic Education and Opportunity Endowment and the Project for Equity, Representation and Governance at Texas A&M University. David Leal would also like to acknowledge the support of the Spencer Foundation/National Academy of Education.

1. Of the 145 original districts in the 1986 survey, several cases could not be included because they fell below 5,000 students by 1999, were consolidated and ceased to exist as independent units, or did not respond to the 2001 survey.

2. What we cannot tell is what percentage of the voters they were. Because many Latinos have not become citizens yet, their voting numbers are lower than their population numbers. Similarly, the younger age of the Latino population means that they compose a smaller percentage of the voting age population than they do of the overall population.

REFERENCES

Chishti, M., & Bergeron, C. (2008, February 15). *USCIS: Backlog in naturalization applications will take nearly three years to clear*. Washington, DC: Migration Policy Institute.

Dee, T. S. (2001). Teachers, race and student achievement in a randomized experiment. *NBER Working Paper Series, Working Paper 8432*. Cambridge: National Bureau of Economic Analysis.

DeSipio, L. (1996). *Counting on the Latino vote*. Charlottesville, VA: University of Virginia Press.

Draper, N. R., & Smith. H. (1981). *Applied regression analysis*. New York: Wiley.

El Nasser, H. (2008, June 30). Births fueling Hispanic growth. *USA Today*. Retrieved June 22, 2010, from http://www.usatoday.com/news/nation/2008-06-29-hispanics_N.htm

Engstrom, R., & McDonald, M. (1981). The election of blacks to city councils. *American Political Science Review, 75*, 344–54.

Garcia, E. (2001). *Student cultural diversity: Understanding and meeting the challenge* (3rd ed.). Boston: Houghton Mifflin.

Goodlad, J. (1990). *Teachers for our nation's schools*. San Francisco: Jossey-Bass.

Henig, J., & Rich, W. (2004). *Mayors in the middle: Politics, race, and mayoral control of urban schools*. Princeton, NJ: Princeton University Press.

Hess, F., & Leal, D. L. (1997). Minority teachers, minority students and college matriculation: A new look at the role-modeling hypothesis. *Policy Studies Journal, 25*, 235–248.

Leal, D. L., Martinez-Ebers, V., & Meier, K. J. (2004). The politics of Latino education: The biases of at-large elections. *Journal of Politics, 66*, 1224–1244.

Lublin, D. L. (1997). *The paradox of minority representation: Racial gerrymandering and minority interests in congress*. Princeton, NJ: Princeton University Press.

Meier, K. J., Eller, W. S., Wrinkle, R. D., & Polinard, J. L. (2001). Zen and the art of policy analysis: A response to Nielsen and Wolf. *Journal of Politics, 63*, 616–629.

Meier, K. J., & Gonzalez Juenke, E. (2005). Electoral structure and the quality of representation: The policy consequences of school board elections. In W. Howell (Ed.), *Besieged: School boards and the future of education*. Washington, DC: The Brookings Institution.

Meier, K. J., & Stewart, J., Jr. (1991). *The politics of Hispanic education: Un paso pa'lante y dos pa'tras*. Albany, NY: State University of New York Press.

Meier, K. J., Wrinkle, R. D., & Polinard, J. (1999). Representative bureaucracy and distributional equity: Addressing the hard question. *Journal of Politics, 61,* 1025–1039.

National Center for Education Statistics. (2003). *Status and trends in the education of Hispanics.* Washington, DC: U.S. Department of Education. Retrieved June 20, 2010, from http://nces.ed.gov/pubs2003/2003008.pdf

Passel, J. S. (2007). *Growing share of immigrants choosing naturalization.* Washington, DC: Pew Hispanic Center.

Passel, J. S., & Cohn, D. (2008). *U.S. population projections: 2005–2050.* Washington, DC: Pew Research Center.

Reyes, P., Scribner, J., & Paredes Scribner, A. (Eds.). (1999). *Lessons from high-performing Hispanic schools.* New York: Teachers College Press.

Riley, R., & Pompa, D. (1998). *Improving opportunities: Strategies from the secretary of education for Hispanic and limited English proficient students.* Washington, DC: Office of Bilingual Education and Minority Languages Affairs, U.S. Department of Education.

Romo, H., & Falbo, T. (1996). *Latino high school graduation: Defying the odds.* Austin, TX: University of Texas Press.

Spring, J. (2000). *American education* (9th ed.). Boston: McGraw-Hill.

Tate, K. (2003). *Black faces in the mirror.* Princeton, NJ: Princeton University Press.

Therrien, M., & Ramirez, R. R. (2001, March). The Hispanic population in the United States: Population Characteristics. *Current Population Reports 20–535.* Washington, DC: U.S. Census Bureau.

U.S. Census Bureau. (2008). *U.S. Hispanic population surpasses 45 million, now 15 percent of total.* Washington, DC: Author. Retrieved June 22, 2010, from http://www.census.gov/newsroom/releases/archives/population/cb09-67.html

U.S. Census Bureau. (2000). Census of the Population. Washington, DC: Author.

U.S. Commission on Immigration Reform. (1997). *Binational study on migration.* Washington, DC: Author.

Valenzuela, A. (1999). *Subtractive schooling.* Albany, NY: State University of New York Press.

CHAPTER 8

Black Empowerment and the Representation of Latinos on Local School Boards

Rene R. Rocha

The present-day political life of racial/ethnic minorities within the United States is the product of a long history of overt and clandestine discrimination. This history, and the social attitudes that stem from it, not only complicates the political relationships between minorities and Anglos, but also between African Americans and Latinos. As a result, inter-minority cooperation seems to be a relatively rare occurrence. The resulting norm of political conflict impacts multiple policy arenas, especially education. Anecdotal evidence suggests that African American-Latino relations are exceptionally tenuous within the educational policy arena (Vaca, 2004). Previous work likewise provides empirical support for the contention that minority groups seldom come together to form mass-level coalitions in school board elections (Rocha, 2007).

Moving beyond a focus on mass-level behavior, this chapter discusses a study that focuses on what kind of relationships develop at the elite level (specifically among elected officials). Within the realm of education policy, this means the elected school-board members who oversee the operation of the vast majority of public schools within the United States. While a study of African-American and Latino legislative cooperation on local school boards allows us to examine race relations within the education system, it may also afford a large degree of generalizability toward other elected officials. After all, nearly 21% of all African-American elected officials served on school boards as of 2000 (Joint Center for Political and Economic Studies, 2000), while a plurality of Latino elected officials, 42%, held such positions (National Association of Latino Elected Officials, 2000). Thus, an examination of the relationships between African Americans and Latinos serving on local school boards speaks to the behavior of a large number of minority politicians generally, and not just the primary political actors within the education policymaking process.

This chapter begins by reviewing what we know about how minorities are substantively represented within legislative bodies, with an emphasis on substantive representation within local legislative bodies. Drawing on insights from studies focusing on inter-minority cooperation and conflict in local politics, it then considers the implications of minority representation for other minority groups. The hypotheses drawn out of this literature are then tested using data provided from the 2001 National Latino Education Study.

MINORITY REPRESENTATION IN LOCAL GOVERNMENT

Since Hanna Pitkin (1967) first developed the descriptive, symbolic, and substantive representation framework, several scholars have studied the interrelationships among these various types of representation. In short, *descriptive representation* occurs when members of a group share some kind of attribute with their public official, such as race or ethnicity. *Substantive representation* occurs when policies or other governmental actions are advanced in a group's interest. One result of Pitkin's framework has been a plethora of studies concluding that descriptive representation usually leads to substantive representation within legislative bodies. While several of these studies focus on the U.S. Congress, others have established this link within local legislative bodies, such as city councils and school boards (see Marschall, 2005; Meier & England, 1984; Mladenka, 1989; Robinson & Dye, 1978; Robinson & England, 1981).

Few studies, however, have extended this literature by examining the implication of minority representation for other minority groups. To some degree, this lack of scholarly attention can be explained by the dominant way substantive representation has been conceptualized. When viewed primarily as policy congruence between representatives and their constituencies, the liberal ideological disposition and Democratic Party affiliation of most African Americans and Latinos tends to result in similar voting patterns, especially at the U.S. Congress level (Lublin, 1997).

Lower levels of government, however, are more likely to face issues that could be considered pragmatic and may not easily be placed on an ideological dimension (Straayer, Wrinkle, & Polinard, 1998). This characterization is compounded within the education system, where nonpartisan governance makes it more difficult for school-board members to form voting blocs that are rooted in ideology. In such settings, a complete understanding of substantive representation must consider not only voting patterns, as most studies of representation in the U.S. Congress or state legislatures do, but also alternative conceptualizations of substantive representation.

Alternative conceptualizations also carry with them different implications relating to African-American and Latino cooperation and conflict. Whereas both African Americans and Latinos typically stand to benefit from redistributive policies, nonlegislative constituent services are more likely to occur within a strict zero-sum context, with particularized benefits for African Americans limiting the benefits that Latinos are able to receive and vice versa. Not surprisingly, such scarcity has been found to foster inter-minority competition over beneficial resources.

Studies that have found positive covariance between socioeconomic indicators across racial/ethnic groups argue that this occurs because income and education, while not limitless, do not occur within a zero-sum context (see McClain & Tauber, 2001; Meier, McClain, Wrinkle, & Polinard, 2004; Meier, Juenke, Wrinkle, Polinard, 2005). Political empowerment variables, such as representation on city councils, are more likely to negatively covary because they exist within a zero-sum context, where increased representation on the part of one group makes it more difficult for other groups to achieve representation.

Within the field of urban politics, one popular measure of the substantive representation of racial/ethnic minorities has been the percentage of municipal employees belonging to such groups. A long stream of literature concludes that as minority political power increases so does the share of public jobs held by minorities (Browning, Marshall, & Tabb, 1984; Campbell & Feagin, 1975; Chandler & Gely, 1995; Dye & Renick, 1981; Eisinger, 1982a, 1982b; Kerr & Mladenka, 1994; Mladenka, 1989; Saltzstein, 1989; Stein, 1986). Generally, these studies find that while minority population size is the primary determinant of public employment, politics does play a critical role. This occurs mainly through minority representation on city council seats— control of the mayoral office is a less consistent predictor of employment (see Kerr & Mladenka, 1994; Mladenka, 1989). Similar relationships also occur within school districts, where research finds that minority representation on school boards is consistently related to the share of minority administrators and teachers (Meier, Stewart, & England, 1989). Saltzstein (1986) has even extended this hypothesis to search for evidence of substantive representation among females, finding that female political empowerment is positively related to female employment in nonclerical and administrative positions. Together, these studies suggest that municipal employment is an extremely useful area of investigation for representation scholars.

In a previous study, McClain (1993) considers the relationship between African-American and Latino municipal employment. Although employment in such positions is, to some degree, a zero-sum situation, McClain

(1993) finds no relationship between African-American and Latino employ-ment. As with political offices, when both groups make gains, they tend to do so at the expense of Anglos. McClain's study, however, does not consider how minority political representation affects the municipal employment of other minority groups, so no conclusions can be drawn regarding African-American and Latino legislative cooperation at the local level.

This chapter takes up this question. More succinctly: Are the positive affects of African-American representation strengthened, weakened, or unaffected by the presence of Latino representation? Conversely: Are the positive affects of Latino representation strengthened, weakened, or unaffected by the presence of African-American representation? These questions also advance current research beyond simple covariance models, resulting in more definitive statements regarding causality. They also allow for an examination of minority-minority relations within the local legislative process, rather than in terms of political inputs or outputs.

MODELING AFRICAN AMERICAN AND LATINO ACCESS TO ADMINISTRATIVE AND TEACHING POSITIONS

The National Latino Education Study

The 2001 National Latino Education Study (NLES) offers unique leverage on this question (Project for Equity, Representation and Governance, 2001). The NLES surveyed every school district in the nation with a student enrollment over 5,000 and yielded a response rate of 96%. This results in a total sample of 1,831 districts across 49 states, 1,672 of which elect their board members. The size and geographic diversity of this sample presents a substantial improvement over samples used in previous studies.

The NLES fell just shy of capturing the universe of urban school districts within the United States, and therefore also offers a nearly complete sample of multiracial school districts as well. Data regarding the demographic makeup of each school district were obtained from the 2000 Census. Census data include the racial composition of the district and the average level of socioeconomic resources (e.g., educational attainment, income, and home ownership) present in each community by race.

Research Questions

Descriptive representation was measured in a relatively straightforward manner through the percentage of school-board seats that each group holds. Considering the contingent nature of the hypotheses, this measure is interacted with a simply dichotomous variable, coded 1 if both African

Americans and Latinos serve on the school board, 0 otherwise. Within the NLES, 113 districts meet this criterion.

Measuring substantive representation, of course, presented a much greater challenge. As mentioned above, urban politics researchers have often used the percentage of municipal employees belonging to some group. Within the educational system, the analogous measure is the percentage of administrators. As with municipal employees, operationalizing the substantive representation of racial/ethnic minorities as the percentage of minority administrators and teachers fits several facets of Eulau and Karps' (1977) framework, including service responsiveness and symbolism. Within education research, a long stream of literature argues that increased descriptive representation among administrators and teachers will positively affect student outcomes, defined both in terms of academic performance and lower levels of "second-generation discrimination" (Hess & Leal, 1997; Meier & Stewart, 1991; Meier, Stewart, & England, 1989; Meier, Wrinkle, & Polinard, 1999). Thus, the argument that such a measure may also be seen as a form of policy responsiveness is applicable within education.

Beyond political explanations of minority employment, the most influential variables determining the percentage of minority administrators should be the size of the available labor pool. For this reason, the study created models to consider the percentage of the population comprised of African Americans/Latinos. Employment within the educational system also requires a college degree, so the models also control for the percentage of African Americans/Latinos who possess at least a bachelor's degree. The same variables should determine the percentage of African-American/Latino teachers within a district; however, representation among teaching faculties may also be a function of the presence of co-ethnics within the administrators. With this in mind, I accounted for the percentage of African-American/Latino administrators when predicting the percentage of African American/Latino teachers within a district. As a final control, I insert a dichotomous variable for those districts in which African Americans or Latinos controlled a majority of seats on the board.

Study Findings

Table 8.1 presents the results for the first series of models, which attempt to determine what influences the percentage of African-American and Latino administrators within a district. The findings indicate that for each point increase in the percentage of the African-American population, African-American representation among school administrators increases .759. In line with the expectation that employment is a function of the available labor pool, an additional boost becomes apparent as the percentage of African Americans holding a college degree increases.

Table 8.1. Black-Latino Cooperation and Conflict in the Hiring of Minority Administrators (OLS Estimates)

Dependent Variable = Percentage of School Administrators That Are:

INDEPENDENT VARIABLE	Black	SE	Latino	SE
Black population	.759**	(0.042)		
Latino population			.333**	(0.023)
Blacks who have a college degree (%)	.018*	(0.009)		
Latinos who have a college degree (%)			.045**	(0.009)
Black school-board members (%)	.172**	(0.036)		
Latino school-board members (%)			.345**	(0.053)
Blacks and Latinos on the board (0,1)	1.100	(1.720)	0.669	(1.999)
Black school-board members X (%)	-0.018	(0.083)		
BLACKS AND LATINOS ON THE BOARD				
Latino school board members "X" (%)			-.205*	(0.101)
Majority black board	7.087*	(3.063)		
Majority Latino board			6.572	(4.243)
Constant	-0.019	(0.309)	-1.708**	(0.276)
N	1361		1372	
R^2	0.79		0.83	

*p < .05, **p < .01

Political representation also increases African-American employment, where capturing an additional seat on a seven-member board appears to increase the percentage of African-American administrators by 2.4%. This study shows no evidence, however, that the presence of Latinos on the school board affects the ability of African Americans to translate descriptive representation into substantive representation in any way.

For Latinos, population numbers appear to matter less. The percentage of school administrators who are Latino increases by a third with each additional point increase in the percentage of the Latino population (where the analogous coefficient for African Americans is .759). However, Latinos do profit from a higher level of college education, indicating that market forces are important for both communities. The finding that Latino administrative employment increases at a higher rate with college education than it does for African Americans (coefficient of .045 for Latinos, compared to .018 for African Americans) is a possible indicator that Latino access to government employment is more influenced by the characteristics of that community.

Latinos appear to benefit just as much from political office holding as they do from their population size, in sharp contrast to African Americans, where population numbers seem to have a much larger influence on employment than office holding. Also differing from the model for African Americans, these results show that the positive relationship between Latino representation on school boards and Latino representation among school administrators *is* contingent upon the presence of African Americans on the board; the positive effect of Latino representation is diminished on boards where African Americans are likewise represented.

This effect is also substantively meaningful. Let us consider a hypothetical seven-member board on which Latinos hold two seats (or approximately 28% of the seats) and all other variables are held at their mean or modal categories. If Latinos do not have to compete with African-American representatives, they can expect to get a boost just shy of 10 percentage points (9.7) in their share of administrative positions. On boards in which Latinos must compete with African-American representatives, Latinos can expect a much more modest boost of 4.6 percentage points, even when controlling for the main effect which indicates that the percentage of Latino administrators tends to be slightly higher within districts in which both groups serve on the board.

Table 8.2 presents the results for a second series of models in order to determine whether school board representation has an effect on hiring minority teachers as it does on minority administrators. Unlike the models presented in Table 8.1, the models for African Americans and Latinos suffer from correlation among the residuals, necessitating the use of Seemingly Unrelated Regressions.

As with administrators, African-American representation among teachers increases with the size of the African-American population, although, unlike the administrator models, the level of education within the African-American community does not have an effect. African-American political representation also increases employment among teachers. The greatest impact on descriptive representation among teachers appears to be the presence of African-American administrators, however, with a one percentage point increase in the number of African-American administrators associated with just under a 0.5 percentage point increase in the number of African-American teachers. As shown in Table 8.1, no evidence indicates that the presence of Latinos on the board affects the ability of African Americans to translate political representation into increased employment within the educational system.

Latino representation among teachers likewise increases with the size of the Latino population, although, like the models for minority administrators,

Table 8.2. Black-Latino Cooperation and Conflict in the Hiring of Minority Teachers (Seemingly Unrelated Regression Estimates)

Dependent Variable = Percentage of School Teacher That Are:				
INDEPENDENT VARIABLE	Black	SE	Latino	SE
Black population	0.276**	(0.019)		
Latino population			0.190**	(0.012)
Blacks who have a college degree (%)	-0.005	(0.008)		
Latinos who have a college degree (%)			0.024*	(0.010)
Black school administrators (%)	0.498**	(0.016)		
Latino school administrators (%)			0.515**	(0.020)
Black school-board members (%)	0.057**	(0.014)		
Latino school-board members (%)			0.103**	(0.018)
Blacks and Latinos on the board (0,1)	-1.079	(0.814)	0.754	(0.788)
Black school-board members X (%)	0.032	(0.029)		
Blacks and Latinos on the board				
Latino school-board members X (%)			-0.133**	(0.028)
BLACKS AND LATINOS ON THE BOARD				
Majority black board	7.455**	(0.991)		
Majority Latino board			0.140	(1.165)
Constant	-0.563**	(0.216)	-0.723	(0.229)
N	1353		1353	
R²	0.87		0.88	

Breusch-Pagan test of independence: χ^2 (Probability), 4.782 (.029)
*p < .05, **p < .01

Latinos appear to benefit from population size to a smaller degree than do African Americans. Latino education, measured as the percentage of Latinos holding a college degree, is also a significant predictor of Latino teachers. Once again, the presence of co-ethnics in administrative positions has the greatest substantive impact. The size of the benefit that Latinos extract from passive representation among administrators is analogous to that African Americans extract (coefficients = .515 and .498 respectively). In addition, Latinos receive a direct benefit from having co-ethnics on the school board, but, as with administrators, the findings also point towards inter-minority competition within the legislative arena of the educational policymaking process.

The positive influence of Latino school-board members is drastically reduced in districts where African Americans serve on the board (note the negative value for the coefficient for the interactive term = –.133, compared to .103 for the main effect). Thus, when it comes to the hiring of both administrators and teachers, we see that Latinos are far less able to translate political gains into employment in districts where they serve on boards alongside African Americans.

CONCLUSION

As residential patterns have changed to create numerous multiracial areas within the United States, so has the potential for the formation of alternative racial coalitions. The possibility now exists for African Americans and Latinos to form political coalitions with one another, promoting the interests of both groups and increasing their mutual political success even when faced with opposition from a conservative Anglo community. But do they?

This chapter focused on the nature of African-American and Latino relations within the legislative component of the education policymaking process. Given that electoral coalitions between African Americans and Latinos are relatively rare (Rocha, 2007), it is not surprising that this study offers no evidence of African-American and Latino legislative cooperation. Indeed, the findings suggest that the presence of Latinos on the board neither positively or negative affects the substantive representation of African Americans. For Latinos, however, political representation has less of a positive impact on the percentage of Latino administrators and teachers when they serve on boards alongside African Americans.

In short, the research reported here offers little hope for those who wish to see minorities work together in order to maximize their political success. Inter-minority competition exists, and Latinos appear to be big losers in this phenomenon. Work by Meier et al. (2004), however, indicates that inter-minority cooperation exists at the bureaucratic level and plays a major role in preventing discrimination against minority students. The question is why inter-minority competition occurs at the legislative stage of policy making within the U.S. education system.

This chapter provides some evidence that scarcity of resources, such as administrative and teaching positions, fosters competition between groups that might otherwise be expected to form cooperative relationships. This finding would seem to confirm the argument made by Meier et al. (2004) that inter-minority competition is most likely to occur in zero-sum situations.

REFERENCES

Browning, R. P., Marshall, D. R., & Tabb, D. H. (1984). *Protest is not enough.* Berkeley, CA: University of California Press.

Campbell, J. D., & Feagin, J. (1975). Black politics in the south: A descriptive analysis. *Journal of Politics, 37,* 129–59.

Chandler, T. D., & Gely, R. (1995). Protective service unions, political activities, and bargaining outcomes. *Journal of Public Administration Research and Theory, 5,* 295–318.

Dye, T. R., & Renick, J. (1981). Political power and city jobs: Determinants of minority employment. *Social Science Quarterly, 62,* 475–486.

Eisinger, P. K. (1982a). Black employment in municipal jobs: The impact of black political power. *American Political Science Review, 76,* 380–392.

Eisinger, P. K. (1982b). The economic conditions of black employment in municipal bureaucracies. *American Journal of Political Science, 26,* 754–771.

Eulau, H., & Karps, P. D. (1977). The puzzle of representation: Specifying components of responsiveness. *Legislative Studies Quarterly, 2,* 233–254.

Hess, F. M., & Leal, D. L. (1997). Minority teachers, minority students, and college matriculation: A new look at the role-modeling hypothesis. *Policy Studies Journal, 25,* 235–248.

Joint Center for Political and Economic Studies. (2000). *Black elected officials: A statistical summary.* Washington, DC: Author.

Kerr, B., & Mladenka, K. R. (1994). Does politics matter? A times series analysis of minority employment patterns. *American Journal of Political Science, 38,* 918–943.

Lublin, D. (1997). *The paradox of representation: Racial gerrymandering and minority interests in congress.* Princeton, NJ: Princeton University Press.

Marschall, M. J. (2005). Minority incorporation and local school boards. In W. G. Howell (Ed.), *Besieged: School boards and the future of education politics.* Washington, DC: Brookings Institution Press.

McClain, P. D. (1993). The changing dynamics of urban politics: Black and Hispanic municipal employment: Is there competition? *Journal of Politics, 55,* 399–414.

McClain, P. D., & Tauber, S. C. (1998). Black and Latino socioeconomic and political competition: Has a decade made a difference? *American Politics Quarterly, 26,* 101–116.

Meier, K. J., & England, R. E. (1984). Black representation and educational policy: Are they related? *American Political Science Review, 78,* 392–403.

Meier, K. J., Juenke, E. G., Wrinkle, R. D., & Polinard, J. L. (2005). Strucutual choices and representational biases: The post-election color of representation. *American Journal of Political Science, 49,* 758–768.

Meier, K. J., McClain, P., Wrinkle, R. D., & Polinard, J. L. (2004). Divided or together? *Political Research Quarerly, 57,* 399–409.

Meier, K. J., & Stewart, J., Jr. (1991). *The politics of Hispanic education.* Albany, NY: State University of New York Press.

Meier, K. J., Stewart, J., Jr., & England, R. E. (1989). *Race, class and education: The politics of second generation discrimination.* Madison, WI: University of Wisconsin Press.

Meier, K. J., Wrinkle, R. D., & Polinard, J. L. (1999). Representative bureaucracy and distributional equity: Addressing the hard question. *Journal of Politics, 61,* 1025–1039.

Mladenka, K. R. (1989). Blacks and Hispanics in urban politics. *American Political Science Review, 83,* 165–191.

National Association of Latino Elected Officials (NALEO). (2000). *National directory of Latino elected officials.* Los Angeles, CA: Author.

Pitkin, H. F. (1967). *The concept of representation.* Berkley, CA: University of California Press.

Project for Equity, Representation, and Governance. (2001). *National Latino education study.* College Station: Texas A&M University. Retrieved June 20, 2010, from http://perg.tamu.edu

Robinson, T. P., & Dye, T. R. (1978). Reformism and black representation on city councils. *Social Science Quarterly, 59,* 133–141.

Robinson, T., & England, R. E. (1981). Black representation and central city school boards revisited. *Social Science Quarterly, 62,* 495–502.

Rocha, R. R. (2007). Black-brown coalitions in local school board elections. *Political Research Quarterly, 60,* 315–327.

Saltzstein, G. H. (1986). Female mayors and women in municipal jobs. *American Journal of Political Science, 30,* 140–164.

Saltzstein, G. H. (1989). Black mayors and police policies. *Journal of Politics, 51,* 525–544.

Stein, L. (1986). Representative local government: Minorities in municipal work force. *American Journal of Political Science, 48,* 694–713.

Straayer, J. A., Wrinkle, R. D., & Polinard, J. L. (1998). *State and local politics* (2nd ed.). New York: St. Martin's Press.

Vaca, N. C. (2004). *The presumed alliance: The unspoken conflict between Latinos and blacks and what it means for America.* New York: Rayo Press.

CHAPTER 9

Anglo Voting on Bilingual Education: The Partisan Nature of the Impact of Proximity to the Border of Mexico

Regina Branton, Gavin Dillingham,
Johanna Dunaway, and Beth Miller

Between 1990 and 2000, the nation's Latino population increased by over half. Nowhere is the growth of the Latino population more visible than in California, where three quarters of the state's population growth occurred within the Latino community during that decade. At the same time, California's foreign-born Latino population increased by 42%. By 2000, foreign-born Latinos accounted for 44% of the state's total Latino population.

California's growing population of foreign-born Latinos intensified the immigration debate (DeSipio & de la Garza, 1998; Sierra, Carrillo, DeSipio, & Jones-Correa, 2000). The political consequences included a series of ballot initiatives specifically targeting both legal and unauthorized immigrants. In 1986, California voters supported Measure 63, which designated English as the state's official language. In 1994, voters supported Proposition 187, which eliminated undocumented immigrant access to social services, such as nonemergency medical care.

By the late 1990s, California's focus shifted to education policy. Approximately 25% of students in the California education system were considered Limited English Proficient (LEP), over 80% of whom were native Spanish speakers. Limited English Proficient refers to foreign-born students or students who have difficulty speaking, understanding, reading, and writing English. The growing LEP population brought the issue of bilingual education into the spotlight. A debate centered on the best method to increase English proficiency and literacy of the LEP population. The 1998 election included Proposition 227, a hotly contested and ultimately successful ballot initiative that aimed to dismantle California's bilingual education program.

In this chapter, we examine the impact of proximity to the U.S.-Mexico border on individual-level voting behavior on California's Proposition 227. Existing research highlights the significant relationship between ethnic context and voting behavior on nativist-type initiatives such as Proposition 227 (Citrin, Reingold, Walters, & Green, 1990; Hero, 1998; Tolbert & Hero, 1996, 1998). However, very little attention has been given to the relationship between proximity to the U.S.-Mexico border and voting behavior on this type of ballot initiative. Thus we considered the impact of proximity to the border of Mexico on Anglo voting behavior on California's Proposition 227, proposing that Anglos residing closer to the border of Mexico are more likely to support the elimination of bilingual education than Anglos residing farther from the border. In addition, we argue that the effect of border distance on voting behavior on Proposition 227 varies as a function of one's partisan affiliation.

CALIFORNIA'S PROPOSITION 227

A long history of bilingual education policy in California preceded Proposition 227. In 1967, California enacted legislation that overturned an 1872 law requiring English-only instruction in schools. This legislation allowed instruction in languages other than English in public schools. The Chacón-Moscone Bilingual-Bicultural Education Act of 1974 required schools to offer language minority students equal education regardless of their proficiency in English. The 1980 Bilingual Education Improvement and Reform Act required schools to provide bilingual instruction.

The first setback to California's bilingual education came in 1986 with the passage of Measure 63. Support for this English-only measure provided the justification necessary for Governor Deukmejian to veto a bill that proposed to extend the bilingual education law. In 1987, the same Governor failed to reauthorize the Chacón-Moscone Act, thus eliminating the formal directive for bilingual education.

In 1994, California voters passed Proposition 187, which sought to deny access to social services, health care, and education to undocumented immigrants. The proposition stipulated that attendance in public schools be limited to citizens and legal residents. On the heels of Proposition 187, the State Board of Education waived bilingual education requirements for four California school districts. A 1998 court case ruled that public schools are not required to offer bilingual education, but must follow the federal guidelines on bilingual education.

The final attempt to eliminate bilingual education culminated in the form of Proposition 227 in 1998. This initiative proposed to eliminate bilingual education in favor of an English Immersion approach, which temporarily places LEP students in a program intended to teach them English quickly. Supporters of Proposition 227 utilized anti-immigrant rhetoric to promote the initiative (Paredes, 2000). The rhetoric focused on bilingual education's alleged role in perpetuating immigrant cultures to the exclusion of assimilation into American culture. As Spanish is the native language of an overwhelming majority of the LEP students in California public schools, many perceived this initiative and the campaign surrounding the initiative to be yet another attack on California's growing Latino community.

IMMIGRATION-RELATED BALLOT INITIATIVES

Proposition 227 is also important in that it speaks to a larger trend in anti-immigrant ballot initiatives. As the immigrant population in the U.S. continues to grow, many states will likely face additional immigration-related ballot propositions. Given the demographic trends and the use of the initiative process to create policies targeting immigrants, it seems important to examine the factors associated with voting on these initiatives. To do so, we rely on the existing work on nativist-oriented—or anti-immigrant—ballot initiatives to develop expectations regarding voting behavior on Proposition 227.

A growing body of research examines the importance of ethnic context for voting behavior on nativist ballot initiatives (Citrin et al., 1990; Hero, 1998; Tolbert & Hero, 1996, 1998, 2001; Valenty & Sylvia, 2004). Citrin et al. (1990) suggest that ethnic context is not related to individual-level support for the English-language initiative. Alternatively, Hero (1998) and Tolbert and Hero (1996, 1998, 2001) find that the presence of both many and few Latinos is associated with heightened county-level support for nativist-oriented ballot initiatives. Finally, Valenty and Sylvia (2004) find that as the ethnic population increases, county-level support for Proposition 187 increases. The extant research therefore offers a mixed view of the relationship between ethnic context and voting on nativist-oriented ballot initiatives.

These discrepant findings might be generated by the tendency to overlook the importance of spatial proximity to the border. Alvarez and Butterfield (2000) revealed a possible relationship between proximity to the Mexican border and voting behavior on California's Proposition 187. They accounted for proximity to the border with a series of dummy variables indicating whether a respondent resided in the city of Los Angeles, a Los Angeles suburb, or in other locations in Southern California, the Central Valley, or Northern California. In this chapter, we utilize a more precise measure of proximity to the border, thus offering a clearer understanding of the importance of spatial location for voting on nativist initiatives.

CONTEXT AND VOTING ON PROPOSITION 227

Based on the extant literature, we can develop hypotheses regarding the impact of environmental characteristics on Anglo voting behavior for Proposition 227. Our basic argument is that spatial proximity to the border enhances the propensity of Anglos to support nativist-oriented policies. However, we also believe this propensity is moderated by partisanship, meaning the effect of proximity to the border is contingent on a person's partisan affiliation. Below, we develop several hypotheses that outline the nature of the relationship between the distance to the border, partisanship, and individual-level voting behavior of Anglos on Proposition 227.

H1: INDIVIDUALS LIVING SPATIALLY PROXIMATE TO THE BORDER ARE MORE LIKELY TO SUPPORT PROPOSITION 227 THAN INDIVIDUALS LIVING AT GREATER DISTANCES FROM THE BORDER. First, we propose that proximity to the border is associated with increased Anglo support for Proposition 227. Anglos residing close to the border are more likely to support the elimination of bilingual education than Anglos living farther from the border. This expectation is based on the idea that those residing closer to the border are more likely to face border issues on a daily basis (Books & Prysby, 1991).

Individuals residing closer to the border are exposed to a plethora of information regarding immigration. In particular, such individuals are continuously exposed to environmental cues and media coverage concerning border and immigration issues. Simply commuting to work can highlight how the border plays a role in one's everyday life. Highways close to the border are often dotted with yellow signs that depict a family running with the warning *Prohibido*. The strong presence of the Border Patrol in areas located closer to the border may reinforce the perception of the influence of the border. Environmental cues can increase the perceived threat among Anglos and thereby lead to heightened ethnic tension and nativist attitudes (Books & Prysby, 1991; Cornelius, 1982).

Alternatively, individuals residing at a greater distance from the border may not receive the magnitude of media information or first-hand images relevant to immigration, thus making the border and border-related issues less salient in everyday life (Books & Prysby, 1991). This rationale is also in accordance with the intergroup conflict research that suggests that exposure to a minority group leads to increased prejudicial attitudes and decreased support for policies providing benefits to the minority group (Bobo, 1988; Glaser, 1994; Key, 1949).

As communications research commonly notes, events occurring "close to home" receive more news coverage in terms of the number of articles and length of articles than events occurring farther away (Adams, 1986; Bendix

& Liebler, 1999; Martin, 1988; Molotch & Lester, 1975). This pattern is reflected in the topics that take center stage among media outlets closer to the border. In areas closer to the border, the media routinely offer more coverage of issues such as unauthorized immigrants, the economic implications of immigration, and drug trafficking across the border than do media outlets farther north (Branton & Dunaway, 2009a; 2009b)

This constant exposure not only heightens the saliency of immigration, but it also leads to negative attitudes toward issues involving the border, immigration, and immigrants. The information conveyed by the media closer to the border often focuses on the negative implications and tends to overlook the benefits of immigration.

H2: REPUBLICANS ARE MORE LIKELY THAN DEMOCRATS TO SUPPORT PROPOSITION 227. Second, we propose that partisan affiliation is associated with voting behavior on Proposition 227. Although ballot initiatives lack partisan labels, recent research highlights the influence of partisan identification on voting behavior on a variety of ballot initiatives (e.g., Banducci, 1998; Bowler & Donovan, 1998; Branton, 2003; Smith & Tolbert, 2001). Voters use information cues typically available to guide their decision making (e.g., Bowler & Donovan, 1998; Lupia, 1994).

In the case of Proposition 227, endorsements from prominent political leaders served as an information beacon for voters. Supporters of the initiative included prominent Republican figures such as Governor Pete Wilson and Los Angeles Mayor Richard Riordan. Opponents of the initiative included Democratic leaders such as President Clinton, Nancy Pelosi, and San Francisco Mayor Willie Brown. Voters may have used these cues to act in a manner consistent with their partisan preferences. Several recent works reveal a significant relationship between partisanship and voting on Proposition 227 (Alvarez, 1999; Smith & Tolbert, 2001; Tolbert & Hero, 2001). Furthermore, this research finds that Republicans tended to support Proposition 227 more than Democrats. Thus, we expect partisan identification to be associated with voting on Proposition 227.

H3: THE INFLUENCE OF SPATIAL PROXIMITY TO THE BORDER ON SUPPORT FOR PROPOSITION 227 HAS A GREATER INFLUENCE ON DEMOCRATS THAN REPUBLICANS. Third, we expect that individual-level partisan affiliation moderates the relationship between proximity to the border and voting behavior on Proposition 227. In other words, border proximity influences individuals differently depending on their partisan affiliation. As noted, we expect Republicans are more likely to consistently support the measure. As such, the influence of proximity to the border among Republicans may be marginal. Although a greater proportion of Democrats opposed this measure, Democrats were less consistent in their voting behavior on this issue. Therefore, we expect proximity to the border to have a more pronounced effect on Democratic support for bilingual education, as it is relevant to border and immigration concerns. As such, we expect the probability of supporting the initiative to decline more rapidly for Democrats than for Republicans as distance to the border decreases.

SUPPORT FOR THE HYPOTHESES

To examine Anglo voting behavior on Proposition 227, we utilized the June 1998 California Poll, 2000 U.S. Census data, and spatially referenced data generated using Geographic Information System (GIS) software. The June 1998 California Poll[1] was chosen for this analysis for two key reasons. First, the survey queried Anglo respondents on how they intended to vote on Proposition 227. Second, the poll asked each respondent his or her county of residence,[2] thereby enabling us to connect respondents to their aggregate-level context. Merging the individual-level survey data and the aggregate-level data accounts for the contextual environment in which respondents reside.

The dependent variable, a respondent's position on Proposition 227, is coded as a dichotomous variable with 1 representing support for Proposition 227 and 0 representing opposition to the proposition.

The key independent variable of interest is spatial proximity to the Mexican border (distance), which is measured using GIS to calculate the distance in miles from the longitudinal and latitudinal center of each county to the Mexico-U.S. border.[3]

The model includes three additional aggregate-level measures: ethnic context, socioeconomic climate, and political environment. The inter-group conflict literature asserts that exposure to a large minority group is associated with increased competition and/or perceived threat between groups for limited resources (e.g., Bobo, 1988; Forbes, 1997; Glaser, 1994; Key, 1949). This argument suggests that Anglos residing in an environment with a large Latino population should exhibit higher levels of opposition for policies benefiting Latinos than would Anglos living in a context with fewer Latinos. Thus, we control for ethnic context with a measure of the percentage of the Latino population within each county.[4]

Several works note the influence of socioeconomic context on racial attitudes and voting behavior on nativist ballot propositions (Branton & Jones, 2005; Huckfeldt & Kohfeld, 1989; Tolbert & Hero 1996, 1998). As such, we control for socioeconomic context with a measure of the percentage of college-educated individuals at the county level.[5] The political environment in which a respondent resides was measured by the Republican Party's vote share in the 1996 presidential election (President Vote). This measure is included to control for the influence of the partisan character of the area in which an individual resides on his/her voting behavior (Campbell, 1987; MacKuen & Brown, 1987).[6]

The model includes several individual-level control variables as well: PID (partisan affiliation), age (measured in actual years), sex (coded 1 if the respondent is female), ideology, and education. Individual-level party identification (PID) is measured as a three-category variable, coded 1 if a respondent is Republican, 2 if independent, and 3 if Democrat. Individual-level ideology is coded 1 if a respondent is conservative, 2 if moderate, and 3 if liberal. Individual-level education ranges from 0 (less than a high school degree) to 4 (greater than a college degree). Finally, the model includes a variable indicating if a respondent has a child in school (coded 1 if the respondent has a child in school). This measure is included to control for potential animosity among Anglo parents toward a program that provides educational resources to a subset of children in the school system.

PROPOSITION 227 VOTING PATTERNS

The dependent variable is a binary response variable. As such, logistic regression is used to estimate the model of voting behavior on Proposition 227.[7] Table 9.1 presents the logit coefficients and corresponding standard errors.

Before we discuss the results of primary interest, note that *education* and *ideology* at the individual level are significantly associated with voting behavior on this proposition. Individual-level education is negatively related, indicating that individuals who are more educated are less likely to vote for the elimination of bilingual education. Further, conservative individuals are more likely to support Proposition 227 when compared to moderate or liberal individuals. The results indicate that age, sex, and having children in school are not significantly related to voting on this initiative.

Further, the findings indicate that residing in a more affluent or more Republican context is associated with heightened support for eliminating bilingual education. Furthermore, Anglos residing in areas with a larger Latino population are more likely to support this policy when compared to Anglos residing in areas with a small Latino population.

Now we move on to the discussion of the variables related to distance from the border (the *Conditional Relationship* variables in Table 9.1). As outlined previously, we hypothesize that the effect of proximity to the border of Mexico on voting behavior on Proposition 227 is conditioned by partisan affiliation. To assess this proposed moderating relationship, the model includes a statistical interaction between partisan affiliation and

Table 9.1. Voting Behavior on California's Proposition 227 Logit Estimates
(Robust Standard Errors)

Covariates	Parameter Estimates	Standard Error
CONDITIONAL RELATIONSHIP		
PID	-.15	(.15)
Distance	.003	(.001)[*]
Distance × PID	-.001	(.000)[**]
CONTEXTUAL ATTRIBUTES		
Ethnic context (percent Latino)	.04	(.02)[*]
Partisan context (presidential vote)	.05	(.01)[***]
College educated	.05	(.02)[*]
INDIVIDUAL-LEVEL ATTRIBUTES		
Age	.01	(.01)
Female	-.37	(.35)
Education	-.32	(.10)[***]
Ideology	-.84	(.20)[***]
School Kids	-.12	(.23)
Intercept	-1.51	(1.98)
Observations	463	
Wald χ^2	182.80[***]	

[*]$p<.05$; [**]$p<.01$; [***]$p<.001$

Source: The data are taken from the June 1998 California Poll, 2000 U.S. Census data, and spatially referenced data generated using GIS. Coefficient estimates are based on logit estimates. Huber/White standard errors are presented in parentheses.

proximity to the border. The interaction is represented by the following simple formula:

$$Y = b1(\text{distance}) + b2(\text{PID}) + b3(\text{distance} \times \text{PID}) \qquad [1]$$

where *distance* represents the distance to the border, *PID* represents partisan affiliation, and *distance × PID* represents the interaction between the two variables.

The first three variables in Table 9.1 represent the interaction in [1]. The significant interaction between *distance* and *PID* confirms H3, indicating that the effect of proximity to the border of Mexico on voting behavior on Proposition 227 is moderated by partisanship. The negative coefficient on the interaction term indicates that across each category of partisan affiliation, the relationship between distance to the border and voting behavior is negative, thus supporting H1. Substantively, this suggests that Democrats, Independents, and Republicans residing closer to the border are more likely to support Proposition 227 compared to Democrats, Independents, and Republicans residing farther north of the border. Further, the interaction parameter estimate supports H3, indicating the effect of distance to the border is more distinct among Democratic than Republican voters.

Based on our analysis, we calculated the probability that an individual with average characteristics (moderate, Anglo, male, of average age, with no children in school, and a high school education), who resides in an average county (including an average-sized Latino population, a mean-level college education, and an average level of support for the Republican presidential candidate in the prior election) would support Proposition 227. Based on this scenario, we calculated the predicted probabilities across the three categories of partisanship for the individual, while allowing spatial distance to the border to vary from the minimum value on the distance variable to the maximum value.

First, in accordance with our first hypothesis, as the distance to the border increases, the probability of supporting the nativist initiative decreases regardless of one's partisan affiliation. Further, Republican respondents are more likely to support Proposition 227 than Independents and Democrats, while Independents are more likely to support the initiative when compared to Democrats, which supports the second hypothesis.

Second, the results support our third hypothesis, indicating that the influence of spatial proximity to the border varies across the three partisan affiliation categories. Although the probability of supporting the initiative as a function of distance to the border declines across each group, the decline is more amplified among Democrats when compared with the other two partisan categories. For example, the probability of support among Democrats drops dramatically from .91 for those closest to the border to .26 for those farthest from the border; while the probability of support among Republicans falls from .93 for those closest to the border to .83 for those farthest from the border. We conclude that the magnitude of support for Proposition 227 among Anglos as a function of distance to the border is contingent on party identification.

Finally, to delineate the simultaneous effect of all the variables in the model, we calculated the predicted probabilities of supporting Proposition 227 for a series of hypothetical voters. We sought to demonstrate the relative magnitude of the model estimates based on tangible scenarios. This enables us to compare the influence of spatial proximity to the border conditioned on partisanship based on actual contextual characteristics of counties located different distances from the border. Each of the estimated probabilities presented in Table 9.2 represents the following hypothetical voter: a moderate Anglo male of average age, with no children in school, who has earned a high school degree.

The first panel in Table 9.2 provides probability estimates for two counties that are characterized by smaller Latino populations. The second panel presents estimates for two counties characterized by moderate-sized Latino populations, and the third panel offers probability estimates for two counties containing large Latino populations. The first case in each scenario shows the estimates for a county that is closer in proximity to the border of Mexico than is the second case. Additionally, within each pairing, the counties are comparable in terms of their socioeconomic and political characteristics. These pairings provide a more refined demonstration of the influence

Table 9.2. Predicted Probabilities of Support for Proposition 227

Location	Distance	Ethnic Context	College Educated	Partisan Context	Republican	Democrat
LOW ETHNIC CONTEXT						
San Luis Obispo	332	16	36	47	.64	.37
Sonoma	649	17	37	30	.37	.08
Difference					.27	.29
MODERATE ETHNIC CONTEXT						
Riverside	106	36	23	46	.70	.58
San Joaquin	649	31	22	45	.51	.17
Difference					.19	.41
HIGH ETHNIC CONTEXT						
Los Angeles	104	45	31	31	.71	.59
Monterey	421	47	29	37	.68	.36
Difference					.03	.23

Note: Distance is the number of miles from the U.S.-Mexico border. Ethnic context represents the percent Hispanic within each county. College educated represented the percent college educated within a county. Partisan context is the percent of Republican Party's vote share in the 1996 presidential election. The Republican and Democrat columns reflect the probability of supporting Proposition 227.

of distance to the border conditioned on partisanship and the importance of ethnic context on individual-level voting behavior.

The estimates across all three panels demonstrate the impact of proximity to the border regardless of partisan affiliation. Consider the probability of supporting Proposition 227 among those residing in areas containing a proportionally smaller Latino population. The difference in support between a voter living in San Luis Obispo and a voter in Sonoma is .29 for Democrats and .27 for Republicans, respectively. Next, the probability of supporting the elimination of bilingual education for a Democrat residing in a county with a moderate Latino population that is close to the border is .41 higher than for a Democrat residing in a county with a moderate Latino population that is farther from the border. Further, the difference for a Republican residing in a county with a moderate Latino population that is spatially closer to the border compared to a Republican residing farther from the border is .19. Finally, consider the difference in support for Proposition 227 for those residing in areas with a large Latino population. The probability of supporting Proposition 227 for individuals that reside in Los Angeles compared to individuals in Monterey is .23 higher for Democrats and .03 higher for Republicans.

A comparison of the predicted probabilities across the three panels elucidates the influence of ethnic context on support for this nativist-oriented initiative. Generally speaking, as one moves from the first panel of probabilities to the second, and the second to the third, the calculations reveal a clear progression. The probability of support is lower for Anglos residing in counties characterized by a low Latino population than among those with a moderate Latino population, which is lower than the probability for those residing in a county with high Latino populations. This pattern suggests exposure to a growing Latino population renders heightened support for a policy that negatively targets this ethnic group.

CONCLUSION

Nationally, the rapid growth of the Latino population has spawned an ever-increasing debate regarding immigrants and immigration-related issues. The subject of immigration has been particularly intense in California in recent decades (DeSipio and de la Garza, 1998; Sierra et al., 2000). The fear that low-skilled, uneducated immigrants are streaming into the United States, taking jobs from legal residents, and placing tremendous pressure on an already strained social services system has driven much of the debate. The salience of this issue has resulted in a series of ballot initiatives that have explicitly targeted both legal and unauthorized immigrants. California's Proposition 227, which successfully dismantled

California's bilingual education program, is one example of these nativist-oriented initiatives.

This chapter examined Anglo voting on Proposition 227 with particular interest in the influence of contextual factors on voting behavior. This study extends the research by examining voting behavior as a function of spatial proximity to the Mexican border. The results lend evidence to the idea that individual-level support for this ballot initiative varies considerably across space and individual characteristics. We believe the findings indicate that attitudes toward immigration and voting behavior on nativist policies are related to one's proximity to the border of Mexico as well as one's political affiliation.

First, although it certainly is the case that the nation as a whole is becoming increasingly more ethnically diverse, this study suggests that proximity to the border retains a unique political importance. The results offer considerable evidence that geographical boundaries matter in the determination of voting on nativist ballot initiatives. Substantively, this suggests that Anglos living closer to the Mexican border are more likely to support Proposition 227 than Anglos living farther from the border, thereby supporting the assertion of Books and Prysby (1991) that international borders act as an important geopolitical contextual factor.

Second, although these spatial and contextual factors are important, they are only part of the story. The findings strongly suggest that the influence of proximity to the border on individual-level behavior is dependent upon partisan predisposition. Republicans, regardless of context or proximity to the border, demonstrate a consistently negative attitude toward immigrants and are likely to support anti-immigrant initiatives. This negative attitude diminishes for Republicans living further from the border, but the change, although significant, is not as large.

In contrast, Democrats appear to be more influenced by this geopolitical factor. Democrats living in close proximity to the border demonstrate far greater support for Proposition 227 than do their Democratic counterparts living in areas that are further from the border. Although Democrats typically have more favorable attitudes toward social policies and immigrant issues than Republicans, these results reveal that context and proximity to the border can trump these attitudes.

These findings hold important implications for future research regarding context and political behavior. First, considering the importance of spatial attributes can extend this research into a number of political and social questions. Second, research that examines the structure of attitudes across racial and ethnic groups, not just Anglo political behavior, will facilitate our understanding of these political behaviors. Finally, future research may explore whether the influence of spatial contextual attributes are consistent across bordering states.

NOTES

1. This random digit dial (RDD) survey, conducted by the Field Institute a week prior to the election, offers a sample of the telephone household population in California. Additional information regarding the sampling technique can be found in the California Field Poll Codebook.

2. The use of the county as a geographic unit of analysis is based on the fact that it is the administrative branch of state government, which oversees redistributive services such as education (National Association of Counties, 2003; Schneider & Park, 1989). Given our focus on the influence of one's contextual environment on voting behavior on this education policy initiative, the relevance of the county makes theoretical and practical sense.

3. We calculate this measure for four crossing points from west to east: Tijuana, Tecate, Mexicali, and Vicente. The shortest distance is then used to represent our measure of distance to the border. Distance to the border ranges from 38 miles to 928 miles. The average distance to the border is 325 miles and the median distance to the border is 242 miles.

4. The observed values of the ethnic context measure range from 4% to 72%. Both the mean and median values of ethnic context (or percent Latino within a county) are 31%.

5. Although there are a variety of potential indicators of socioeconomic context, education level has been proven to be a very reliable indicator of aggregate-level socioeconomic status (Huckfeldt & Sprague, 1995; Oliver & Mendelberg, 2000).

6. The model of voting behavior on Proposition 227 was estimated both with and without these two aggregate-level control variables. A comparison of these two sets of results indicated that the inclusion of these variables did not have a substantive (or statistical) influence on the relationship between the two key environmental characteristics and voting behavior on Proposition 227.

7. The use of individual and aggregate-level data (multilevel data) can present problems due to serial dependence within clusters (counties) and heteroscedasticity across clusters. There are several methods that address the statistical problems associated with clustered data (see Steenbergen & Jones, 2002). We utilize the Huber/White/sandwich estimation (Huber, 1967), which adjusts the variance-covariance matrix to correct for heteroscedasticity and serial dependency.

REFERENCES

Adams, W. (1986). Whose lives count? TV coverage of natural disasters. *Journal of Communication, 36*, 113–22.

Alvarez, R. M. (1999, January). *Why did Proposition 227 pass?* Paper presented at the Center for U.S.–Mexican Studies, University of California–San Diego.

Alvarez, M., & Butterfield, T. (2000). The resurgence of nativism in California? The case of proposition 187 and illegal immigration. *Social Science Quarterly, 81*, 167–179.

Banducci, S. (1998). Direct legislation: When is it used and when does it pass? In

S. Bowler, T. Donovan, & C. Tolbert (Eds.), *Citizens as legislators: Direct democracy in the United States.* Columbus, OH: Ohio State University Press.

Bendix, J., & Liebler, C. (1999). Place, distance, and environmental news: Geographic variation in newspaper coverage of the spotted owl conflict. *Annals of Association of American Geography, 89,* 658–676.

Bobo, L. (1998). Group conflict, prejudice, and the paradox of contemporary racial attitudes. In P. Katz, & D. Taylor (Eds.), *Eliminating racism: Profiles in controversy.* New York: Plenum Press.

Books, J. W., & Prysby, C. L. (1991). *Political behavior and the local context.* New York: Praeger Publishers.

Bowler, S., & Donovan, T. (1998). *Demanding choices: Opinion and voting in direct democracy.* Ann Arbor, MI: University of Michigan Press.

Branton, R. (2003). Examining individual-level voting behavior on state ballot propositions. *Political Research Quarterly, 56,* 367–377.

Branton, R., & Dunaway, J. (2009a). Slanted newspaper coverage of immigration: The importance of economics and geography. *Policy Studies Journal, 37,* 257–273.

Branton, R., & Dunaway, J. (2009b). Spatial proximity to the US-Mexico border and newspaper coverage of immigration issues. *Political Research Quarterly, 62,* 298–302.

Branton, R., & Jones, B. (2005). Reexamining racial attitudes: The conditional relationship between diversity and socio-economic environment. *American Journal of Political Science, 49,* 359–372.

Campbell, J. (1987). The revised theory of surge and decline. *American Journal of Political Science, 31,* 965–979.

Citrin, J., Reingold, B., Walters, E., & Green, D. (1990). The "official English" movement and the symbolic politics of language in the United States. *Western Political Quarterly, 43,* 535–559.

Cornelius, W. (1982). Interviewing undocumented immigrants: Methodological reflections based on fieldwork in Mexico and the U.S. *International Migration Review, 16,* 378–411.

DeSipio, L., & de la Garza, R. O. (1998). *Making Americans, remaking America: Immigration and immigrant policy.* Boulder, CO: Westview Press.

Forbes, H. (1997). *Ethnic conflict.* New Haven, CT: Yale University Press.

Glaser, J. (1994). Back to the black belt: Racial environment and white racial attitudes in the south. *Journal of Politics, 56,* 21–41.

Hero, R. (1998). *Faces of inequality: Social diversity in American politics.* New York: Oxford Press.

Huber, P. (1967). The behaviour of maximum likelihood estimates under nonstandard conditions. *Proceedings of the Fifth Berkeley Symposium on Mathematical Statistics and Probability, 1,* 221–233.

Huckfeldt, R., & Kohfeld, C. W. (1989). *Race and the decline of class in American politics.* Chicago: University of Illinois Press.

Huckfeldt, R., & Sprague, J. (1995). *Citizens, politics, and social communication.* New York: Cambridge University Press.

Key, V. O., Jr. (1949). *Southern politics in state and nation.* Knoxville, TN: University of Tennessee Press.

Lupia, A. (1994). Shortcuts versus encyclopedias: Information and voting behavior in California insurance reform elections. *American Political Science Review*, *88*, 63–76.

MacKuen, M., & Brown, C. (1987). Political context and attitude change. *American Political Science Review*, *81*, 471–490.

Martin, S. (1988). Proximity of event as factor in selection of news sources. *Journalism Quarterly*, *65*, 986–989.

Molotch, H., & Lester, M. (1975). Accidental news: The great oil spill as local occurrence and national event. *American Journal of Sociology*, *81*, 235–260.

National Association of Counties. (2003). *National Association of Counties: About counties*. Retrieved September 1, 2009, from http://www.naco.org/Content/NavigationMenu/About_Counties/County_Government/CountyOverview.pdf

Oliver, J. E., & Mendelberg, T. (2000). Reconsidering the environmental determinants of racial attitudes. *American Journal of Political Science*, *44*, 574–589.

Paredes, S. M. (2000). How Proposition 227 influences the language dynamics of a first and second-grade mathematics lesson. *Bilingual Research Journal*, *24*, 179–199.

Schneider, M., & Park, K. O. (1989). Metropolitan counties as service delivery agents: The still forgotten governments. *Public Administration Review*, *49*, 345–352.

Sierra, C. M., Carrillo, T., DeSipio, L., & Jones-Correa, M. (2000). Latino immigration and citizenship. *PS: Political Science and Politics*, *33*, 535–540.

Smith, D., & Tolbert, C. (2001). The initiative to party: Partisanship and ballot initiatives in California. *Party Politics*, *7*, 781–799.

Steenbergen, M., & Jones, B. (2002). Modeling multilevel data structures. *American Journal of Political Science*, *45*, 218–237.

Tolbert, C., & Hero, R. (2001). Dealing with diversity: Racial/ethnic context and social policy change. *Political Research Quarterly*, *54*, 571–604.

Tolbert, C., & Hero, R. (1998). Race/ethnicity and direct democracy: The contextual basis of support for anti-immigrant and official English measures. In S. Bowler, T. Donovan, & C. Tolbert (Eds.), *Citizens as legislators: Direct democracy in the United States*. Columbus, OH: Ohio State University Press.

Tolbert, C., & Hero, R. (1996). Race/ethnicity and direct democracy: An analysis of California's illegal immigration initiative. *Journal of Politics*, *58*, 806–818.

Valenty, L., & Sylvia, R. D. (2004). Thresholds for tolerance: The influence of racial and ethnic population composition on the vote for California Propositions 187 and 209. *Social Science Journal*, *41*, 433–446.

CHAPTER 10

The Politics of Bilingual Education Expenditures in Urban School Districts

David L. Leal and Frederick M. Hess

This chapter[1] investigates the factors that determine urban school district expenditures on bilingual education programs. It represents a step forward in the research on urban politics and school policymaking because it pinpoints the independent effects of political and other factors on funding for a specific public policy.

The issue of bilingual education has long been dominated by normative arguments about the best approaches to second language instruction for non-English speakers. Shortchanged in this debate has been an understanding of the political, demographic, and fiscal determinants of bilingual education spending. How much freedom do school districts have in setting their spending policies? Is funding driven by need or is need only one factor among many? Do local political factors play any role, as they might serve to increase or decrease funding beyond need or capacity? Is Latino representation on school boards, for example, associated with increased money for bilingual education? This chapter seeks to provide some insight into these important public policy questions.

THE HISTORY OF BILINGUAL EDUCATION IN AMERICA

The history of bilingualism in America is more complex than is commonly known. The use of more than one language by a community has been part of the American social and political landscape for more than 2 centuries (Kloss, 1977). The Continental Congresses of 1774–1789, for example, regularly published documents in German and French as well as in English (Gonzalez, Brusca-Vega, & Yawkey, 1997). In the classroom, an 1839

Ohio law allowed for instruction in German, English, or both, according to the wishes of parents (Crawford, 1991), and similar laws were passed in other states with large numbers of non-English speakers, such as Louisiana and New Mexico (Ambert & Melendez, 1985). At the turn of the century, 600,000 elementary schoolchildren received all or part of their education in German (Kloss, 1977), "probably a larger proportion than receive Spanish-English instruction today" (Attinasi, 1998, p. 274).

A confluence of political and social developments in the late 1800s and early 1900s brought renewed hostility to languages other than English (Higham, 1963). First, an unprecedented wave of immigration from 1890 to 1914 led the United States to focus on assimilating new ethnic groups into American culture (Crawford, 1992). In addition, World War I led to hostility to the German language, at the time a leading second language (Heath & Ferguson, 1981). By 1923, 34 states required English to be the only language of classroom instruction, leading to a "sink or swim" policy of English immersion (Brisk, 1998).

In 1968, President Lyndon B. Johnson signed the Bilingual Education Act (BEA) and committed the federal government to helping students with limited English skills (Birman & Ginsburg, 1983). The BEA remains the major piece of national legislation on bilingual education, although amendments were passed in 1974.

The courts played an important role in the bilingual debate. *Lau v. Nichols* (1974), a class action suit brought by Chinese American students in San Francisco, asserted a denial of "education on equal terms" because of their limited English skills. The U.S. Supreme Court ruled that students who did not know English were "foreclosed from any meaningful education" and ordered school districts to remedy the situation (*Lau v. Nichols*, 1974).

Such federal interventions were necessary preconditions to the reestablishment of bilingual education, as most immigrant populations lack the political resources to institute such a program in their local schools. One notable exception was the group of refugees who fled to Florida from Cuba after the 1959 revolution. These refugees, many of whom were education professionals, were the catalysts for the introduction of a 1961 Spanish-English bilingual program in the Miami–Dade County public schools (Crawford, 1991).

Today, while bilingual education has often been associated with Spanish instruction, the students served by federal Limited English Proficiency (LEP) programs speak over 100 languages. Nevertheless, 80% of children who originally benefited from Title VII were Spanish speaking (Porter, 1990) and currently three quarters of LEP students are Hispanic (Congressional Research Service, 1999).

ANALYZING EXPENDITURES

This chapter examines which factors are statistically associated with bilingual education expenditures. The data in this study were collected from the 1992 Council of Urban Boards of Education (CUBE) study, which included 62 cities, and the 1990 U.S. Census, which was organized by school districts in the 1994 *School District Data Book* (see original journal article for more information).

The data were analyzed using ordinary least squares (OLS) regression. The dependent variable is a district's per-pupil spending on bilingual education. This figure was obtained by dividing the amount each district spent on K–12 bilingual programs by the total district enrollment as reported by the census.

The Potential Role of Latino Representation

We first considered the percentage of local school-board members who are Latino, calculated from the CUBE study. The percentages of women, Latinos, African Americans, and Asian Americans on each school board were calculated from the CUBE study, which reported total school-board membership and the number of women and minority board members in each district. Because bilingual education is considered by most Latino activists to be of critical importance to the Latino community for both educational and cultural reasons, we expect that the greater the power of Latinos on a school board, the larger district expenditures on bilingual education.

Such support for bilingual education is longstanding. One of the leading Latino advocacy organizations, the Mexican American Legal Defense and Education Fund (MALDEF), began filing suits on behalf of bilingual education advocates in the 1970s. When describing the strategies of Latino political activists, San Miguel (1987) found the following:

> After 1975 bilingual education came to be viewed as the most appropriate instrument for attaining equality in society. Bilingual education was considered the key for ameliorating historic problems in schools with large numbers of Spanish-speaking children. This comprehensive approach of instructing Spanish-speaking children implied a fundamental reassessment of the support, governance, administration, and content of the public schools as well as an increase of state and federal intervention on their behalf and a call for greater participation by the community in educational matters. (pp. 215–216)

More recently, the position of the Latino political community on this issue was in evidence during the debate over Proposition 227 (described in more detail in Chapter 3), the 1998 California ballot initiative to end bilingual education. Two of the most influential Latino organizations, the National Council of La Raza (NCLR) and MALDEF, opposed 227 and filed suit against it after the election. On the federal level, the Congressional Hispanic Caucus, composed of the Latino Democratic members of Congress, continues to support increased funding for bilingual education programs.[2]

Previous research suggests that Latino school-board members do not impact educational policy outcomes. Fraga, Meier, and England (1986) noted that "Although Hispanic access to school board seats and teaching positions (passive representation) is important in and of itself, such access is more important if it has policy implications (active representation)" (p. 861). They investigated the impact of Latino school-board members on seven education policy variables, such as student suspensions and college attendance, and found that the percentage of school-board members who are Latino did not have a direct impact on these policies, although Latino board members did influence the hiring of Latino teachers, and Latino teachers were shown to have an impact on two policy outcomes.

The Potential Role of Asian-American Representation

The possibility that the percentage of Asian Americans on local school boards might influence bilingual spending was likewise tested. Because Asian Americans make up the second largest percentage of bilingual education students after Latinos, it would be remiss to include only the percentage of Latino school-board members. Asian Americans helped precipitate federal involvement in bilingual education through the Lau case and the Asian Legal Foundation joined Latino groups in lawsuits against Proposition 227.

The Potential Role of African-American Representation

We considered the percentage of school-board members who are black because previous research suggests that African Americans may not be sympathetic to bilingual spending. Falcon (1988) noted that African Americans in New York City did not support bilingual programs because they were primarily concerned with desegregation and feared a diversion of resources. Furthermore, McClain (1993) and McClain and Karnig (1990) found that African Americans and Latinos tended to gain socioeconomically and politically in tandem, except for the cases where African Americans were a majority or plurality of the city population. In these instances, Latinos did less well. Meier and Stewart (1991), however, found that while blacks did not oppose Latino school-board candidates, Latinos did appear to oppose black candidates.

The Potential Role of Gender

The fourth political variable we considered is the percentage of women on the school board. Previous research has revealed the greater willingness of women to fund programs for the disadvantaged and needy (Klein, 1984; Cook & Wilcox, 1991), so we tested whether the percentage of women had an impact on this particular issue. The literature also shows that female state legislators are more sympathetic than their male colleagues toward social and family issues (Thomas & Welch, 1991; Kathlene, 1995) and differ especially on the issue of abortion (Berkman & O'Connor, 1993). There is little research, however, on gender differences in local political bodies. If significant, this variable would indicate one example where political will overcomes the various economic constraints under which local governments operate.

Other Possible Factors

Median family income is most likely a political and not simply an economic capacity measure. Wright, Erikson, and McIver (1987) found that, "ironically, state income is positively related to state opinion liberalism, even though the wealthiest individuals tend to be the most conservative . . . state income is a proxy for liberal policy preferences" (p. 988). Other control variables include student enrollment in bilingual education programs, state and local per-pupil expenditures, and federal per-pupil expenditures.

FACTORS INFLUENCING EXPENDITURES

Table 10.1 indicates that the percentage of school-board members who are Latino has a statistically and substantively significant impact on bilingual spending. Even when controlling for demand for bilingual education programs, the presence of more Latino members on a school board has a positive impact on funding for a program that many consider to be of vital interest to this community. Substantively, every 10% increase in Latino school-board members leads to an extra 16 dollars spent per student on bilingual education.[3]

Fraga, Meier, and England (1986), however, showed that a greater number of Latino school-board members did not directly impact seven education policy outputs, although bilingual education was not examined. They concluded, "the findings suggest that Hispanics are in a subordinate political position and are thus unable to affect educational policy to their benefit" (p. 870). Our data do not contradict their findings, but they do suggest that

Table 10.1. Regression of Model on Per-Pupil Bilingual Education Expenditures

Variable Name	Coefficient (Standard Error)	Probability
Constant	-167.417 (50.899)	0.002**
Students enrolled in bilingual education programs (%)	165.482 (105.040)	0.122
Latinos on school board (%)	157.515 (51.279)	0.004**
Asian Americans on school board (%)	320.571 (120.029)	0.010**
Blacks on school board (%)	8.769 (37.590)	0.817
Women on school board (%)	55.961 (34.479)	0.111
Median income (in thousands)	3.786 (1.528)	0.017*
State and local dollars per student (in hundreds)	1.841 (0.650)	0.007**
Federal dollars per student (in hundreds)	-3.102 (7.084)	0.663
Adjusted R^2	0.51	—
Observations	56	—

$^*p \leq .05,\ ^{**}p \leq .01.$

Latino school-board members may play a direct role only in issues at the core of their agenda, like bilingual education, and play a more limited role in other issues. These politicians may, in effect, conserve their political ammunition for the most important battles.

The percentage of black school-board members was statistically insignificant, while the research of Falcon (1988), as well as McClain and Karnig (1990) and McClain (1993), might suggest a negative correlation. This finding is not enough to conclusively argue that African American and Latino school-board members do not have policy differences on bilingual education, but it does suggest that such conflicts may not apply in urban school districts.

Asian-American representation on school boards did have a positive impact on bilingual spending, as anticipated. Because Asian Americans are the second largest group of students using this program, it makes sense that Asian-American school-board members would work to increase levels of funding. Substantively, a 10% increase in representation leads to an extra 32 dollars spent per student for bilingual programs.

One tentative finding is that female school-board members may be more supportive of bilingual education than male members. Increasing a school board from 0% female to 25% female may boost per-pupil bilingual spending by almost 15 dollars. This contributes some evidence toward the notion, as discussed above, that female and male legislators possess different public policy priorities.

Median family income also appears to be important. This could simply reflect the depth of the local tax base, whereby districts with higher income levels can spend more on schools, and therefore more on bilingual education. However, for statistical reasons that we will not explore here (although see original journal article), the likelier explanation is that districts with higher family incomes are making different choices than other districts about which programs to fund with a given amount of money. The most likely explanation is therefore the Wright et al. (1987) finding that median family income acts as a proxy for liberal policy preferences.

CONCLUSIONS

In this chapter, we discussed the factors that determine a substantial share of the spending for a specific education program. We found that for bilingual education expenditures, systematic factors account for almost half of the variance between the urban districts examined.

The key finding is the positive impact of the political measures. The percentages of Latinos and Asian Americans on local school boards were both associated with increases in funding for bilingual education, a program most Latinos and Asian Americans (although not all) consider critical to their communities.

These results differ somewhat from those of Fraga, Meier, and England (1986), which showed that a larger percentage of Latino school-board members did not directly impact seven education policy outputs. They did not consider bilingual education, however, so direct comparisons were not possible. Taken together, these two findings may suggest that Latino school-board members play a direct role in issues at the core of their agenda, such as bilingual education, but play a more limited role in other areas.

There has been little work on the impact of women on local political bodies, but the literature on the policy impact of women in legislatures shows that they are more supportive of social and family programs. Our data similarly show that the percentage of women on school boards may be associated with increased funding for bilingual education.

Another hint of how policy preferences may influence spending is found in the median family income variable. Even after controlling for per-pupil expenditures, wealthier districts spent more on bilingual education than did lower-income districts. Districts with higher family incomes are therefore making different choices about which programs to fund with a given amount of money. The most likely explanation suggested by the political science literature is that median family income acts as a proxy for policy liberalism, with relatively liberal communities more willing to divert funds to bilingual programs. This is additional intriguing evidence of how policy preferences may impact policy outcomes.

NOTES

1. This is an edited version of an article that originally appeared as "The politics of bilingual education expenditures in urban school districts" in *Social Science Quarterly*, *81*(4), December 2000, 1064–1072. Please see the original article for additional information about methodology and data.

2. There has been some discussion of whether the overall Latino population supports bilingual education. This chapter, however, concentrates on the implications of Latino political power for bilingual education, not on whether Latino school board members adequately represent their constituents. Latino opposition to bilingual education was likely overstated in any case; exit polls show that on Election Day, 63% of the Latino vote was against Proposition 227 (Pyle, McDonnell, & Tobar, 1998). In addition, a poll conducted by Spanish-language media institutions in Los Angeles reported that 88% of Latino parents with children in bilingual programs in that city believed they were beneficial (Crawford, 1998).

3. This amount has a greater impact than might be immediately apparent. The reason is that it represents the amount spent per capita across an entire school district on all children, while bilingual education programs affect a smaller population.

REFERENCES

Ambert, A., & Melendez, S. E. (1985). *Bilingual education: A sourcebook*. New York: Garland.

Attinasi, J. J. (1998). English only for California children and the aftermath of Proposition 227. *Education*, *119*, 263–283.

Berkman, M., & O'Connor, R. (1993). Do women legislators matter? Female legislators and state abortion policy. *American Politics Quarterly*, *21*, 102–124.

Birman, B. F., & Ginsburg, A. L. (1983). Introduction: Addressing the needs of language minority children. In K. Baker, & A. de Kanter (Eds.), *Bilingual education: A reappraisal of federal policy* (pp. ix–xxi). Lexington, Mass.: Lexington Books.

Brisk, M. E. (1998). *Bilingual education*. Mahwah, N.J.: Lawrence Erlbaum.

Congressional Research Service. (1999). *Bilingual education: An overview*. Washington, DC: Author.

Cook, E. A., & Wilcox, C. (1991). Feminism and the gender gap: A second look. *Journal of Politics*, *53*, 1111–1122.

Crawford, J. (1991). *Bilingual education: History, politics, theory, and practice*. Los Angeles: Bilingual Education Services.

Crawford, J. (1992). *Hold your tongue: Bilingualism and the politics of equal opportunity.* New York: Addison Wesley.

Crawford, J. (1998). *Proposition 227 and the future of bilingual education in California.* Paper presented at California State University, Long Beach, CA.

Falcon, A. (1988). Black and Latino politics in New York City: Race and ethnicity in a changing urban context. In F. C. Garcia (Ed.), *Latinos and the political system* (pp. 171–194). Notre Dame, IN: University of Notre Dame Press.

Fraga, L., Meier, K., & England, R. (1986). Hispanic Americans and educational policy: Limits to equal access. *Journal of Politics, 48*(8), 50–76.

Gonzalez, V., Brusca-Vega, R., & Yawkey, T. (1997). *Assessment and instruction of culturally and linguistically diverse students with or at risk of learning problems.* Needham Heights, MA: Allyn and Bacon.

Heath, S. B., & Ferguson. C. A. (Eds.). (1981). *Language in the USA.* Cambridge, UK: Cambridge University Press.

Higham, J. (1963). *Strangers in the land: Patterns of American nativism 1860–1925.* New York: Atheneum.

Kathlene, L. (1995). Alternative views of crime: Legislative policymaking in gendered terms. *Journal of Politics, 57,* 696–723.

Klein, E. (1984). *Gender politics.* Cambridge, MA: Harvard University Press.

Kloss, H. (1977). *American bilingual tradition.* Rowley, MA: Newbury House.

Lau v. Nichols, 414 U.S. 563, 94 5. Ct. 786 (1974).

McClain, P. D. (1993). The changing dynamics of urban politics: Black and Hispanic municipal employment—Is there competition? *Journal of Politics, 55,* 399–414.

McClain, P., & Karnig, A. (1990). Black and Hispanic socioeconomic and political competition. *American Political Science Review, 84,* 477–509.

Meier, K., & Stewart, J. (1991). *The politics of Hispanic education.* Albany, NY: State University of New York Press.

National Center for Education Statistics. (1994). *School district data book.* Washington, DC: U.S. Department of Education.

Porter, R. P. (1990). *Forked tongue: The politics of bilingual education.* New York: Basic Books.

Pyle, A., McDonnell, P., & Tobar, H. (1998, June 4). The Latino vote: Voter participation doubled since '94 primary. *Los Angeles Times,* p. A1.

San Miguel, G. Jr. (1987). *Let them all take heed: Mexican-Americans and the campaign for educational equality in Texas 1910–1981.* Austin, TX: University of Texas Press.

Thomas, S., & Welch, S. (1991). The impact of gender on activities and priorities of state legislators. *Western Political Quarterly, 44,* 445–456.

Wright, G., Erikson, R., & McIver, J. (1987). State political culture and public opinion. *American Political Science Review, 81,* 797–813.

CHAPTER 11

Extending Beyond Dropouts:
College Preparation in Texas High Schools

Carl Doerfler

Consider two high schools in Texas. Palm trees surround the first; barbed wire encircles the second. At the first school, dedicated teachers come in on Saturday to help Advanced Placement students with their physics problems; at the second school, teachers refuse to attend curriculum-planning meetings unless they receive additional pay. Administrators walk the halls during passing periods at the first school, calling students by name and inquiring politely into their social lives; administrators hide in their offices during passing periods at the second, hoping they will not be physically harmed. One school prepares students well for college; the other school does not.

The differences in these schools cannot be attributed to differences in funding, location, or the ethnicity of their students. Funding levels are similar, they are both located in suburban areas, and Latino students are the majority in both schools. In this chapter, I attempt to answer why the first school is able to prepare Latino students well for college while the other cannot.[1]

The college aspirations literature supports the assertion that a student's peers, parents, abilities, and schools attended influence the decision to pursue a higher education (see, for example, Hossler, Schmit, & Vesper, 1999). Our study focuses on school characteristics in order to examine public policy implications. If our society is determined to identify and remove the perceived and actual barriers to college attendance among Latino students, then this is the natural place to begin. If research can demonstrate that certain school practices lead to better college preparation, then the findings will inform public policy debates and improve the decisions of public policy makers (see Elmore, 1996).

We also choose to focus on school characteristics because of the impact they can have on a student's peers, parents, and abilities. For example, while an educational institution cannot choose a student's friends, it can provide an opportunity to interact with certain other students by either aggressively tracking gifted students through college-prep courses or by offering only a limited core curriculum required for all students. These school-level decisions, while not forcing students to befriend any given individual, obviously influence student interactions in classes and peer-group development.

THE IMPORTANCE OF A COLLEGE EDUCATION FOR LATINOS

Because society benefits greatly when minority students attend college, it is imperative for society to address the issue of college preparation among Latino students. For example, survey evidence suggests that students acquire valuable skills at college that help them to better interact with members of other races. College graduates are more likely to vote and utilize new technologies and less likely to engage in criminal activities (see Bowen & Bok, 1998; and Hossler, Schmit & Vesper, 1999) for informative reviews on the benefits of college attendance. Bowen and Bok (1998) pointed out that the

> active recruitment of minority students that began in the 1960s was motivated by more than a conviction that the enrollment of a diverse student body would improve the educational process for everyone. It was also inspired by a recognition that the country had a pressing need for well-educated black and Hispanic men and women who could assume leadership roles in their communities and in every facet of national life. (p. 156)

Minority communities have a critical need for talented, educated individuals to assume leadership roles. The situation becomes even more acute when we acknowledge that government programs and policies greatly affect disadvantaged communities, yet members of these communities are less likely to participate in the political process (Leighley, 2001). In other words, according to Bowen and Bok (1998):

> [I]mportant opportunities exist for highly trained minority managers and professionals in meeting the pressing needs in predominantly minority communities. At present, minority groups are disadvantaged in government and politics because they are less likely to vote than the rest of the population. This is especially true in poor communities, where voting rates have been falling for three decades and are now far below the national average. Because these communities have such a vital stake in public policies involving health care, welfare, law enforcement, job training, education, and other areas, it is especially important that they have well-trained, articulate leaders to represent them in the political arena. (p. 12)

The need for college-educated, well-trained Latino leaders will become even greater in the future. Census projections indicate that by 2050, minority groups will comprise about 48% of the U.S. population, with Latinos being the largest such group (U.S. Census Bureau, 2000). If capable members of these minority groups do not assume leadership positions in the United States of the future, confidence in government may wane in minority communities. Without elected officials to represent them, minorities may increasingly believe that they are unable to influence the workings of government through normal political processes.

THE STATE OF COLLEGE PREPARATION FOR LATINOS: DETERMINING THE SUCCESSFUL AND UNSUCCESSFUL DISTRICTS

Texas is an ideal state in which to study college preparation among minority students. It includes a large number of school districts, many with large Latino and African-American student populations. As a first step, the research team identified school districts that are doing an excellent job of preparing Latino students for college. While people are certain to disagree about specific elements of the definition, we suggest that a district does an excellent job of preparing minority students for college if it is successful at the following: 1. getting large percentages of minority students to take the SAT and the ACT, 2. increasing the average SAT and ACT scores of minority students, 3. enrolling minority students in Advanced Placement (AP) courses, and 4. getting minority students to take AP tests.

Using these four measures as our dependent variables, we then ran a number of education production function statistical models using data provided by the Texas Education Agency (TEA) (which ranks the districts from the highest performing to the lowest performing). School districts face different constraints, such as the amount of tax dollars available to them. Education production functions (discussed below) allow us to take these factors into account in order to better assess how a district is serving the college prep needs of Latinos given the constraints within which they are operating (Burtless, 1996). The primary control variables in our models were 1. financial resources available to the district, such as instructional expenditures per pupil and total budgeted revenue per pupil; and 2. student characteristics, such as the percentage of low-income students and the percentage of special education students. After running all the models, we totaled the standardized residuals. Schools that did much better than our models predicted they would, given the constraints within which they were operating, received high scores; schools that did much worse received low scores.

After identifying the highest-performing districts in the state, we identified low-performing districts that were geographically located nearby. The team reasoned that geographic proximity would allow me to study schools that are operating in somewhat similar environments but are experiencing radically different results in terms of preparing Latino students for college. The study also includes several schools that are doing an outstanding job of preparing students for Texas' standardized test of basic skills,[2] but are doing an average job of preparing students for college. We arranged interviews with school administrators, such as counselors, assistant principals, or deans of curriculum, at various schools in the districts. A total of 22 interviews were conducted, typically lasting between 1 and 2 hours.

At the beginning of each interview, educators at high-achieving schools were told that we were conducting a study on college aspirations among minority students. We explained the statistical models we had used, informing them that based on these models they were doing an outstanding job of preparing minority students for college. We then asked what strategies they employed to help them attain such outstanding results.

Educators at low-achieving schools were also told that we were conducting a study on college aspirations among minority students, but we did not tell them that their school had done a poor job at preparing students for college based on the results from our statistical models. Not only would this have been rude, it would likely have produced a defensive response and limited the amount of information our respondents would be willing to give. We therefore told the interviewees that we were visiting schools to find out what they were doing well in order to prepare minority students for college and to find out what challenges they faced in the college preparation process. Although this meant that our prompt was different from that given at high-performing schools, we felt that it was the most tactful and ethical way to proceed.

THE VIEWS OF THE SCHOOLS

The next section describes three of the interviews in some detail to give the reader a flavor for each school. The first interview is from a high-performing school. The second interview is from a school that is doing an outstanding job of preparing students for Texas' standardized test of basic skills but an average job of preparing students for college. The third interview is from a low-performing school. These three schools will serve as archetypes for each category of school that they represent. Then, in the following section, I will use the information gained from all of our interviews to make generalizations about how secondary schools can successfully prepare Latino students for college.

Southeast Texas—Interviewee: Dean of Curriculum

The first interview was conducted at the high school that has had the most success preparing minority students for college in the state according to the statistical analysis. The student population is approximately 40% white, 35% Hispanic, and 25% African American. According to the dean of curriculum, the teachers at the high school share the belief that education is the key to opportunity. In harmony with this belief, teachers and administrators make an active effort to track students into the highest and most challenging courses they can.

The curriculum is aligned from Kindergarten to grade 12, with the expectation that students will eventually take the highest-level classes that the district offers. This means that first-grade math teachers are laying the foundation for all students to take calculus-level courses in high school. Since the ultimate goal in mathematics courses is to prepare as many students as possible for calculus, teachers attempt to introduce elements of calculus into their lesson plans and discussions whenever possible. Teachers recognize that not all students will eventually take calculus, but they also recognize that, although this is the student's choice, the teacher's job is to make every opportunity available to every student. Teachers point out to students who choose to forego higher-level mathematics courses that they have closed off certain future opportunities. In addition, counselors meet with students at least twice a year.

Teachers have embedded SAT and other test-taking strategies (such as helping students to develop a college-level vocabulary as early as possible) in the entire curriculum. Although some people may consider this "teaching to the test," these teachers feel they are attempting to ensure that what they are teaching kids is aligned with how they are going to be assessed. The teachers recognize that, right or wrong, high test scores are necessary if students want to attend prestigious schools; if students do not do well on the SAT or the ACT, then they may not have that opportunity.

In harmony with their belief that every student should have every opportunity to pursue high academic goals, educators at this high school find pre-AP and AP classes are more valuable than classes for "gifted" students. In AP classes, students participate in challenging classes regardless of their gifted status, and AP classes count towards college credit. In addition, the high school pays for every student who desires to take the PSAT. This makes every student eligible for national merit scholarships and gives them practice taking standardized, high-stakes tests. Counselors meet with students individually after they receive the PSAT results to discuss what the results mean and to suggest areas of improvement.

PSAT and SAT preparation courses are offered for elective credit. Although the dean of curriculum said that very few students ("less than 1%")

actually take the course, offering a test preparation course for credit is one of many examples that illustrate this high school's commitment to academic excellence and putting learning first.

When asked why he thought their high school was so successful, the dean responded that they have "no silver bullets"—it is not just one thing that they do; it is everything they do. The culture of continuous improvement is another important aspect of this school's success: Educators here constantly examine what they do in an attempt to improve their effectiveness through in-house surveys and surveys to parents and recent graduates.

Factors beyond the school's control certainly affect their students' decisions to prepare for and attend college to some degree. For example, although Greater East Texas Services provides readily accessible loan information, and the major university in the area undoubtedly influences many students' decisions to prepare for and eventually attend college, this high school sends many more minority students to college than a nearby comparable school district. This fact leads us to believe that many of this high school's characteristics, other than proximity to a major university, are influencing students' decisions to prepare for and eventually attend an institution of higher learning.

Houston, Texas—Interviewee: Head Counselor

The second school provides an excellent example of a school that is doing an outstanding job of preparing students for the Texas Assessment of Knowledge and Skills (TAKS), but an average job of preparing students for college. Not surprisingly, this school has made performance on the TAKS their top priority.

Commitment to the TAKS begins with scheduling; as the head counselor stated, their "big secret is the way we schedule our kids." The school uses an accelerated block schedule; students attend four 90-minute classes a day, 5 days a week. In the 9th and 10th grades, students take math and English courses all year, preparing them to be in top form when they take the TAKS toward the end of their 10th-grade year.

Students who do not pass the math and/or English portions of the TAKS in the 10th grade must take corresponding TAKS remediation courses. The school also offers summer tutorials and summer TAKS preparation courses. If they have not passed the TAKS, the school contacts parents by letter and by phone to ensure student attendance. Counselors tenaciously attempt to reach students and parents who do not initially respond.

For students who are struggling with the math portion of the TAKS, the school offers a self-paced computer program called "Success Maker" that goes back to first-grade math concepts. As students display concept mastery, the program proceeds to the next, more challenging concept. Although the computer program appears to primarily utilize "skill and drill" pedagogical techniques, a teacher is in the room to help students with any problems and to help explain math concepts.

One reason the school obtains such outstanding results on the TAKS is because it does an excellent job of communicating with parents and emphasizing its importance. The school holds a TAKS night, during which parents are given information about the test. Parents can also use the school's computers to take release tests of the TAKS to understand what their children are facing. In addition, because the school has a number of teachers who are fluent in English and Spanish (as well as a number of other languages), communication problems with parents rarely arise. It takes advantage of this fortunate situation by holding a special TAKS night for ESL students, where information is presented in both Spanish and English, and study tips are sent home with parents in both languages. The school offers TAKS preparation courses with ESL teachers after school on a tutorial basis, for which students earn high school credit.

The list of special efforts the school makes to help students score well on the TAKS goes on and on:

- teachers work twice a week during their preparation period in TAKS tutorials to help struggling students
- students are taken from elective classes once or twice a week to receive additional TAKS preparation
- students are given incentives such as free pizza, movie passes, and candy to attend after-school TAKS tutorials
- the school holds "TAKS Saturday" two weeks before the real test (providing breakfast and a pizza lunch) so students can work on a computer with release TAKS tests or one-on-one sessions with teachers
- students do "TAKS warm-ups" (comprised of several practice TAKS questions from previous tests) during the first few minutes of every class period in 9th and 10th grade
- teachers record student practice test scores in a logbook, and students receive additional instruction during tutorials if they perform poorly on questions covering any specific concept
- several weeks before the TAKS, school staff (a TAKS specialist, assistant principal, area superintendent, or another administrator) pulls students out of class one at a time in order to go over their logbook and encourage them to attend tutorials to address any deficiencies, adding a pep talk.

This school is apparently doing an outstanding job of helping students perform well on the TAKS. The teachers and administrators have gone above and beyond the call of duty in helping students master the basic skills the TAKS measures. The teachers and administrators obviously possess the organizational and pedagogical skills necessary to help students perform well on a test the state of Texas uses to accredit schools.

If the state of Texas decided to use SAT and ACT scores in addition to TAKS scores when accrediting schools, thereby encouraging schools such as this one to place as much emphasis on SAT and ACT preparation as they do on TAKS preparation, one wonders what a dedicated, talented staff at a school such as this would be capable of achieving. Unfortunately, the emphasis on the TAKS has derailed certain activities and strategies meant to prepare students for college. For example, while their block scheduling appears optimal for preparing students for success on the TAKS, the head counselor noted that since going on the block schedule, the school "has seen a drop in SAT and ACT scores because students are not taking math and English until their later years in school." Another danger of the block schedule is that if students do go on to college but have not taken a math class since the 10th grade, they are usually placed into remedial math, costing additional time and money.

Fort Worth, Texas—Interviewees: Academic Counselor and Vocational Counselor

The third school is a school in crisis. Although its student population is similar to school #1 in terms of race, ethnicity, and average family income, students here are much less likely to go on to college; and teachers and other staff seem discouraged, demoralized, and depressed.

Prior to my interview with the academic counselor, the vocational counselor spoke with me briefly and showed me around the school of about 840 students. He introduced me to the baseball coach, who informed us that only 11 players had shown up at the last game, which they lost 16 to nothing. The coach was distraught about the lack of commitment among his players and noted that one of the students had a very good reason why he could not make it to the game—he had just been arrested. After telling us further tales of woe, the coach said, "No wonder I drink so much," and then rushed off to class. Seemingly a likable person, the coach appeared visibly discouraged by the sense of hopelessness permeating the school.

The academic counselor, whom I spoke with next, shared this sentiment. The academic counselor had only been at the school for about 4 years, and said that prior to his arrival, the school placed little to no emphasis on high academic achievement. The year before he arrived, only two AP courses were taught, only four students took an AP test, and none of those students scored above a 3 (the cut-off score on a 5-point scale). Discouraged by these abysmal numbers, the academic counselor requested that at least five AP courses be offered the next year; nearly all of the students failed these courses, however, because they did not have the academic foundation necessary to succeed on the AP exams. The counselor recognized that he was going to have to address the problem of vertically aligning the curriculum from Kindergarten to grade 12 with the expectation that students will eventually take AP courses if the AP program was to be successful. He said that this proved to be a formidable task for a variety of reasons.

To begin with, the administration's decision to focus on the TAKS left the school with little administrative commitment to preparing students for success in AP courses or for high scores on the SAT or the ACT. The long-range goal of preparing students to attend college was not a high priority for this administration. He suggested that if schools were judged and rated by how many AP courses kids take, how well they do on the SAT or ACT, and so forth, then schools would reorder their priorities and place more emphasis on improving these measures of success.

Another obstacle to vertical alignment was the administrative task of getting all of the teachers of a given subject in the same place at the same time, made more difficult because the teachers in the district were not enthusiastic about altering the curriculum. The counselor stated that many of the teachers had a curriculum with which they were comfortable, and they did not want to change. This lack of enthusiasm led to complaints and to the desire to be paid for any extra time spent on planning the new curriculum.

In addition, the counselor observed that very few parents think that it is realistic for their children to attend college, which presents another obstacle to vertical curriculum alignment. Consequently, parents make few demands on the school to prepare their children well for college, and students appear all too willing to participate in the game of low expectations.

With most students, teachers, administrators, and parents willing to accept low academic achievement, one wonders where the impetus for change might emerge, and if any proposals for change would be effective until broader support exists. For example, the school moved to a block schedule a number of years ago in an attempt to improve academic achievement, but the teachers simply used the same methods and covered the same material in 90 minutes that previously fit into 50 minutes. After realizing that block scheduling was not working effectively, the school moved back to 50-minute periods. One attempt at reform down, but perhaps an infinite number left to go.

SUCCESSFUL STRATEGIES

Educators at the highest-performing districts in the state almost universally acknowledged that increasing the number of students who go on to college was an explicit goal of the district; they also agreed that a broad segment of the community enthusiastically supported this goal, from the superintendent to the classroom teachers to the parents. As a result of establishing this general goal, districts identified and established a series of subtasks to help prepare students more fully for college attendance, such as improving SAT and ACT scores and increasing the number of students who take AP courses. In order to increase the number of students taking the SAT and the ACT, high-performing school districts implemented a number of innovative strategies.

Payment Strategies

As mentioned in the case study above, the highest-performing district in the state pays for all of its students to take the PSAT rather than the SAT, making all students eligible for National Merit Scholarships and giving students practice with the basic SAT format. When the PSAT results are returned, counselors meet individually with each student to explain exactly what the results mean to allow students to identify their weaknesses while they still have time in high school to improve them.

After schools have encouraged students to take AP classes, many districts encourage students to take the AP tests by paying for the exam. The state of Texas already pays a portion of the fees; successful districts typically pay whatever portion remains. One extremely successful district even awards Advanced Placement Scholarships that pay students for passing scores; the higher the score, the more money the student receives. If a student earns a 3 or 4 on an AP exam, the district pays that student $100. If a student earns a 5, the district pays that student $200. One can only imagine how getting paid for passing AP exams influences student attitudes toward high academic achievement.

Other important strategies include paying for all students to take a college-entrance exam at least once and making efforts to establish the high school as a test site. Although middle-class adults might not see the fee as a major obstacle to taking the SAT or ACT, these districts pay the fee for all students in order to help many students take the test who otherwise would not have. Offering the school as a test site not only increases the number of students taking the test, but educators suggested that it also improved student scores because students were familiar and comfortable with their surroundings and did not have to travel to a distant, unfamiliar test site.

Improving Information Dissemination and Test Preparation

By increasing the number of students who take the SAT or the ACT, high schools also increase the number of students who receive information directly from colleges. Colleges obtain lists of students who took the SAT or

ACT from the test providers and mail information about the college to the students and invite them to apply. Students therefore become more aware of available options and more confident as colleges ask them to apply.

In order to improve student performance on the SAT or ACT, high-performing districts typically offer test-preparation courses for local credit. The most experienced and talented math and English teachers in the district typically teach these courses. Several educators mentioned that only a small percentage of the students were taking these courses in their schools and that they would like to see more students enroll in them, which makes their effect on the average SAT or ACT scores questionable; we believe these courses have a larger effect than many people realize, not only because they directly improve the scores of the small number of students taking the test, but because they signal to students, parents, and teachers that the district places a high priority on test preparation in particular and on preparing students for college in general.

Vertical Alignment and Advanced Placement

School districts that have been successful at increasing the number of students taking AP courses have vertically aligned their curriculum from Kindergarten through grade 12 with the expectation that all students will eventually take AP courses in high school. If students are unable to meet this expectation, they are then moved into a lower track. This action shows commitment beyond the rhetoric most schools use, but it comes at a clear dollar and time cost to the district in terms of the resources needed to offer a wide range of AP courses. In order for a district to align the curriculum in the anticipation that all students will eventually take AP Calculus, Physics, Chemistry, U.S. History, European History, and so on, school districts must actually offer these courses. The most successful districts do.

In addition to vertically aligning the curriculum, successful districts make active efforts to inform parents about the benefits of AP courses. The successful high school highlighted in the case study discussed holds an AP information night every year; all students and parents are encouraged to attend, and many do. Counselors and AP teachers stress how the AP curriculum is challenging yet interesting, and how passing scores on AP tests can earn students college credits, which saves parents money. Counselors and teachers also stress that all students are welcome to take AP courses; while students must meet certain selection criteria in order to participate in gifted courses, no selection criteria exist for enrollment in AP courses beyond the desire to participate. Educators at several successful schools commented that many parents, particularly recent immigrants, those who dropped out of high school, and those who did not attend college, are unaware of the benefits of the AP program.

Block Scheduling

In order to improve student performance in AP courses and on AP tests, almost all successful schools have implemented *block scheduling*, which nearly doubles class time to 90 minutes. Educators in schools that utilize block scheduling noted that the AP teachers love it because it gives them enough time to explore topics in depth without undue interruption. Educators also frequently mentioned that science teachers find the block format extremely beneficial because it gives students enough time to perform lab procedures and discuss the results. We found the enthusiastic support for block scheduling, particularly among science teachers, extremely noteworthy. Educators reported that block scheduling reduces the amount of time spent on administrative duties in the day (such as taking role, making announcements, and so forth), which increases the amount of time students spend on task. Education research supports the conclusion that student achievement increases as the amount of time spent on task increases (Murphy, 1986).

This format demands a great degree of preparation and pedagogical expertise from teachers, however. In order to maintain student interest and increase the level of learning, teachers need to vary their instructional strategies, perhaps using three or four different strategies within the given 90 minutes; a teacher who lectures for the full 90 minutes is doomed. Successful teachers often vary their instructional strategies across a variety of dimensions, including teacher/student-centered instruction and structured-unstructured strategies. While the most talented teachers will adjust their instructional techniques according to the needs of their particular students, much of the literature on minority academic achievement suggests that students in urban settings benefit from "structured learning environments" (Murphy, 1986, p. 504).

The finding that minority students benefit from structured learning environments assumes increasing importance when linked with the finding that science teachers enjoy the block scheduling format the most. Science labs provide a structured learning environment that allows students to become actively involved in the learning process. In other words, labs can provide hands-on, student-centered, active reinforcement of abstract concepts originally presented through teacher-centered instructional techniques. Labs thus allow science teachers to vary their pedagogical techniques while still providing a structured learning environment. These general principles regarding effective instructional strategies gleaned from the experiences of science teachers can benefit teachers in other content areas as well. Apparently, the most successful teachers in the most successful schools use a variety of instructional strategies and learning techniques while still maintaining the structured learning environments associated with high academic achievement among minorities.

CHALLENGES DISTRICTS CONTINUE TO FACE

The most successful districts have clearly made a commitment to preparing students for success on college entrance exams and for success in AP courses, and they devote time and resources in order to meet this commitment. The least successful districts have not made such a strong commitment. Interestingly, many of the educators interviewed in the low-performing districts said that they would like to place a higher emphasis on preparing students for college, but they often faced opposition from top-level administrators. Some administrators interviewed were hesitant to place higher emphasis on preparing students for college because they do not want to take any emphasis away from preparing students for the TAKS. Perhaps if the state of Texas expanded the number of criteria used to accredit schools in order to include some measures of college preparation, schools would alter their priorities accordingly.

Focusing on the TAKS rather than on preparing students for college is not the only characteristic that separates low-performing schools from high-performing schools. Another characteristic of successful schools is that talented, innovative, and committed teachers and administrative staff are key ingredients for student success. Compliments between teachers and administration were unrestrained in the schools that had higher rates of graduation and college entrance, while they were few and far between in the low-performing schools. Innovative programs and policies are less effective and sometimes counterproductive when the teaching staff is ill-prepared to implement them or the administration does not provide the resources or support required to make them work.

For example, when visiting top-performing schools, we frequently heard administrators boast about teacher excellence, for example: "We have a heck of a staff," "We just have great teachers," and "I would compare our teachers to any in the state." When visiting low-performing schools, counselors and other administrators rarely said anything positive or negative about the teachers, most often preferring to say nothing at all. Occasionally, however, administrators would be more critical. A counselor at one school claimed that most of the teachers were comfortable with the status quo and were reluctant to adopt more effective teaching practices. For example, although the school changed to a 90-minute block schedule a number of years ago to improve academic achievement, the teachers simply used the same teaching methods they had used during 50-minute periods, covering the exact same material. After realizing that block scheduling was not working effectively, the school moved back to 50-minute periods. The experience of this school suggests that certain programs, policies, and procedures by themselves will not boost student academic achievement. Teachers and other academic staff must buy in to the program in order to implement them to achieve the desired results. Programs alone will not guarantee good results; talented teachers alone will not produce good results. The highest-performing schools have both.

The schools that are highly committed to preparing Latino students for college do more than simply help students succeed on the measures of college preparation used in this study. The schools that are the most successful at preparing Latino students for college also: 1. encourage students to enroll in dual credit classes, 2. encourage students to attend college and increase student enthusiasm, and 3. increase the amount of college and financial aid information given to parents.

Large percentages of students participated in dual credit classes in the successful schools in this study. Dual credit classes allow students to take challenging courses while still in high school, for which they receive credits both toward their high school diploma and toward a college degree. Many of the most successful schools have excellent dual credit arrangements with local community colleges, and several offer dual credit courses on the high school campus, whereby their own qualified high school teachers teach the courses (in order for high school teachers to be qualified, they must meet the hiring standards of the cooperating community college, which usually means that they have received at least some graduate school education). These educators identified several benefits of dual credit courses.

First, they provide students with a challenging intellectual experience that helps them develop the higher-order thinking skills that help them to do well on college entrance exams and are essential to long-term success in college. Second, dual credit courses familiarize students with the college experience and give them confidence that they can handle a college-level curriculum. For many students, particularly those who come from families where parents and siblings have not attended college, dual credit courses appear to be an excellent way of introducing students to the college experience.

Third, dual credit courses allow students to save money. By working toward a college degree while still in high school, students are able to graduate from college earlier, thus reducing opportunity costs. In addition, the cooperating community college courses for which they receive credit have very modest fees, and many of the highest-performing districts in our study pay the fees for the students if they pass the courses. Given that a high percentage of Latino students come from impoverished backgrounds, the importance of reducing the costs of attending college becomes critical.

Taking dual credit and community college courses is an excellent way for students to reduce college costs. High-performing schools recognize, however, that they need to encourage students to consider a range of post-secondary education options. Therefore, they encourage students to consider attending 4-year universities through a variety of strategies. Strategies to increase enthusiasm for attending 4-year universities vary from school to school; what seems to be important is not the exact nature of the strategy used, but rather that it instills in students a palpable enthusiasm for attending college. For example, one school on the Texas-Mexico border comprised almost entirely of Latino students takes every student in the top 10% of the senior class on a district-paid trip to visit Texas A&M and the University of Texas. For many students, it is their first time leaving the Rio Grande Valley. The counselor who takes the students every year says that the students always have a wonderful time, and when they return to the high school, they tell the other students about the highlights of the trip.

Successful schools also employ a variety of strategies to increase parental knowledge about college and financial aid options. For instance, successful schools send college information home in both Spanish and English. Successful schools also work hard to help students qualify for financial aid, including holding special "financial aid nights" when counselors and other school officials help parents and students fill out financial aid forms. In some districts, accountants attend these events and help recent immigrants file their taxes promptly so that they can qualify for financial aid in time to help their son or daughter attend college.

CONCLUSIONS

Throughout the state of Texas, some school districts do an excellent job of preparing Latino students for college, devoting a considerable amount of time, energy, and resources to this task; some do not. Interestingly, the districts that provide the best college preparation for Latino students have not made Latino students a priority alone; rather, they have made *all* students their priority. This does not mean that these districts coerce students into thinking that attending a 4-year university is their only postsecondary option; rather, they ensure that all students have had every educational opportunity made available to them. These districts concentrated on preparing students for college; the school's agenda (or lack thereof) did not limit them or force them to pursue other post-secondary options.

NOTES

1. I would like to thank Dr. Kenneth Meier for his invaluable assistance with this project and for use of the dataset assembled under his direction.

2. Educators and administrators regularly referred to the Texas Assessment of Academic Skills (TAAS), which had at that time recently been changed to the Texas Essential Knowledge and Skills (TEKS). Throughout the text, I will refer to the Texas Assessment of Knowledge and Skills (TAKS) test to acknowledge its more recent title.

REFERENCES

Bowen, W. G., & Bok, D. (1998). *The shape of the river: Long-term consequences of considering race in college and university admissions.* Princeton, NJ: Princeton University Press.

Burtless, G. (1996). *Does money matter? The effect of school resources on student achievement and adult success.* Washington, DC: Brookings Institution.

Elmore, R. F. (1996). Getting to scale with good educational practice. *Harvard Education Review, 66*(1), 1–26.

Hossler, D., Schmit, R., & Vesper, N. (1999). *Going to college: How social, economic, and educational factors influence the decisions students make.* Baltimore: Johns Hopkins University Press.

Leighley, J. (2001). *Strength in numbers? The political mobilization of racial and ethnic minorities.* Princeton, NJ: Princeton University Press.

Murphy, D. M. (1986). Educational disadvantagement: Associated factors, current interventions, and implications. *Journal of Negro Education, 55*(4), 495–507.

U.S. Census Bureau. (2000). *National population projections.* Retrieved July 9, 2004, from http://www.census.gov/population/projections/nation/summary/np-t4-g.txt

CHAPTER 12

Latinos in Higher Education: Why the Politics Matter

Alisa Hicklin

A number of political scientists have made considerable progress in advancing our understanding about how political and bureaucratic institutions contribute to Latino K–12 education. Despite the significant attention given to Latino student achievement in the K–12 system, substantially less attention has been devoted to the politics of Latino higher education, such as the factors that affect Latino student collegiate enrollments. This is surprising, given how often we hear about this issue in state legislatures, on university campuses, and in the media.

Much of the attention has circulated around recent Supreme Court decisions, particularly how they affect university admissions policies, and how certain policies are weighed against the changing measure of constitutionality. Noticeably absent from these studies is the consideration of how other institutions (such as state legislatures or bureaucratic agencies) affect these policy outcomes. Research on other higher education policy areas, such as budgeting and oversight, consider a host of possible determinants, with significant focus placed on state legislative bodies and top state bureaucratic agencies.

State governments play a critical role in the success of public universities, serving as the primary overseer in policy, funding, and accountability. The state legislature determines the level of public funding that each university will receive through the specification of a funding formula, and it allocates a significant amount of money throughout grant programs, individual projects, and other avenues. Legislatures also have the ability to regulate tuition, to set statewide admissions policies, and to advance numerous policies in the K–12 system that will affect the students who eventually feed into universities.

Similarly, each state has a bureaucratic agency that has some measure of control over the public universities, although the extent to which these agencies affect policy varies across states. The agency's responsibilities range from simple planning and coordination in some states to considerable control over personnel, budgets, policies, and curriculum in other states. Throughout the nation, these agencies vary significantly in their structure and level of autonomy. The amount of control these agencies have should affect education policy in the state, as most legislative initiatives must be filtered through the state agency as they are applied to individual universities.

Because most of the scholarly literature that deals with issues of Latinos in higher education focuses primarily on the *benefits* of diversity, we know little about the factors that affect levels of minority enrollment (U.S. Commission on Civil Rights, 2002; Bowen, Bok, & Loury, 2000; Duderstadt, 2000; Hurtado & Cade, 2001). In addition, the majority of studies only include a handful of universities, most of which are elite, Ivy League institutions, concentrated in specific geographic areas (Chapa & Lazaro, 1998; Horn & Flores, 2003; Post, 1998; Simmons, 1982; Welch & Gruhl, 1998). Because of this focus on elite institutions, we have very little knowledge about what affects the other 80% of college students in the higher education system. Critical differences in size, selectivity, and scope have not been incorporated into much of the research, and, as a result, the limited research that we have is even more limited by its inapplicability to the majority of universities.

This chapter considers a number of state and institutional factors in an effort to understand how state governments affect one of the more salient goals of many universities: increased representation of Latino students, also termed *increasing diversity*. In an effort to investigate the higher education policy environment, I draw from other policy research, including many of the forces determined to be significant predictors of other policy outcomes, especially in the K–12 education arena. Specifically, this chapter will consider the effects of minority legislative representation, bureaucratic structure, judicial interventions, and university-specific characteristics. This investigation is an effort to discover which state and university-level factors influence minority student enrollment at American public universities.

PREDICTING POLICY OUTCOMES

A substantial literature within the fields of political science and public policy would suggest that varying levels of representation and bureaucratic structures at the state level should have a significant effect on policy outcomes (Lowry, 2001; Meier, 2000; Pitkin, 1967; Preston, 1978). Incorporating the literature on descriptive representation, bureaucratic structure, and the effect of political interventions will generate new hypotheses and research designs for analyzing higher education. This method has proven to be useful in the study of K–12 education, but it has not yet been successfully applied to higher education.

Legislative Representation

Because state governments control public universities, differences among state legislatures should have some effect on each state's universities. Theories of representation suggest that increased representation of minority groups in a decision-making body (descriptive representation) often translates into policies that increasingly favor the represented minority group, known as substantive representation (Mansbridge, 1999; Phillips, 1993; Pitkin, 1967). This relationship is found to be an important factor in improving educational outcomes for minority students in the K–12 system; increased minority representation in the decision-making organization (the school board) is positively associated with increased student performance (standardized test scores, attendance, graduation rates) for minority student groups (Fraga, Meier, & England, 1986; Meier, Stuart, & England, 1989; Meier & Stewart, 1991). Because of the similarity between the two systems, one would expect the same relationship to exist in higher education.

For universities, the elected body would be the state legislature and a "better policy outcome" for the particular minority group(s) would be an increase in minority student enrollment. This literature provides the foundation for hypothesis one (H1): Increased Latino representation in the state legislature will positively affect Latino student enrollment at public universities.

Bureaucratic Structure

The link between legislated policy intentions and street-level policy outcomes is the bureaucratic agency. For public higher education, each state has an agency that is responsible for some measure of state university oversight. These agencies vary in their structure, especially with respect to centralization and amount of control. Some states have very centralized autonomous boards, called governing boards, many of which have control over daily decisions made at each university, including personnel, budgeting, and curriculum. In these states, universities are bound by rules and regulations set at the state level and carried out at the university level. Other states have various types of coordinating boards, a less authoritative entity that has some control over university policies, but not to the extent of governing boards. Coordinating boards often take care of much of the lobbying and master planning for the state, leaving most of the decision-making discretion to universities administrators.

The distribution of bureaucratic discretion through varying structures has been shown to significantly affect how legislative objectives are translated into policy. Many authors consider more centralized, autonomous bureaucracies to be hardwired at the time of their creation, affected less by the changing views of the legislature over time (Epstein & O'Halloran, 1999; Huber & Shipan, 2002; McCubbins, Noll, & Weingast, 1989; O'Halloran, 1999). In higher education, this would mean that universities with more autonomous governing boards, having been established at a time when fewer minorities were represented, would negatively affect minority student enrollment figures.

Other studies have considered how the centralization of the bureaucracy helps translate legislative preferences into policy outcomes more efficiently. This body of work has shown that more centralized bureaucracies positively affect the relationship between increased minority representation and policy outcomes that are favorable to minorities (Hawes & Hicklin, 2004), and that structure affects many aspects of higher education policy (McLendon, 2003; Nicholson-Crotty & Meier, 2003; Richardson, Bracco, Callan, & Finney, 1999).

In the case of minority representation, the structure of the chief bureaucratic agency could therefore have an independent effect on minority enrollment or could have an interactive effect, moderating the relationship between increased minority legislative representation and increased minority student enrollments. These expectations are the basis for hypotheses two (H2, that increased centralization of the chief bureaucratic agency should be negatively associated with Latino student enrollment) and three (H3, that increased centralization of the chief bureaucratic agency should positively increase the effect of Latino legislative representation on Latino student enrollments).

Restrictions on Using Race in Admissions Policies

For the last 40 years, interest groups, politicians, and educational institutions have battled over methods designed to ensure equitable access to education for all groups of American students. Affirmative action policies have been enacted at a number of universities, some of which are very aggressive in recruiting minority students and using their racial background as a factor in determining admissions and financial aid. Some members of majority groups have attacked these policies as reverse discrimination, and the courts and legislatures have struck many of them down. The constitutionality of including race in admissions has not been a clear-cut issue. Instead, the constitutionality of such programs depends on the location of the university, the year, and the nuances of how the policy was formed and carried out. Arguments regarding the appropriateness of including race in admissions have taken place both in the courts and in state legislatures, but the outcomes of the battles have virtually identical constraints on institutions. Because of the similarities between the judicial and legislative constraints, they will be reviewed separately, but in the empirical analysis, they will be combined into one variable that indicates when universities are restricted from incorporating race.

JUDICIAL INTERVENTIONS. The most recent and politically salient political interventions are the court cases addressing the use of race in admissions policies. *Bakke* (*Regents of University of California v. Bakke*, 1978), *Hopwood* (*Hopwood v. Texas*, 1996), and the Michigan cases each altered the ability of universities to include race as a factor in determining admissions and financial aid. The Supreme Court's *Bakke* decision set a precedent of ambiguity that has plagued universities ever since. It articulated both sides of the debate—views supporting policies aimed at raising minority student enrollment levels—as well as views objecting to policies that allow a person's race to be formally incorporated into policy decisions.

Hopwood, the 1996 ruling of the Fifth Circuit Court of Appeals, restricted all use of race in admissions decisions for public universities in Louisiana, Mississippi, and Texas, thereby eliminating those universities' ability to attract minority students through race-based admissions policies. Because of *Bakke*'s ambiguity and *Hopwood*'s limited jurisdiction, American universities were left without a common standard until 2003, when the Supreme Court ruled again on the use of race in admissions policies. The Michigan cases (*Grutter* [*Grutter v. Bollinger*, 2003] and *Gratz* [*Gratz v. Bollinger*, 2003]) lifted the *Hopwood* ban on race, but still placed some restrictions on how a university chooses to incorporate race into admissions.

LEGISLATIVE POLICIES. In response to *Hopwood* and before the *Grutter* and *Gratz* decisions, while the constitutionality of using race was exceptionally vague, many states that were not bound under the Fifth Circuit Court passed laws that precluded the use of race in admissions. California's Proposition 209 and Florida's "One Florida" policy restricted institutions from incorporating race into admissions. These laws limited many institutions in their pursuit of diversity, and each state received considerable criticism. Some of the criticism focuses on accusations of increasing minority student segregation among universities and increased educational disenfranchisement due to lower levels of minority student enrollment. Some laws substituted other policies that attempted to increase diversity without giving preference to certain groups.

This study will test the effect of these judicial interventions and state restrictions on race through hypothesis four (H4, that restricting the use of race in admissions is negatively associated with levels of Latino student enrollment).

University Characteristics

Some of the more interesting questions about how state-level factors affect policy outcomes are not focused on their direct effects, but on how the relationship between state-level factors and policy outcomes is moderated by university-specific characteristics. One of most substantial differences between universities is their level of selectivity. Selectivity, a measure of competitiveness or prestige, affects almost every facet of a university, including type of students, mission, curriculum, faculty, and budgets. Not considering how differences in institutional selectivity play a role in policy would be to ignore a critical component of the higher education policy environment. This is why the existing literature on affirmative action in university admissions is so limited in its generalizability. Studying only Ivy League and flagship universities ignores the importance of varying levels of selectivity.

Previous research has shown that the institution's level of selectivity has a significant moderating effect on the relationship between race restrictions and minority enrollments for universities bound under *Hopwood* and California's Proposition 209 (Hicklin, 2004). Because the inclusion of race into admissions is intended to give minority students a more competitive edge in gaining admissions, those universities with open enrollment policies would not see the inclusion of race as a means to increase minority enrollment. If everyone who meets the minimum requirement is accepted, the value of that extra edge is limited. Alternatively, if a university is very selective, any advantage is significant. Because most previous research does not include universities of varying selectivity, we know little about how these differences affect outcomes. This relationship will be tested for all American public universities through hypothesis five (H5, that the effect of race restrictions on minority student enrollment depends on the institution's level of selectivity).

Other institutional-specific characteristics were included in the study I conducted as well. Because public universities compete in a market (though not a free market) for minority students, some measure of cost should be included. However, it is important to note that it has only been in the last few years that many states have deregulated tuition. Compared with the difference between public and private schools, which can exceed $30,000 a year, differences among public universities are almost negligible. This is changing because state budgets have not been able to keep up with the increasing costs of education, and some public universities have been forced to generate a greater percentage of their budget through tuition and fees. For the sake of model specification, tuition was included as a control variable.

Finally, in the case of minority student enrollments, we know that many public universities have identified serving Latino students as their primary mission. These universities have been designated Hispanic-Serving Institutions (HSIs). Although the Historically Black Colleges and Universities

(HBCU) designation carries more weight, the HSI designation does have some importance within the minority community and often allows universities to receive special funds. This designation was also taken into account.

THE APPROACH OF THE STUDY

The data for this project were compiled from numerous federal and state sources.[1] For a methodological discussion, see the second footnote.[2] The dataset includes all American public, 4-year universities from 1990–2001 that offer a bachelor degree. The original dataset included 594 universities over 11 years (with some exceptions), resulting in 5,772 data points. The dataset used in estimation (after dropping those with missing data) included 4,213 data points.

The dependent variable, enrollment, is measured as the percentage of Latino undergraduate students in an institution. There is some debate over whether to use the percentage of students who are Latino, the total number of Latinos in college, the change from year to year, or the ratio of Latino college students to Latino high school students. Because the more politically salient issue is the percentage of college enrollment that consists of Latino students, this is the better choice, especially given the particular interest in the political side of this issue.

This study considers state-level and university-level factors that may influence minority enrollment. To test hypothesis one, I include minority legislative representation, which is measured by the percentage of Latino representatives in both chambers of a state legislature. A variable for state bureaucratic structure represents the degree of centralization and autonomy held by the state's chief higher education agency (1 = an autonomous, centralized governing board, 0 = a decentralized coordinating or planning board).

Another variable represents when state universities are restricted from using race in admissions policies, whether from the courts or the state government (1 = restricted, 0 = unrestricted). This variable is used to explore the relationship between a university's level of selectivity and minority enrollment levels. Selectivity is a 6-point measure based on *Barron's Profile of American Colleges'* (2000) measure of competitiveness; the categories include noncompetitive, less competitive, competitive, more competitive, highly competitive, and most competitive.

Three control variables are included as well, which take into account additional relevant factors. Although public universities are bureaucratic institutions, they also compete in the market, which encourages them to spend substantial amounts of time and money improving their reputations. In the case of minority enrollment, many universities are well known for being receptive or hostile to minority students. In an effort to account for some of the reputation effect, I added two control variables. First, I include a dummy variable for those universities designated as *Hispanic-Serving Institutions* (HSI). This variable is included in an effort to catch some measure of reputation. Second, I include a lagged dependent variable because I incorporate data from 10 consecutive years. Although universities receive new students each year, the undergraduate enrollment numbers are largely a function of previous enrollments. This also raises the bar for achieving significance, resulting in more conservative estimates. Finally, in an effort to control for the market forces that often affect college-going decisions, I include a variable for cost, operationalized as the annual in-state tuition and fee costs per student; it is centered on the state mean in an effort to account for some cost-of-living issues.

STUDY FINDINGS

First, the study indicated support for hypothesis one, that increased Latino representation in the legislature does indeed result in higher levels of Latino enrollment (see Table 12.1). This is consistent with previous research in K–12 education, which found that greater levels of Latino school board representations are associated with substantive policy outcomes that are important to Latino communities—ranging from greater shares of Latino teachers to increased bilingual education funding (Hess & Leal, 2000; Leal, Martinez-Ebers, & Meier, 2004). This paper therefore adds additional support to the argument that Latino descriptive representation is of both symbolic and substantive significance.

Although minority representation does affect enrollments, there seems to be no support for the idea *that structure matters in this system*. As such, neither hypothesis two nor hypothesis three is supported. There are a number of possibilities as to why this may be the case. The obvious conclusion would be that state higher education agencies either do not vary enough or do not have enough control to make any difference. However, it is possible that this nonfinding could be because of recent growth in Latino representation in legislatures. The ability to make these changes requires that some group in the legislative body holds real power and foresight, enabling them to make decisions that would ensure future political payoffs. It is quite possible that Latinos are just now at the point where they are gaining the seniority, experience, and political capital to invest in these long-term payoffs.

The test of hypotheses four and five (restricting the use of race in admissions is negatively associated with levels of Latino student enrollment; the effect of race restrictions on minority student enrollment depends on the institution's level of selectivity) produce notable results. The independent

Table 12.1. Determinants of Latino Student Enrollment

Dependent Variable	Percentage of Student Undergraduate Enrollment Who Are Latino
Latino legislative representation	0.0354** (2.534)
Bureaucratic structure	0.0141 (1.050)
Representation / Structure	-0.0053 (0.928)
Restrictions on race	0.2554** (2.146)
Selectivity	0.0061 (0.882)
Race restrictions / Selectivity	-0.1552*** (3.954)
HSI	0.4255*** (4.664)
Tuition	-0.0380* (1.921)
Lagged dependent variable	1.0075*** (142.603)
Constant	0.0425** (2.147)
N	4213

*p < .01, **p < .05, ***p < .10

effect of restricting the use of race in admissions is puzzling, prima facie. Restricting minority students from using their racial background as a "plus" in admissions results in the counterintuitive, *positive* correlation with enrollment levels for Latinos. However, once considering a university's level of selectivity (via the model's interaction term), the effect of including race in admissions becomes contingent on the university, and for many universities, the relationship changes direction. As the university's level of selectivity increases, the more the university is negatively affected by their inability to include race into admissions. As a result, restrictions on the use of race result in a redistribution of Latino students throughout the state. Latino students who would have attended flagship universities, instead opt for second-tier universities; and those students who would have attended the midsize universities decide to enroll in smaller, regional schools.

Smaller universities benefit from diversity efforts when elite universities are unable to use race-inclusive admissions policies to attract more minority students. However, this positive relationship only exists for the least selective universities. Universities with moderately selective admission standards would not be affected by the ability to include race, while competitive universities feel the negative effects of the state-level restrictions. These findings negate hypothesis four (restricting the use of race in admissions is negatively associated with levels of Latino student enrollment) but strongly support hypothesis five (the effect of race restrictions on minority student enrollment depends on the institution's level of selectivity).

For Latino students, less expensive (often regional) universities have an advantage in attracting minority students relative to other, more expensive universities in the state. This may be due to family financial constraints, a relative lack of knowledge of the higher education system, or possibly the location of selective universities (Perez, 2002). Latino students may also want to stay near their hometown, which would limit the options available to them.

Similarly, the variables for reputation are both positive and significant, with HSI status and the lagged dependent variable both substantively large and statistically significant. This is not surprising. In the case of HSIs, this distinction is a more recent development in higher education. States have just recently initiated special funding opportunities for these institutions, thereby offering HSIs more opportunities to recruit students and add to the quality of their institutions. These recent developments, along with the rapidly increasing Latino population, may account for the independent effects of both the lagged dependent variable and the HSI status.

Last, the significance of the past year's enrollments shows that the gains and losses caused by the above factors, no matter the size, become embedded in the system, thereby increasing or holding back progress over time. This suggests the importance of understanding how these factors affect Latino higher education enrollment and seeking policy solutions for educational obstacles.

CONCLUSION AND RECOMMENDATIONS

The most important conclusion in this chapter is that political dynamics can make a considerable difference in Latino higher education. In discussing the underrepresentation of Latinos in universities, it is often said that the fault lies primarily with the K–12 system. Numerous studies do show that Latinos are systematically disadvantaged in the K–12 school system through their overrepresentation in the poorer school districts and discriminatory tracking and disciplinary policies (Meier & Stewart, 1991), resulting in inequitable educational opportunities for Latino youth.

However, the findings in this chapter suggest that variations in state government policies and institutions also matter for Latino students. Latino representation in higher education is not only a function of Latino legislative representation but also the legal context, such as restrictions on the use of race in admissions, as well as selectivity and tuition cost.

This suggests that government may have a key role to play in Latino higher education. In addition to taking into account the factors discussed above, there may be other useful ways for state policy makers to improve outcomes. For example, if a relatively large number of qualified Latino students are underplacing themselves (choosing not to attend college when they are capable) due to family constraints, lack of information, or lower aspirations, the state may have an opportunity to intervene. Legislatures could fund special projects targeted at Latino families to inform parents about the college-going process, and a state's higher education agency could launch more aggressive programs aimed at motivated (and motivating) Latino students in high school.

More generally, the higher education policy arena suffers from a lack of knowledge about how political institutions shape educational processes and outcomes in public universities. Compared to the research on K–12 education, research on higher education has a long way to go. States and universities are investing vast resources to bolster system abilities to ensure equity and further diversity efforts. Understanding what factors affect these issues, and, equally important, what factors do *not* make a difference, can help decision makers formulate the policies that will be most efficient and most effective in bringing about real change and positive progress.

NOTES

1. Student enrollment data, tuition data, and HSI status is drawn from the Department of Education's Integrated Postsecondary Education Data System (IPEDS) from 1990–2001 (IPEDS 2004). University selectivity is based on the competitiveness measure in *Barron's Profile of American Colleges* (Barron's 2000). State Latino legislative representation is drawn from the National Association of Latino Elected and Appointed Officials (NALEO, 2004). Legislative and judicial restrictions regarding race during this study's time period were collected from various other sources. Private universities, community colleges, technical/vocational schools, professional schools, exclusively upper-level schools, and remote campuses were excluded from the analysis. The statistical software used in this analysis dropped those universities missing data for any variable in the analysis from the dataset.

2. Because these data are drawn from two levels of aggregation (state and university), this chapter employs a multilevel approach, using hierarchical linear modeling to calculate model estimates. The structure of the data (universities clustered by states) makes Ordinary Least Squares (OLS) an inefficient estimator because it violates the assumption that individual errors are independent, resulting in artificially low standard errors. The key hypotheses in this study also rely on the hierarchical relationships between states and universities, calling for a multilevel modeling approach.

I estimated the random-intercept portion of the model using all of the state-level determinants. In addition, to test for the interactive effect of restrictions on using race (a state-level factor) and institutional selectivity (a university-level factor), I estimated a random slope model.

One of the advantages of using hierarchical modeling is that it allows us to determine how much of the variance can be attributable to state-level factors and how much is left to university-level characteristics. Unlike similar studies of African-American enrollments where the state-level indicators account for only 2% of the variance (Hicklin & Meier, 2005), this model attributes 12% of the variance to state-level factors. Substantively, this means that the states do have a considerable impact on levels of enrollment and that the politics of the issue can make a real difference.

REFERENCES

Barron's Profile of American Colleges (24th ed.). (2000). New York: Barrons Educational Series.

Beyond Percentage Plans: The Challenge of Equal Opportunity in Higher Education. (2002). U.S. Commission on Civil Rights. Retrieved May 8, 2005 from http://www.usccr.gov/pubs/percent2/percent2.pdf

Bowen, W., Bok, D., & Loury, G. C. (2000). *The shape of the river*. Princeton, NJ: Princeton University Press.

Chapa, J., & Lazaro, V. A. (1998). Hopwood in Texas: The untimely end of affirmative action. In G. Orfield, & E. Miller (Eds.), *Chilling admissions: The affirmative action crisis and the search for alternatives*. Cambridge, MA: Harvard Education Press.

Duderstadt, J. (2000). *A university for the 21st century*. Ann Arbor, MI: University of Michigan Press.

Epstein, D., & O'Halloran, S. (1999). *Delegating powers: A transaction cost politics approach to policy making under separate powers*. Cambridge, UK: Cambridge University Press.

Fraga, L. R., Meier, K. J., & England, R. (1986). Hispanic Americans and education policy: Limits to equal access. *Journal of Politics, 48*, 850–876.

Gratz v. Bollinger, 539 U.S. 244. (2003).

Grutter v. Bollinger, 539 U.S. 306. (2003).

Hawes, D., & Hicklin, A. (2004, April). *Trickle-down representation: Passive representation and higher education*. Paper presented at the Midwest Political Association Conference. Chicago, IL.

Hess, F., & Leal, D. (2000). The politics of bilingual education expenditures in urban school districts. *Social Science Quarterly, 81*, 1064–1072.

Hicklin, A. (2004, September). *The effect of race-based admissions in public universities: Debunking the myths about Hopwood and Proposition 209*. Paper presented at the American Political Science Association Conference. Chicago, IL.

Hicklin, A., & Meier, K. J. (2005). *Diversity in higher education: The role of state governments*. Unpublished manuscript.

Hopwood v. Texas, 78 F.3d. 932. (1996).

Horn, C. L., & Flores, S. M. (2003). *Percent plans in college admissions: A comparative analysis of three state's experiences*. The Civil Rights Project. Retrieved February 18, 2005 from http://www.civilrightsproject.harvard.edu

Hurtado, S., & Wathington Cade, H. (2001). Time for retreat or renewal? Perspectives on the effects of Hopwood on campus. In D. Heller (Ed.), *The states and public higher education policy: Affordability, access, and accountability* (pp. 100–120). Baltimore, MD: The John Hopkins University Press.

Huber, J. D., & Shipan, C. R. (2002). *Deliberate discretion? The institutional foundations of bureaucratic autonomy.* Cambridge, UK: Cambridge University Press.

Leal, D., Martinez-Ebers, V., & Meier, K. J. (2004). The politics of Latino education: The biases of at-large elections. *Journal of Politics, 66,* 1224–1244.

Lowry, R. (2001). Governmental structure, trustee selection, and public university prices and spending: Multiple means to similar ends. *American Journal of Political Science, 45,* 845–861.

Mansbridge, J. (1999). Should blacks represent blacks and women represent women? A contingent yes. *Journal of Politics, 61,* 3.

McCubbins, M., Noll, R., & Weingast, B. (1989). Structure and process, politics and policy: Administrative arrangements and the political control of agencies. *Virginia Law Review, 75,* 431–482.

McLendon, M. K. (2003). State governance reform of higher education: Patterns, trends, and theories of the public policy process. In J. C. Smart, & W. G. Tierney (Eds.), *Higher education: Handbook of theory and research. XVIII* (pp. 57–144). New York: Agathon Press.

Meier, K. J. (2000). *Politics and the bureaucracy: Policymaking in the fourth branch of government* (4th ed.). Fort Worth, TX: Harcourt Brace.

Meier, K. J., & Stewart, J. (1991). *The politics of Hispanic education.* Albany, NY: State University Press of New York.

Meier, K. J., Stewart, J. Jr., & England, R. (1989). *Race, class, and education.* Madison, WI: University of Wisconsin Press.

NALEO. (2004). *National Association of Latino Elected and Appointed Officials.* http://www.naleo.org

Nicholson-Crotty, J., & Meier, K. J. 2003. The politics of structure in higher education: Bureaucracy and access to education. *Educational Policy, 17,* 98–120.

Perez, A. (2002, September 26). Hispanics must raise the bar. *Black Issues in Higher Education, 19,* 37.

Phillips, A. (1993). *Democracy and difference.* University Park, PA: Pennsylvania State University Press.

Pitkin, H. (1967). *The concept of representation.* Berkeley, CA: University of California Press.

Post, R. (1998). Introduction: After Bakke. In R. Post, & M. Rogin (Eds.), *Race and representation: Affirmative action* (pp. 13–28). New York: Zone Books.

Preston, M. (1978). Black elected officials and public policy: Substantive and symbolic representation. *Policy Studies Journal, 7,* 196–201.

Regents of the University of California v. Bakke, 438 US 265. (1978).

Richardon, R. C., Bracco, K. R., Callan, P. M., & Finney, J. E. (1999). *Designing state higher education systems for a new century.* Phoenix, AZ: Oryx Press.

Simmons, R. (1982). *Conflict and change in higher education after Bakke.* Cambridge, MA: Schenkman.

Swail, W. S., Cabrera, A. F., & Lee, C. (2004). *Latino youth and the pathway to college.* A report for the Education Policy Institute at the USC Annenberg School for Communications.

U.S. Census Bureau. (2001). *Statistical abstract of the United States*. Available http://
    www.census.gov/prod/www/statistical-abstract-us.html

U.S. Department of Education. (2004). *Integrated Postsecondary Education Data
    System (IPEDS)*. Retrieved March 17, 2004 from http://nces.ed.gov/IPEDS/

Welch, S., & Gruhl, J. (1998). *Affirmative action and minority enrollments in medi-
    cal and law schools*. Ann Arbor, MI: University of Michigan Press.

CHAPTER 13

The Future Politics of Latino Education

Kenneth J. Meier

Numerous studies—including those described in this book—have documented the educational disparities that negatively affect Latinos. The consistent theme of this volume is that some of these inequities have their origin in politics. How much of the difference can be attributed to the political process is unclear. However, the persistent finding that the education of Latinos is linked to a variety of political variables (such as political resources and representation) means that any policy actions intended to correct Latino educational inequities need to also recognize the forces that limit Latino political action. Politics, even in education, cannot be divorced from policy or from the implementation of policy. Politics can also be the vehicle for addressing education problems as Latinos gain greater access to the political system and make their preferences felt throughout the education system.

This chapter looks back at the findings in the volume, not to summarize them, but rather to use them as a springboard for setting an agenda for future studies of Latino education politics. In doing so, several questions are posed: If the political landscape of America has changed so dramatically, why has school board politics remained so similar? How does macro politics (that is, the broader political system) including but not limited to the macro politics of education and education reform, affect Latinos specifically? What are the current forms of institutionalized discrimination? What is the politics of policy implementation as it affects Latino students? What can be learned about Latino education by going beyond the study of K–12 education? How might studies of Latino education be improved?

UNCHANGING ELECTORAL POLITICS

The structure of the independent school district is designed to create barriers to political influence. Although this structure limits some political influences rather than all of them (Wirt & Kirst, 2005), it means that elections for the school board are the primary vehicle for outside policy change at the local level. Despite the massive change in the demographics of major urban school districts in the last 20 years, the comparative study of educational representation in 1986 and 2001 shows no real changes. The translation of Latino population into representation on the school board remains low, and at-large elections remain a significant barrier. One indication of the reason for this unchanging politics was reported by Rocha in Chapter 8 concerning the key role that immigration plays in the coalitions among Latinos, Anglos, and African Americans. Because large immigrant populations are associated with lower levels of Latino representation, the continued influx of immigrants not only means coalition partners will find Latinos a less attractive coalition partner, but that the translation of Latino population into Latino votes will remain extremely problematic. The field needs additional studies of how Latinos in some districts overcome these barriers to electoral representation and how one incorporates immigrants into the political process.

Although at-large elections have been the central concern of educational policy scholars for several decades, they are not the only structure that influences electoral outcomes. A wide variety of factors can affect turnout, especially the relative turnout of Latinos to members of other groups. Rocha examines the impact of partisan elections and shows that Latinos achieve far greater representation in partisan systems than in nonpartisan ones, exactly what would be expected given the higher levels of turnout in partisan elections. Election timing is also likely to matter, as some school districts hold elections on the regular November election day, and others hold them separately, at times when other campaigns are not active.

Representation can also be nonelectoral. Previous studies show that it also matters if Latinos hold administrative positions and teaching positions (Leal, Martinez-Ebers, & Meier, 2004). The literature almost always assumes that the process of representation is top down with school boards determining administrators and administrators hiring teachers, yet the only systematic studies of this phenomena indicate that the relationship is likely reciprocal (Meier & Smith, 1994; Meier & O'Toole, 2006). If that is true, then current models of bureaucratic representation are underspecified and need to incorporate this reciprocal relationship, and we need to determine how administrative representation grows independently of political representation. The second promising area is to focus directly on policy. Meier, McClain, Wrinkle, & Polinard (2004) found that the zero-sum competition between Latinos and African Americans for representation became a positive-sum relationship in terms of policy. How one translates this competition over electoral representation into cooperation in setting policy needs to be investigated more fully.

MACROPOLITICS

Although Latinos are central to the politics of the United States, major political issues are often debated and resolved without considering how they might affect Latinos, even though there are clear impacts. The authors in this volume noted that noneducation issues, such as welfare reform or the efforts to restrict immigrants from gaining various policy benefits, have had a detrimental impact on Latino education. Branton and coauthors (Chapter 9) showed that the initiative, a majoritarian process adopted long before immigration became a major issue, provided a vehicle for anti-immigrant and anti-Latino sentiment. Hamann's report on Dalton, Georgia, described in Chapter 6, illustrated how the same situation can be framed in different ways. Issue framing is an area with substantial work in political science that could be fruitfully applied to questions of Latino education. How an issue is framed is central to the various theories of politics such as Schneider and Ingram's (1997) social construction theory, Baumgartner and Jones' (1993) policy equilibrium theory, as well as classical theories of politics (Schattschneider, 1960). Moving this literature to Latino education policy would benefit both the study of Latino politics and the study of public policy framing generally.

Within the realm of education policy, the same aphorism applies—policies adopted without consideration of the educational status of Latinos can have major ramifications. With the launch of the recent wave of education reform after the 1983 publication of A Nation at Risk (NCEE, 1983) through the implementation of the federal No Child Left Behind Act, a whole series of education reforms have been adopted, many at the national level, that have created an extensive accountability system built around standardized tests. No Child Left Behind, in fact, specifically requires that schools and school districts administer standardized tests and tabulate data by racial and ethnic group.

This volume addressed some of these recent education reforms. In Chapter 3, Greene and Winters showed that the elimination of social promotion in Florida had very similar positive effects on Latino, Anglo, and African-American students. In Chapter 4, Polinard and coauthors demonstrated that charter schools spur public schools to improve performance, including the performance of Latino students. Alternative certification processes appear to have no impact. This is a nice start on the study of Latinos and education reform, but one needs to be aware that the basic ground rules for these reforms can vary greatly. Texas has a charter school law that creates large incentives to serve disadvantaged populations (and thus could improve public school scores simply by removing students not likely to do well in public schools; see Bohte, 2004); other states have less restrictive charter laws that might or might not detrimentally affect Latino students. Similarly, how well Latino students in charter schools do compared with their cohorts in public schools or their fellow charter school enrollees is yet to be examined. Similar studies of other educational reforms are greatly needed.

INSTITUTIONAL DISCRIMINATION

This differential impact of various education reforms suggests that students of Latino politics need to spend time studying the implementation of these policies. Many policies are neutral on their face, but the structures of the policies or the implementation of the policies can create an institutionalized form of discrimination. The administration of standardized tests to Latino students, for example, is a two-edged sword. Valenzuela and Maxcy in Chapter 1 raised the issue of test exemptions and how by exempting Latinos or by excluding their scores Latino students are denied equal educational opportunities. Others have charged that standardized tests are culturally biased and thus underestimate the performance of Latino students; this underestimation, then, generates a variety of negative educational results (e.g., grouping and tracking) that further limits a Latino student's access to quality education. An alternative view might be that testing and the test-score gaps bring to the surface the failure of the schools to educate Latino students and thus could provide the political ammunition to support some redistributive reforms.

Recognizing the implementation aspect of education policy implies that neutral policies can be implemented in ways detrimental to Latinos and other students but also that policies that are perceived to negatively affect Latinos might be moderated or overcome by administrators and teachers concerned with equity for Latino students. Hamann's introduction of scripts in Chapter 6 is relevant here simply because the political script adopted by the school board might vary a great deal from the administrative script used by the superintendent and other administrators; both might be different from the street-level implementation script of the teachers (see Lewis & Ramakrishnan, 2007). Teachers and administrators have vast discretion and can often shape policies in unintended ways.

THE POLITICS OF IMPLEMENTATION

Questions regarding who is tested and what types of assessment are used raise the issue of policy implementation. A truism of public policy in general that applies quite clearly to education policy is that the actual implementation of policies is often more important than the policies that are promulgated. Policies that prohibit social promotion, for example, are efforts to limit the discretion of teachers and administrators in the implementation process. Initial testing policies in Texas were subverted by the use of exemptions for students classified as limited English or assigned to special education (Bohte & Meier, 2000).

Even within a rigid system of performance appraisal based on standardized tests, school districts still have vast discretion on which of the various multiple indicators of education that should be stressed. The often-pronounced tradeoff is between emphasis on standardized tests and emphasis on citizenship or emphasis on college-bound training. Despite the pressures to perform on standardized tests, schools vary in how much emphasis they place on this particular performance indicator versus attendance, dropouts, college prep classes, and so forth. Unfortunately, little research is being done on the myriad of performance indicators in regard to Latino education and what, if any, tradeoffs are made among these indicators.

Several authors stressed the important role of Latino teachers in the education of Latino students. Despite this emphasis, we lack a fundamental understanding of how Latino teachers affect Latino students. Four possible ways appear in the literature—by using pedagogical techniques more attune to Latino students, by making decisions on grouping and tracking, by influencing Anglo teachers and administrators to change policies or behavior, and by simply serving as role models. Separating out these various forms of influence would do a great deal to demonstrate how school systems can overcome a shortage of Latino teachers that is likely to grow larger.

BEYOND K–12 EDUCATION

The overwhelming attention in education policy generally as well as Latino education specifically is on K–12 education. This volume presented two studies that demonstrated that an examination of other areas of education is also useful. Chapter 11 by Doerfler illustrates both the use of alternative indicators of education success and how programs interact with people. A series of programs such as challenging classes, integrated curricula, and block schedules are linked to more Latino college matriculation; but such programs only work in districts that have the ability to make use of these techniques. Chapter 11 suggests that more research should be done on how much programs matter separate from the people who implement them.

Hicklin's chapter on higher education (Chapter 12) introduces an extensive database on higher education to the study of Latino education policy. She demonstrates that many of the K–12 factors also play a role in higher education—political representation, structures, macro policies, and so forth. A series of questions such as how the representation of faculty matters, the role of the cost of education, the competition between public and private universities, and the contribution of individual administrative leadership can be studied with both admissions data and other data on completion rates of students. Examining colleges is not the only other education forum that needs analysis. We know little about how Latinos fare in pre-K programs or under various GED policies.

THE NEED FOR BETTER RESEARCH DESIGNS

These five areas do not exhaust the potential areas of additional research on Latino education politics. Also important in the study of Latino education policy is the use of better research designs that will allow schools to provide some definitive answers to policy makers. As an illustration, in many cases control groups or comparisons are needed. In Chapter 2, Staudt argues that the emphasis on standardized tests has resulted in a lack of citizenship education in two Texas districts, although other work (Godwin & Kemerer, 2002) shows that public schools generally fail in this regard for all students. The failure of public schools to teach democratic values is important; whether this failure is especially important in regard to Latinos needs to be established.

A second illustration is the need to be able to make clear causal linkages. Many contend that standardized tests or other policies create tradeoffs that will lower the level of education (for Latinos or for others). Yet for the most part these arguments rely on the face validity of the argument rather than systematic analysis. Because education operates with a variety of overlapping production functions (that is, the resources that are used to teach basic literacy also eventually contribute to college-bound students), schools and districts that do well on standardized tests usually do well on college admissions and higher end indicators. We need systematic analysis, such as the correlated errors techniques developed in other policy literatures (Martin & Smith, 2005), that clearly demonstrates where and when actual tradeoffs occur.

A third illustration is the need to study both short- and long-term effects of policy reforms. Short-term impacts can often dissipate over time, and second-order consequences can often take some time to show up. The emphasis on timing of impacts should be augmented with an emphasis on examining subgroups of Latino students. The children of immigrants likely face a different set of educational problems than the children of citizens. Policies could also have gender implications as well as impacts that might be different for the Latino community compared to other communities. Extensive work on the various national origin groups among Latinos would also be useful.

In short, there is much to do in the study of the politics of Latino education policy. The issues involving Latinos in education are likely to continue to grow in importance as the size of the Latino community continues to grow. To truly understand the politics of education in the contemporary United States, one needs to understand the politics of Latino education.

REFERENCES

Baumgartner, F. R., & Jones, B. D. (1993). *Agendas and instability in American politics*. Chicago: University of Chicago Press.

Bohte, J. (2004, November). Examining the impact of charter schools on performance in traditional public schools. *Policy Studies Journal, 32*, 501–520.

Bohte, J., & Meier, K. J. (2000, March/April). Goal displacement: Assessing the motivation for organizational cheating. *Public Administration Review, 60*, 173–182.

Godwin, R. K., & Kemerer, F. R. (2002). *School choice tradeoffs: Liberty, equity, and diversity*. Austin, TX: University of Texas Press.

Leal, D. L., Martinez-Ebers, V., & Meier, K. J. (2004). The politics of Latino education: The biases of at-large elections. *Journal of Politics, 66*(11), 1224–1244.

Lewis, P. G., & Ramakrishnan, S. K. (2007). Police practices in immigrant destination cities. *Urban Affairs Review, 42*(6), 874–900.

Martin, S., & Smith, P. (2005). Multiple public service performance indicators. *Journal of Public Administration Research and Theory, 15*, 599–613.

Meier, K. J., McClain, P. D., Wrinkle, R. D., & Polinard, J. L. (2004). Divided or together? Conflict and cooperation between African-Americans and Latinos. *Political Research Quarterly, 57*, 399–409.

Meier, K. J., & O'Toole, L. J., Jr. (2006). Political control versus bureaucratic values: Reframing the debate. *Public Administration Review, 66*, 177–192.

Meier, K. J., & Smith, K. B. (1994). Representative democracy and representative bureaucracy: Examining the top down and the bottom up linkages. *Social Science Quarterly, 75*, 790–803.

National Commission on Excellence in Education. (1983). *A nation at risk: A report to the nation and the secretary of education, United States Department of Education*. Washington, DC: U.S. Department of Education. Retrieved June 22, 2010, from http://www2.ed.gov/pubs/NatAtRisk/index.html

Schattschneider, E. E. (1960). *The semi-sovereign people*. New York: Holt, Reinhart and Winston.

Schneider, A. & Ingram, H. (1997). *Policy design for democracy*. Lawrence: University of Kansas Press.

Wirt, F. M., & Kirst, M. W. (2005). *The political dynamics of American education* (3rd ed.). Richmond, CA: McCutchan Publishing Corporation.

About the Contributors

John Bohte is an associate professor of political science and MPA Program Director at the University of Wisconsin-Milwaukee. He has published in numerous public administration journals and is coauthor (with Kenneth J. Meier and Jeffrey L. Brady) of *Applied Statistics for Public and Nonprofit Administration*, now in its eighth edition.

Regina Branton is an assistant professor of political science with the University of North Texas. Her research interests focus on the behavioral, electoral, and institutional implications of racial and ethnic diversity in the United States. Her current research examines the influence of race and ethnicity on congressional elections, the importance of spatial context on media coverage of immigration, and how media coverage of immigration influences public opinion.

Gavin Dillingham is a Ph.D. candidate at Rice University. He currently works as an analyst for the city of Houston in their economic development policy analysis group. Gavin's research interests include public policy analysis and political institutions. His substantive policy interests are in immigration policy and urban economic development.

Carl Doerfler is an assistant professor of political science at the University of Montevallo, a public liberal arts college in Alabama. He earned his Ph.D. at Texas A&M University, where he was part of the Texas Educational Excellence Project, which researched questions of equity and representation in education. His current research interests include education policy and minority representation.

Johanna Dunaway is an assistant professor of political science and mass communication at Louisiana State University. Her current research projects include papers on the institutional determinants of information quality in political news coverage, influences on news media coverage of female electoral candidates, and local news coverage of Latino immigration and its influence on public opinion.

Jay P. Greene is endowed chair and head of the Department of Education Reform at the University of Arkansas. He is also a fellow with the George W. Bush Institute. Greene conducts research and writes about education policy, including topics such as school choice, high school graduation rates, accountability, and special education. He is the author of *Education Myths* (2005). Greene has been a professor of government at The University of Texas at Austin and the University of Houston. He received his B.A. in history from Tufts University in 1988 and his Ph.D. from the Government Department at Harvard University in 1995.

Edmund "Ted" Hamann is an associate professor in the Department of Teaching, Learning, and Teacher Education at the University of Nebraska–Lincoln and an affiliated researcher at the Centro Interdisciplinario de Estudios de Educación y Superación de Pobreza (CIESESP) at Mexico's Universidad de Monterrey. He studies school reform and educational policy formation in reaction to the growth in English learners and/or immigrant newcomer school enrollment. He also studies the schooling of students in Mexico who have prior experience in U.S. schools. In addition to more than 30 journal articles and book chapters, his works include *Alumnos transnacionales: Las escuelas mexicanas frente a la globalización* (co-author, 2009), *The Educational Welcome of Latinos in the New South* (2003), and *Education in the New Latino Diaspora* (co-editor, 2002).

Frederick M. Hess is an educator, political scientist, and author who studies a range of K–12 and higher education issues. He is the author of influential books on education, including *The Same Thing Over and Over, Education Unbound, Common Sense School Reform, No Child Left Behind Primer*, and *Spinning Wheels*. He is also editor of the new volume *Stretching the School Dollar* and author of the *Education Week* blog *Rick Hess Straight Up*. His work has appeared in scholarly and popular outlets such as *Teachers College Record, Harvard Education Review, Social Science Quarterly, Urban Affairs Review, American Politics Quarterly, Chronicle of Higher Education, Phi Delta Kappan, Educational Leadership, U.S. News & World Report, The Washington Post*, and *National Review*. He serves as executive editor of *Education Next*, is on the Review Board for the Broad Prize in Urban Education, and is on the boards of directors of the National Association of Charter School Authorizers, 4.0 Schools, and the American Board for the Certification of Teaching Excellence. A former high school social studies teacher in East Baton Rouge, Louisiana, he has also taught at the University of Virginia, the University of Pennsylvania, Georgetown University, Rice University, and Harvard University. He holds an M.A. and Ph.D. in government from Harvard University, as well as an M.Ed. in teaching and curriculum.

Alisa Hicklin is an assistant professor of political science at the University of Oklahoma. Her research interests include higher education policy, minority policy issues, and public management; and she teaches courses in public administration and education policy. Her most recent work has appeared in the *Review of Policy Research* and will appear in *Public Administration Review*. Her most recent work has appeared in the *Journal of Politics*, the *Journal of Public Administration Research and Theory*, and *Policy Studies Journal*.

Eric Gonzalez Juenke is an assistant professor of political science at the Michigan State University. His current research examines how racial minorities turn their preferences into policy in the face of institutional constraints, entrenched majority interests, and policy incrementalism. His other research interests include the effects of minority representation in legislative and bureaucratic institutions, policy change, inter-institutional interactions over time, and the crossnational analysis of education. He received his B.A. (1999) and M.A. (2002) in Political Science from the University of North Texas, and his Ph.D. (2005) from Texas A&M University.

David L. Leal is an associate professor of government, faculty associate of the Center for Mexican-American Studies, and director of the Irma Rangel Public Policy Institute at The University of Texas at Austin. His primary academic interest is Latino politics, and his work explores a variety of questions involving public policy, public opinion, and political behavior. He has published over 40 journal articles and book chapters on these and other topics. He is also the co-editor of *Latinos and the Economy* (2010), *Beyond the Barrio: Latinos and the 2004 Elections* (2010), *Immigration Policy and Security* (2008), and *Latino Politics: Identity, Mobilization, and Representation* (2007). Leal was a Spencer/National Academy of Education postdoctoral fellow, an American Political Science Association (APSA) congressional fellow, and a member of the APSA Task Force on Religion and American Democracy. He is currently a member of the editorial boards of *American Politics Research*, *Social Science Quarterly*, and *State Politics & Policy Quarterly*. He received his Ph.D. from Harvard University and B.A. from Stanford University.

Melissa Marschall is associate professor of political science at Rice University. Her research interests include urban politics, education policy, and minority political incorporation. She is coauthor of *Choosing Schools: Consumer Choice and the Quality of American Schools* (2000). Her work has appeared in journals such as *American Political Science Review, American Journal of Political Science, Political Research Quarterly, Political Behavior, Educational Policy, Policy Studies Journal*, and *Social Science Quarterly*.

Valerie Martinez-Ebers is professor of political science at the University of North Texas and vice president of the American Political Science Association. Her teaching interests and research areas of expertise include race, ethnicity and politics; public policy; political tolerance; and the politics of rock-n-roll music. She was one of the principal investigators for the Latino National Survey funded by Ford, Carnegie, Russell Sage, Hewlett, Joyce, Rhode Island, and National Science Foundations. Many of Martinez's publications are on the consequences of education policies for minority students, but she also has publications on Latino/a politics, women in politics, aging policy, and methods of survey research. Three of her more recent publications include *Perspectives on Race, Ethnicity and Religion: Identity Politics in the United States, Politicas: Latina Public Officials in Texas*, and "*Su Casa* Es *Nuestra Casa: Latino Politics Research and the Development of American Political Science*," published in the *American Political Science Review*. She also is a coauthor of "Should They Dance With the One Who Brung 'Em? Latinos and the 2008 Presidential Election," in *PS: Political Science and Politics* (2008).

Brendan D. Maxcy is an associate professor of Educational Leadership and Policy Studies at the Indiana University School of Education. He is co-director of the Urban Principalship Program at Indiana University–Purdue University Indianapolis

(IUPUI). His research uses qualitative methods and critical theories to explore educational policies and school leaders' responses to these. In addition to work on U.S. schooling, he studied leadership in schools contending with national educational reforms and intense regional unrest in the border provinces of southern Thailand. He has published in *Educational Administration Quarterly, Urban Education, Educational Policy* and *Educational Management, Administration & Leadership*.

Kenneth J. Meier is the Charles H. Gregory Chair in liberal arts and distinguished professor of political science at Texas A&M University. He also holds an appointment as a professor of public management in the Cardiff School of Business, Cardiff University (Wales). A former editor of the *American Journal of Political Science*, Meier has eclectic research interests, which cover a wide range of subfields in political science, including a long-standing focus on questions of race, equity, and democratic inclusion. Dr. Meier is the author or coauthor of 16 books, 30 book chapters and monographs, and 150 journal articles and essays. His books include *The Politics of Hispanic Education* (1991), *Bureaucracy in a Democratic State* (2006), *The Politics of Sin: Drugs, Alcohol, and Public Policy* (1994), and *Politics, Policy, and Organizations* (2003). He is currently directing a study of the politics of educational equity using the 1,800 largest school districts in the United States.

Beth Miller is an assistant professor of political science at the University of Missouri–Kansas City. Her research focuses on the importance of psychological processes for the way we think about politics. Specifically, her research focuses on the ways memory structures and processes affect public opinion and political behavior.

Jerry Polinard is professor and chair of the Department of Political Science at the University of Texas–Pan American (UTPA). He received his Ph.D. from the University of Arizona. He taught at Lamar University and Oklahoma State University before coming to the UTPA in 1972. He has held visiting appointments at the University of New Mexico, the University of Arizona, The University of Texas at Austin, Texas Lutheran, and Texas A&M–Corpus Christi. He is the author and coauthor of publications on Mexican-American political behavior and political redistricting.

Rene R. Rocha is assistant professor of political science at the University of Iowa. He received his B.A. from the University of Texas–Pan American and his Ph.D. from Texas A&M University. His current research projects include a study on how residential context influences Latino politics and an assessment of the competition or cooperation between blacks and Latinos in electoral and policy areas (focused on education policy).

Paru Shah is an assistant professor of political science at Macalester College in St. Paul, Minnesota. Her major areas of research and interest include racial and ethnic politics, urban politics, and the intersection of race and urban education politics. Her recent publications (with Melissa Marschall) include "Keeping Policy Churn Off the Agenda: Urban Education and Civic Capacity" (*Policy Studies Journal*, 2005) and

"The Attitudinal Effects of Minority Incorporation: Examining the Racial Dimensions of Trust in Urban America" (*Urban Affairs Review*, 2007). Her recent publications have appeared in the *American Journal of Political Science, Social Science Quarterly*, and *American Politics Research*.

Kathleen (Kathy) Staudt received a Ph.D. in political science from the University of Wisconsin in 1976. She founded the Center for Civic Engagement at the University of Texas at El Paso and directed it for 10 years. Staudt teaches political science and education courses about schools in communities, borders, policy analysis, leadership, and democracy. She has published fourteen books, several of which focus on the U.S.-Mexican border, including *Pledging Allegiance: Learning Nationalism in El Paso-Juárez* (with Susan Rippberger, 2003); *Free Trade? Informal Economies at the U.S.-Mexico Border* (1998); *Fronteras No Más: Toward Social Justice at the U.S.-Mexico Border* (with Irasema Coronado, 2002); and *Violence and Activism at the Border: Gender, Fear, and Everyday Life in Ciudad Juárez* (2008). She was the lead editor for *Human Rights along the U.S.-Mexico Border* (2009). Staudt collaborated with colleagues at El Colegio de la Frontera Norte in Ciudad Juárez for *Cities and Citizenship at the U.S.-Mexico Border: The El Paso del Norte Region* (2010), which includes two chapters on the business model in education, standardized testing, and international competitiveness themes in the binational region. Staudt is active in community-based organizations, nonprofit agencies, and public schools.

Angela Valenzuela is the associate vice president for School Partnerships, serving as director of the Texas Center for Education Policy at The University of Texas at Austin, a university-wide research and policy center that operates at local, state, national, and international levels to advance equity and excellence in public elementary, secondary and higher education. She currently serves as the national director for the National Latino Education Research Agenda Project (NLERAP). NLERAP embarks on a national project to establish teacher education institutes in five regions of the country, such as the Southwest region which includes Texas. She is also a professor in the Departments of Curriculum and Instruction and Educational Administration at the College of Education at The University of Texas at Austin. Her research and teaching interests are in the sociology of education, race and ethnicity in schools, urban education reform, educational policy, immigrant youth in schools, and U.S.-Mexico relations. She is the author of *Subtractive Schooling: U.S. Mexican Youth and the Politics of Caring* (1999), winner of both the 2000 American Educational Research Association Outstanding Book Award and the 2001 Critics' Choice Award from the American Educational Studies Association. Her most recent book, *Leaving Children Behind: How "Texas-style" Accountability Fails Latino Youth* (2004), examines high-stakes testing policy in Texas. Valenzuela received her doctorate from Stanford University.

James P. Wenzel is an associate professor of political science at the University of Texas–Pan American. His research interests are in the areas of judicial politics and civil liberties. His research has appeared in journal such as *American Politics Research* and *Social Science Quarterly*.

Marcus A. Winters is an assistant professor in the Leadership, Research, and Foundations Department in the College of Education at the University of Colorado, Colorado Springs. He has conducted several studies on a variety of education policy issues including grade retention, performance pay for teachers, and the effects of school choice on public school systems.

Robert D. Wrinkle, a native of South Texas, is professor of political science and director of the Center for Survey Research at the University of Texas–Pan American, where he has been for a number of years. He is the coauthor of *Electoral Structure and Urban Policy: The Impact on Mexican-American Communities* (1994), and has published in the *American Journal of Political Science, Journal of Politics*, and *Political Research Quarterly*, among other journals. His interests include studying Latino political attitudes and behavior, public policy, and education politics, as well as attending major track and field meets.

Index

A designation of "n" follows a page number when the reference is to a note.

This index uses the term Latino *rather than* Hispanic *in keeping with the editors' and authors' preference, except in cases of established phrases and formal names.*